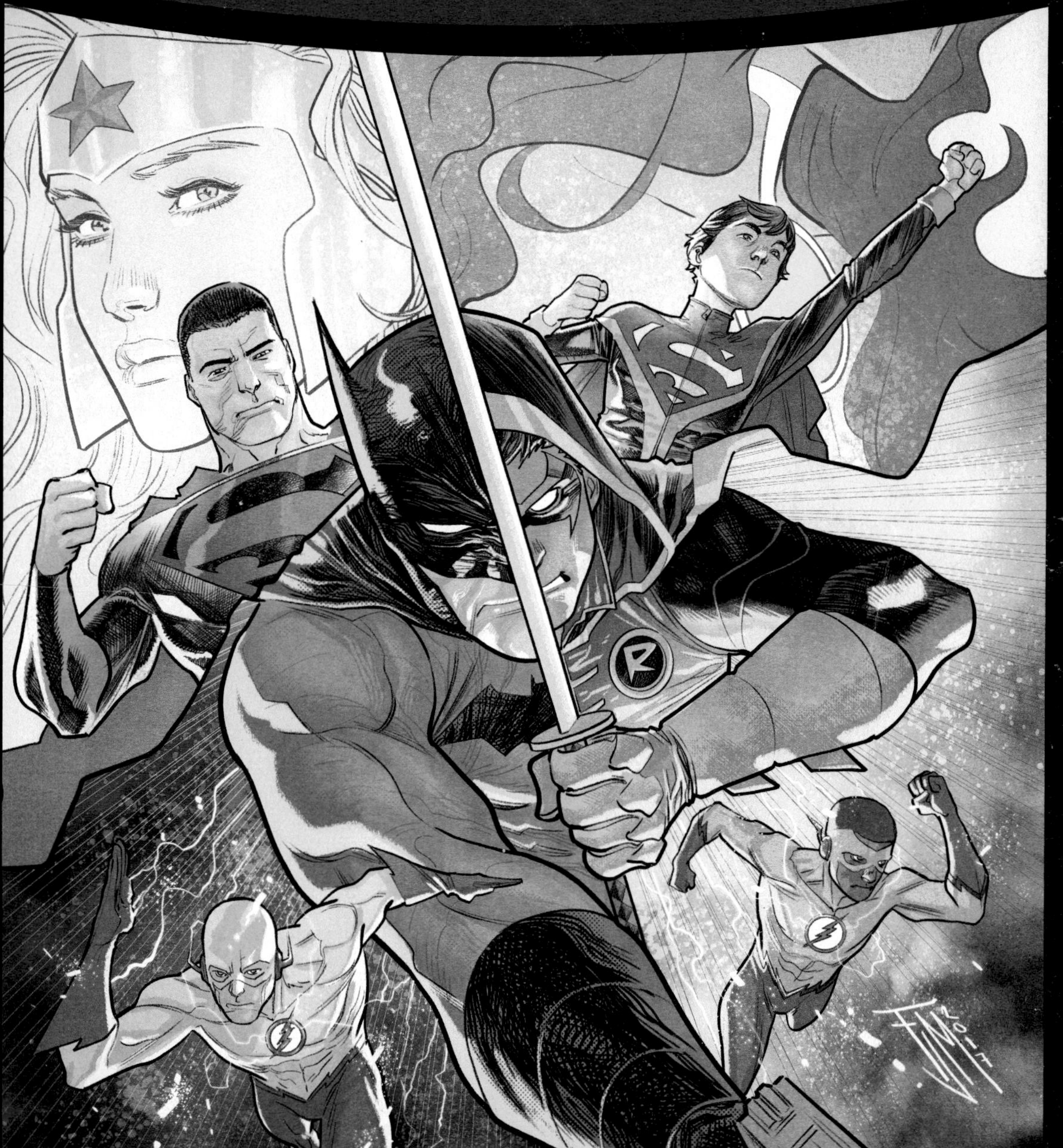

SUPER SONS OF TOMORROW

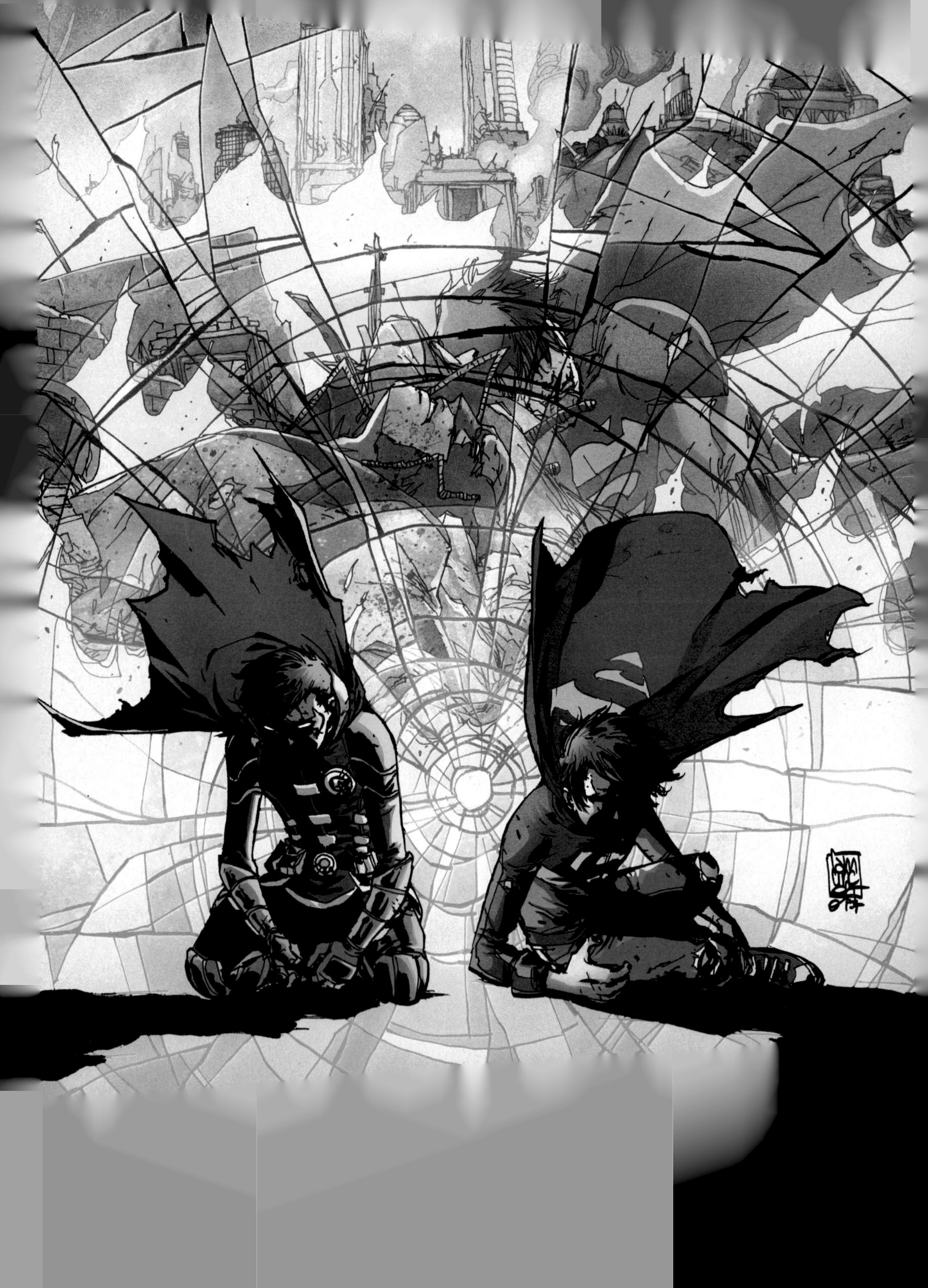

SUPER SONS
OF TOMORROW

PETER J. TOMASI
PATRICK GLEASON
writers

JORGE JIMENEZ * **RYAN BENJAMIN**
RICHARD FRIEND * **ED BENES** * **SERGIO DAVILA**
VICENTE CIFUENTES * **TYLER KIRKHAM**
artists

ALEJANDRO SANCHEZ * **GABE ELTAEB**
DINEI RIBEIRO * **TOMEU MOREY**
colorists

ROB LEIGH * **COREY BREEN**
letterers

FRANCIS MANAPUL
collection cover artist

SUPERMAN created by **JERRY SIEGEL** and **JOE SHUSTER**
SUPERBOY created by **JERRY SIEGEL**
By special arrangement with the Jerry Siegel family

ALEX ANTONE PAUL KAMINSKI Editors - Original Series
BRITTANY HOLZHERR JESSICA CHEN Associate Editors - Original Series * **ANDREA SHEA** Assistant Editor - Original Series
JEB WOODARD Group Editor - Collected Editions * **TYLER-MARIE EVANS** Editor - Collected Edition
STEVE COOK Design Director - Books * **CURTIS KING JR.** Publication Design

BOB HARRAS Senior VP - Editor-in-Chief, DC Comics
PAT McCALLUM Executive Editor, DC Comics

DIANE NELSON President * **DAN DiDIO** Publisher * **JIM LEE** Publisher * **GEOFF JOHNS** President & Chief Creative Officer
AMIT DESAI Executive VP - Business & Marketing Strategy, Direct to Consumer & Global Franchise Management
SAM ADES Senior VP & General Manager, Digital Services * **BOBBIE CHASE** VP & Executive Editor, Young Reader & Talent Development
MARK CHIARELLO Senior VP - Art, Design & Collected Editions * **JOHN CUNNINGHAM** Senior VP - Sales & Trade Marketing
ANNE DePIES Senior VP - Business Strategy, Finance & Administration * **DON FALLETTI** VP - Manufacturing Operations
LAWRENCE GANEM VP - Editorial Administration & Talent Relations * **ALISON GILL** Senior VP - Manufacturing & Operations
HANK KANALZ Senior VP - Editorial Strategy & Administration * **JAY KOGAN** VP - Legal Affairs * **JACK MAHAN** VP - Business Affairs
NICK J. NAPOLITANO VP - Manufacturing Administration * **EDDIE SCANNELL** VP - Consumer Marketing
COURTNEY SIMMONS Senior VP - Publicity & Communications * **JIM (SKI) SOKOLOWSKI** VP - Comic Book Specialty Sales & Trade Marketing
NANCY SPEARS VP - Mass, Book, Digital Sales & Trade Marketing * **MICHELE R. WELLS** VP - Content Strategy

SUPER SONS OF TOMORROW

DC Comics, 2900 West Alameda Ave., Burbank, CA 91505
Printed by LSC Communications, Kendallville, IN, USA. 5/25/18. First Printing.
ISBN: 978-1-4012-8239-4

Library of Congress Cataloging-in-Publication Data is available.

PEFC Certified

Printed on paper from
sustainably managed
forests, controlled
sources

PEFC/29-31-337   www.pefc.org

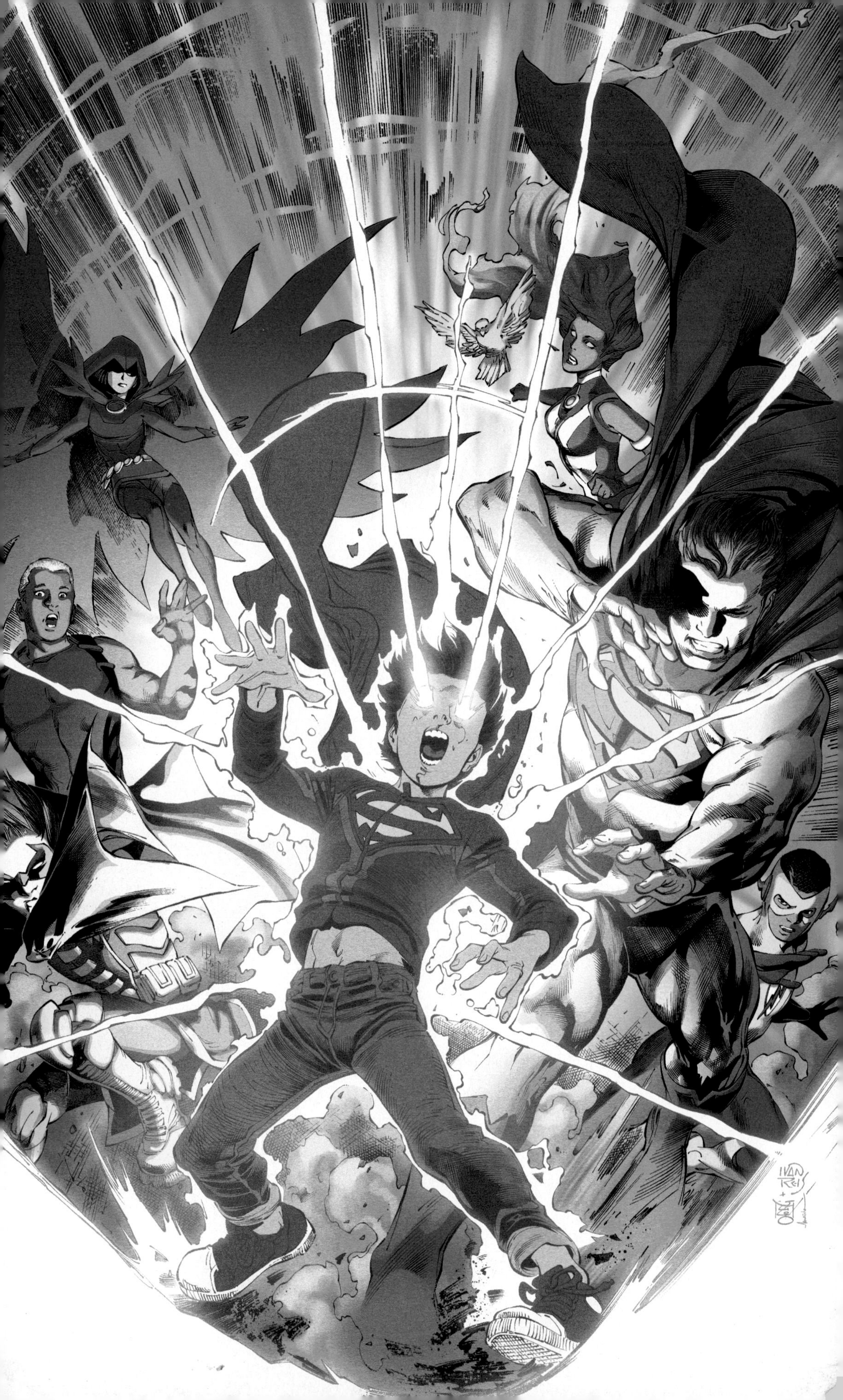

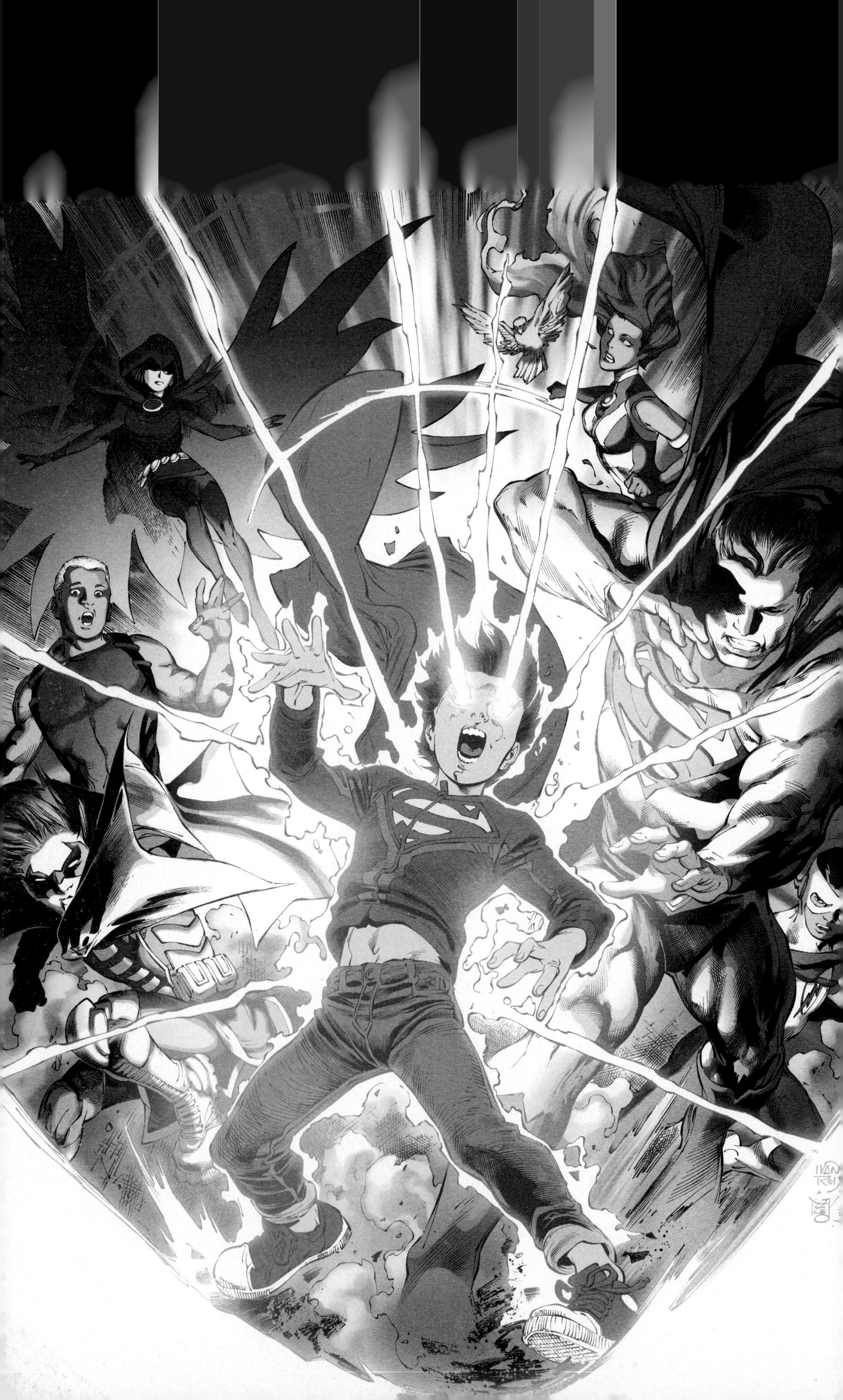

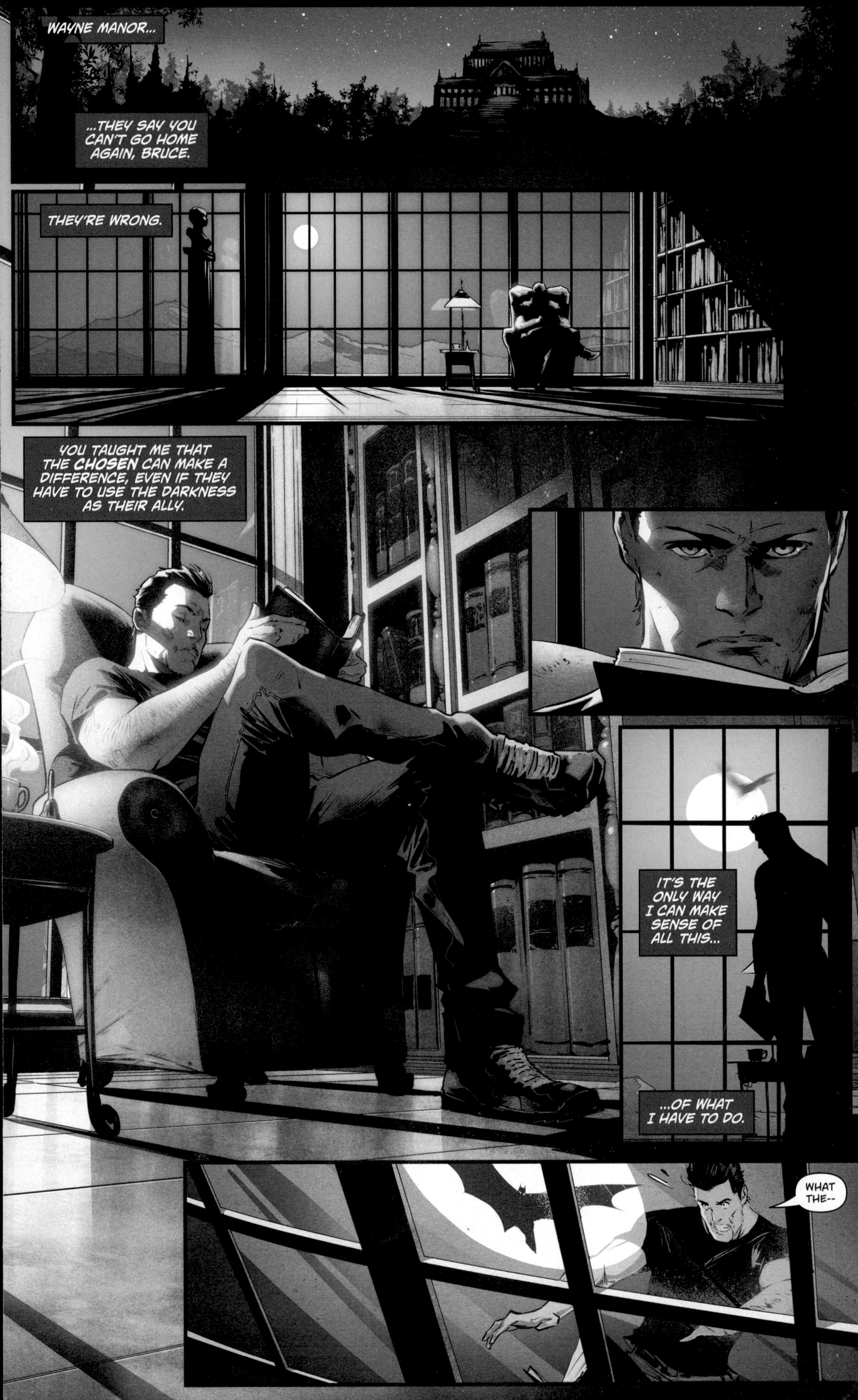
WAYNE MANOR...
...THEY SAY YOU CAN'T GO HOME AGAIN, BRUCE.
THEY'RE WRONG.
YOU TAUGHT ME THAT THE CHOSEN CAN MAKE A DIFFERENCE, EVEN IF THEY HAVE TO USE THE DARKNESS AS THEIR ALLY.
IT'S THE ONLY WAY I CAN MAKE SENSE OF ALL THIS...
...OF WHAT I HAVE TO DO.
WHAT THE--

HELLO, BRUCE!
TIM?!
Super sons
of TOMORROW Part 1
DARK
of the
SON
PETER J. TOMASI and PATRICK GLEASON writers/JORGE JIMENEZ artist
ALEJANDRO SANCHEZ colorist/ROB LEIGH letterer
IVAN REIS, JULIO FERREIRA & MARCELO MAIOLO cover
BRITTANY HOLZHERR and JESSICA CHEN associate editors
ALEX ANTONE and PAUL KAMINSKI editors
EDDIE BERGANZA and BRIAN CUNNINGHAM group editors

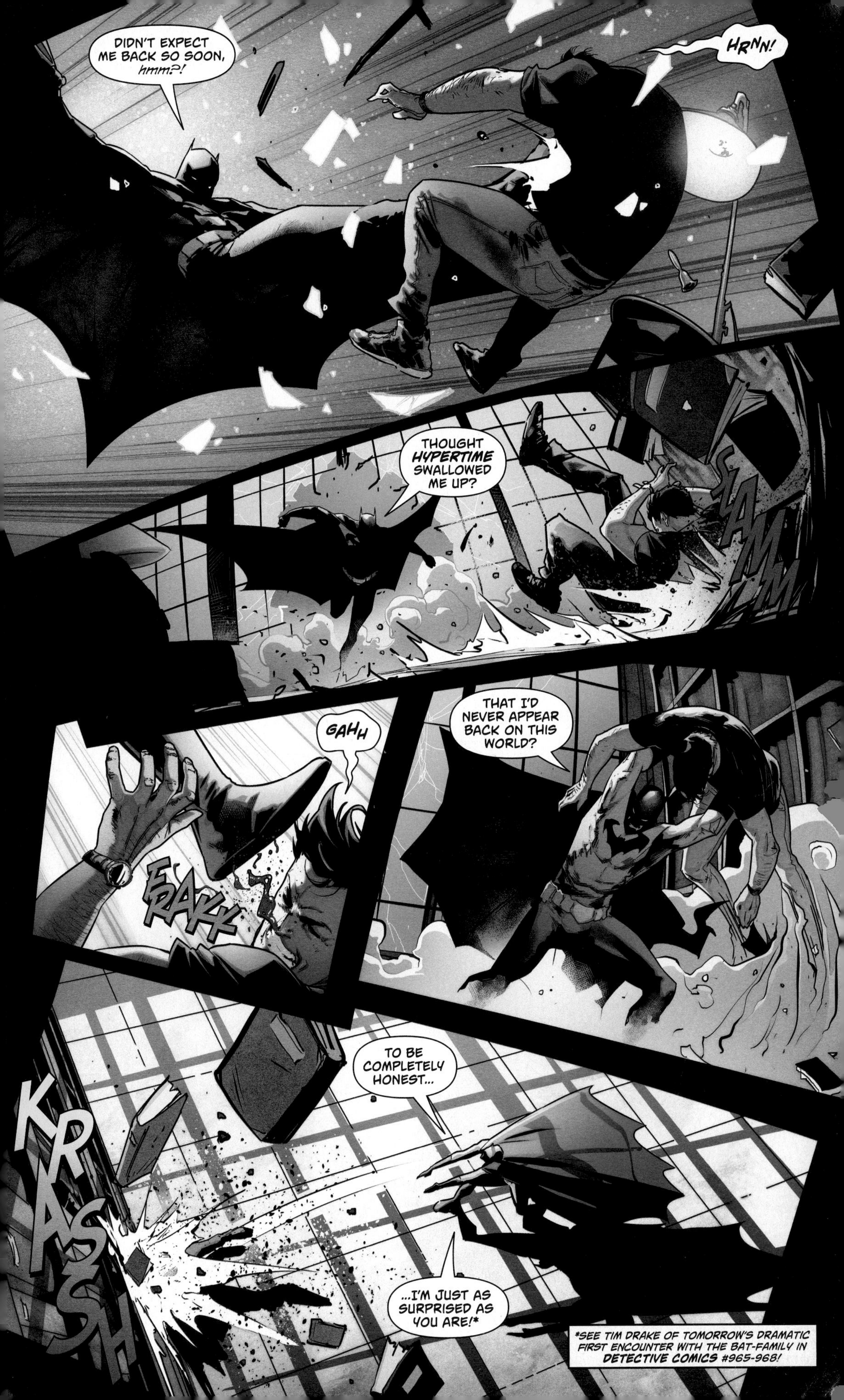
DIDN'T EXPECT ME BACK SO SOON, *hmm?!*
HRNN!
THOUGHT **HYPERTIME** SWALLOWED ME UP?
GAHH
FRAKK
THAT I'D NEVER APPEAR BACK ON THIS WORLD?
KRASH
TO BE COMPLETELY HONEST...
...I'M JUST AS SURPRISED AS YOU ARE!*
*SEE TIM DRAKE OF TOMORROW'S DRAMATIC FIRST ENCOUNTER WITH THE BAT-FAMILY IN **DETECTIVE COMICS** #965-968!

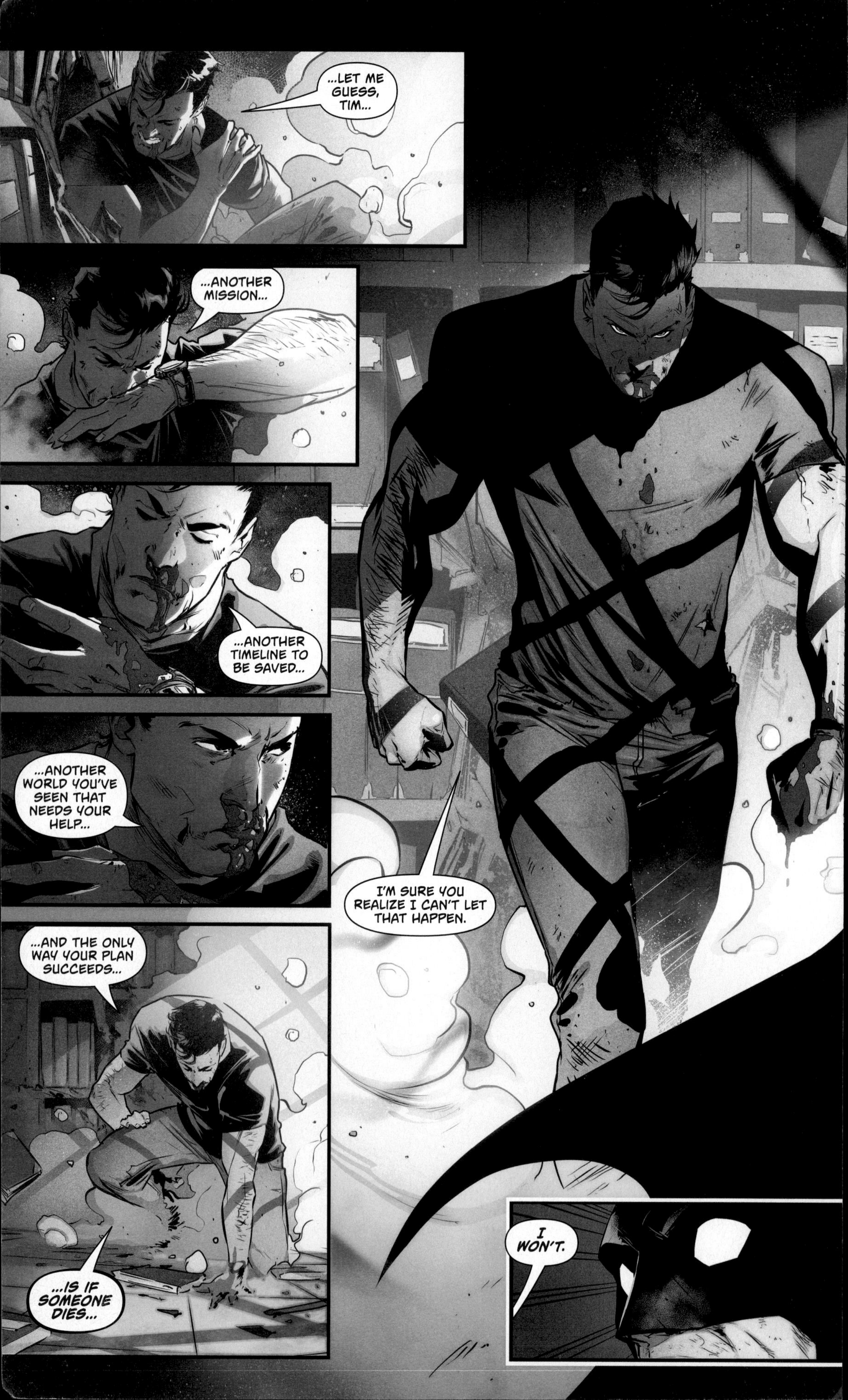
...LET ME GUESS, TIM...
...ANOTHER MISSION...
...ANOTHER TIMELINE TO BE SAVED...
...ANOTHER WORLD YOU'VE SEEN THAT NEEDS YOUR HELP...
...AND THE ONLY WAY YOUR PLAN SUCCEEDS...
...IS IF SOMEONE DIES...
I'M SURE YOU REALIZE I CAN'T LET THAT HAPPEN.
I WON'T.

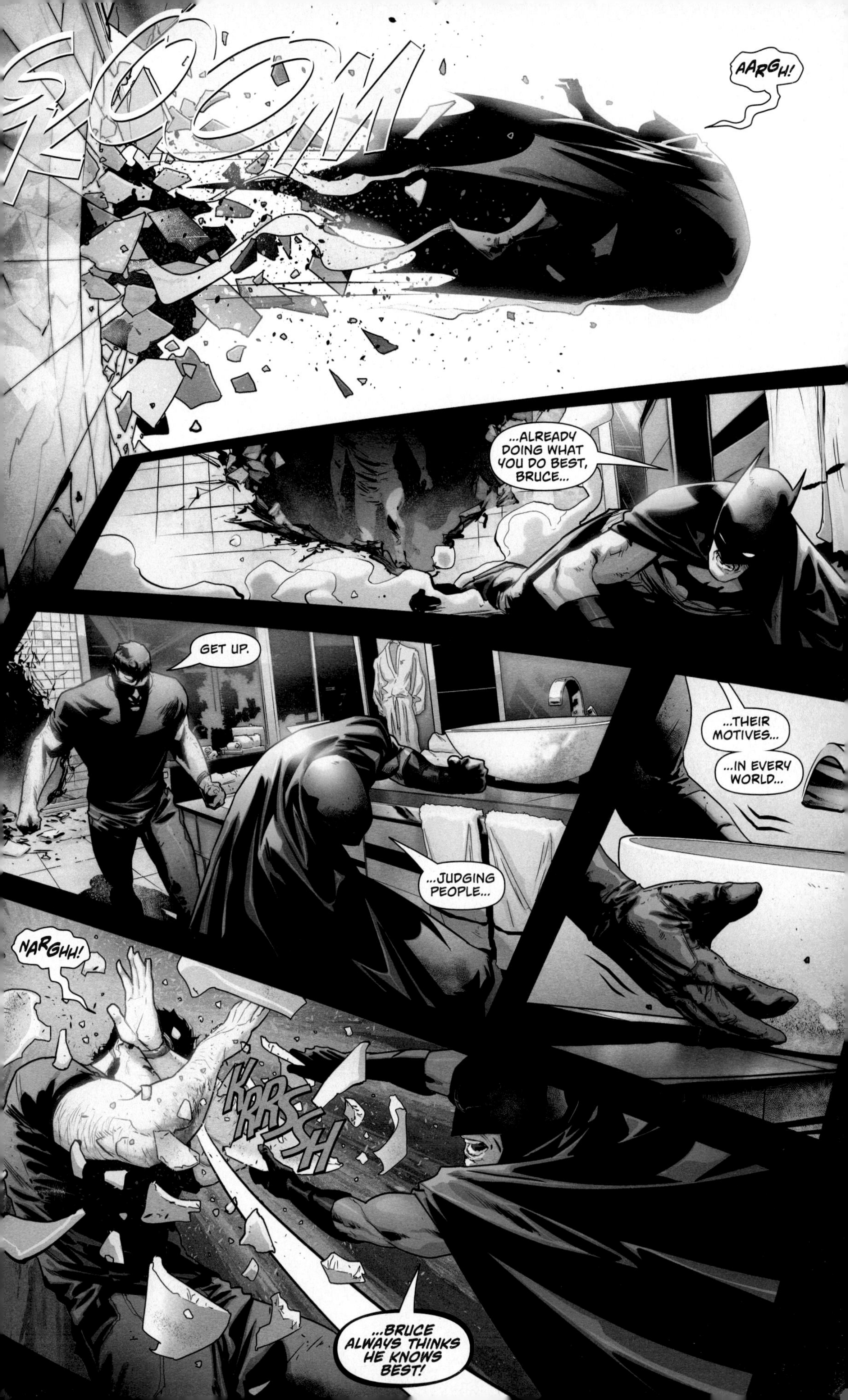
SKOOM
AARGH!
...ALREADY DOING WHAT YOU DO BEST, BRUCE...
GET UP.
...JUDGING PEOPLE...
...THEIR MOTIVES...
...IN EVERY WORLD...
NARGHH!
KRRSCH
...BRUCE ALWAYS THINKS HE KNOWS BEST!

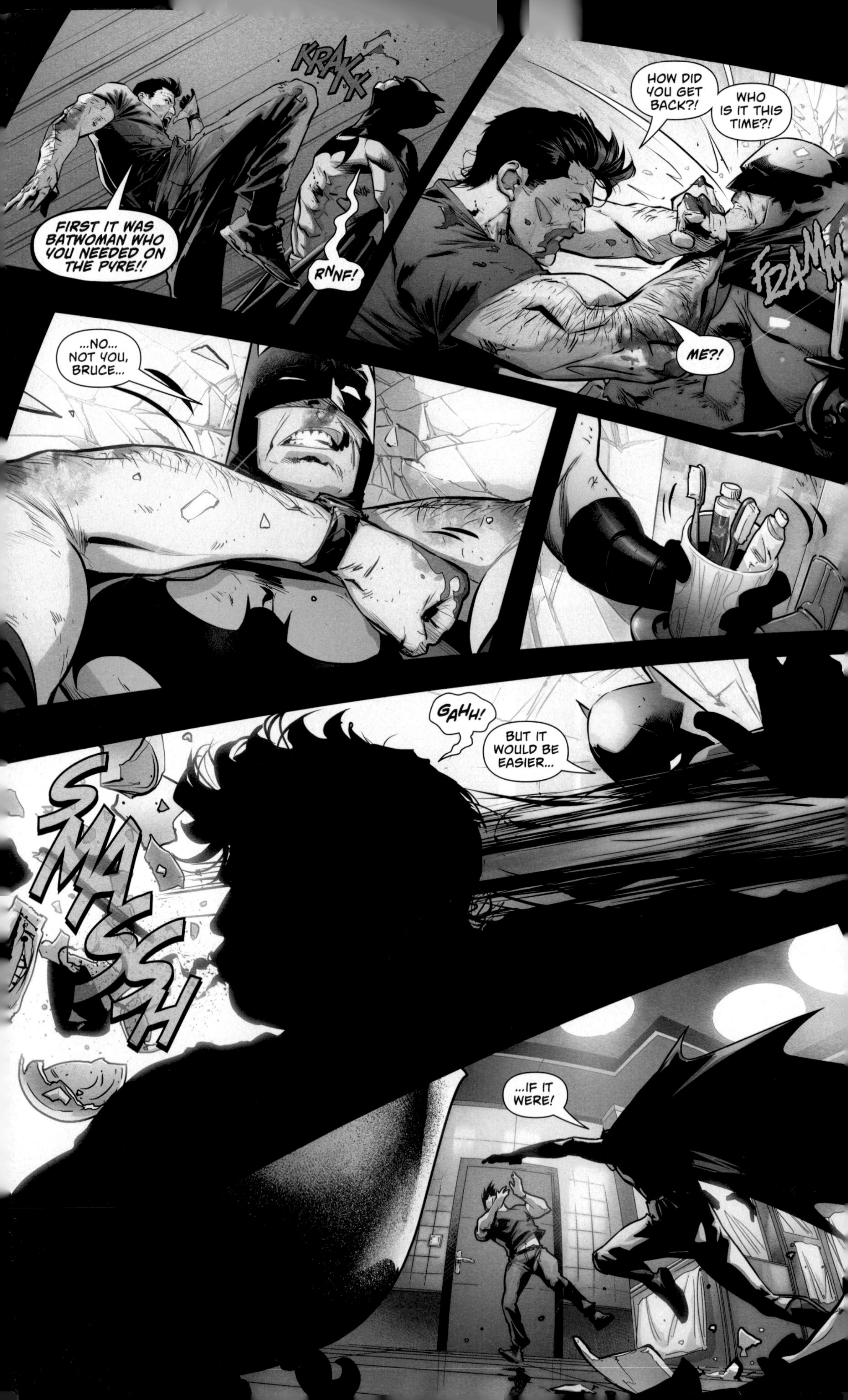
KRAKK
FIRST IT WAS BATWOMAN WHO YOU NEEDED ON THE PYRE!!
RNNF!
HOW DID YOU GET BACK?!
WHO IS IT THIS TIME?!
FRAM
ME?!
...NO... NOT YOU, BRUCE...
GAHH!
BUT IT WOULD BE EASIER...
SMASSH
...IF IT WERE!

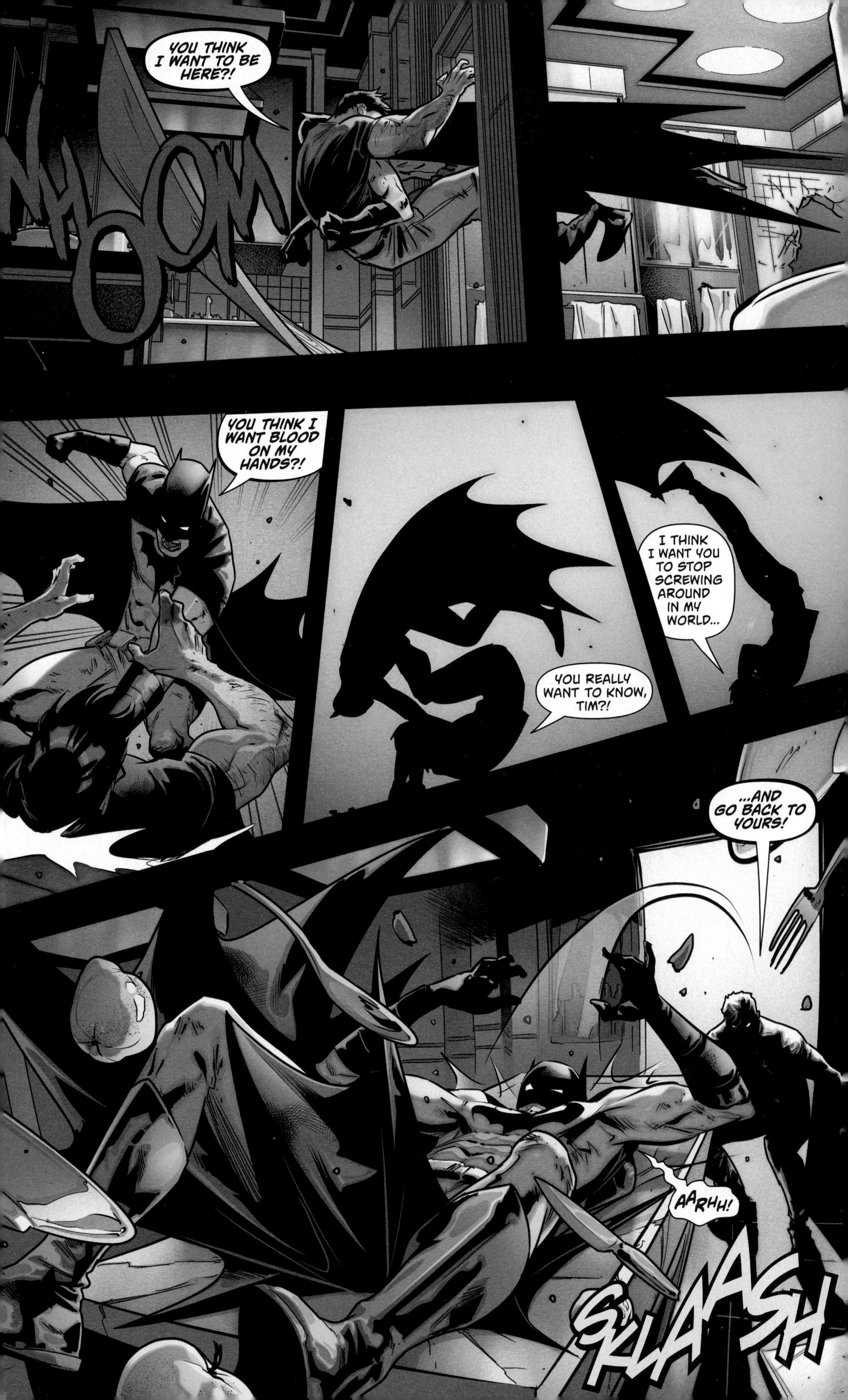
YOU THINK I WANT TO BE HERE?!
WHOOOM
YOU THINK I WANT BLOOD ON MY HANDS?!
I THINK I WANT YOU TO STOP SCREWING AROUND IN MY WORLD...
YOU REALLY WANT TO KNOW, TIM?!
...AND GO BACK TO YOURS!
AARHH!
SKLAASH

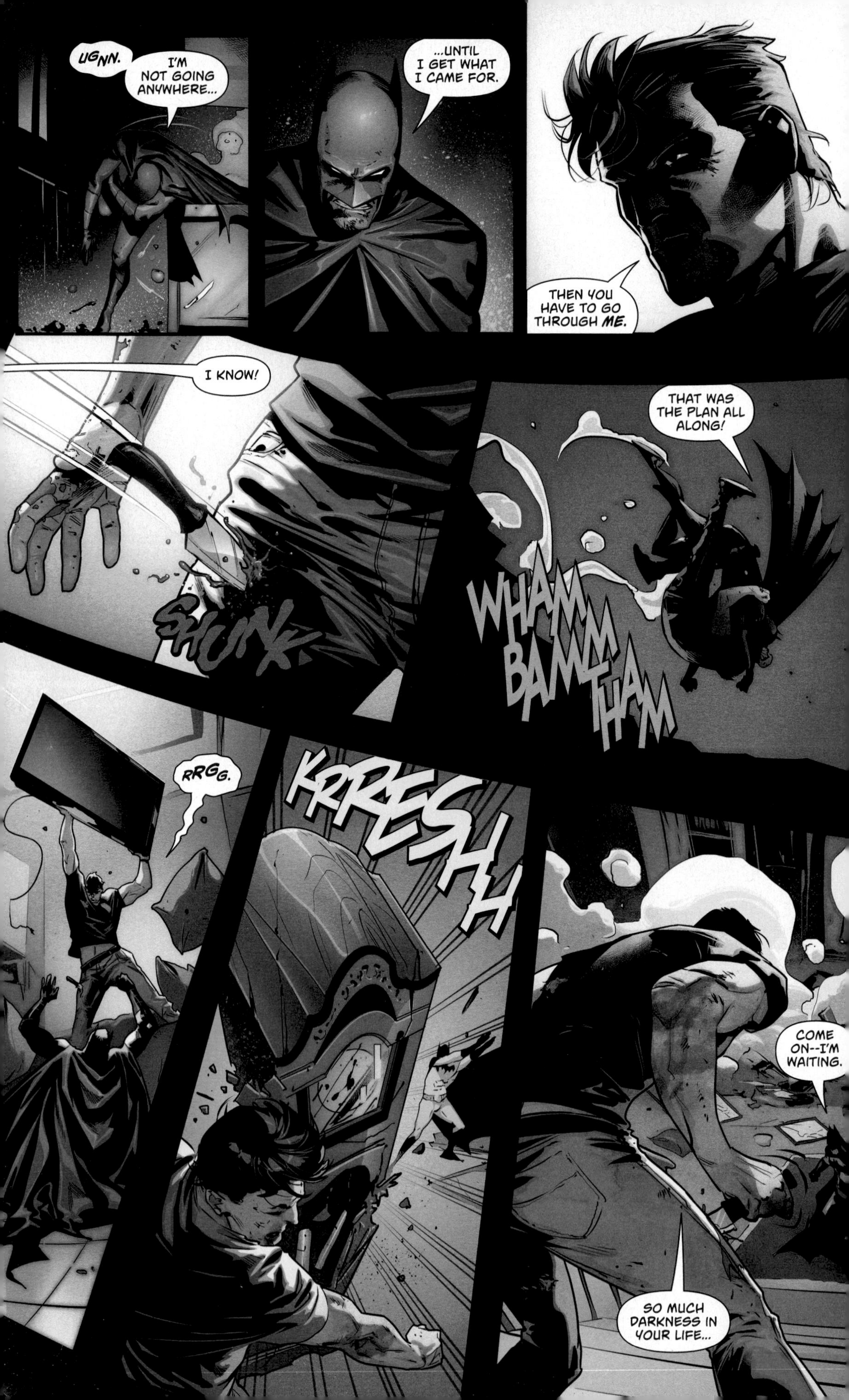
UGNN.
I'M NOT GOING ANYWHERE...
...UNTIL I GET WHAT I CAME FOR.
THEN YOU HAVE TO GO THROUGH ME.
I KNOW!
SHUNK
THAT WAS THE PLAN ALL ALONG!
WHAMM BAMM THAM
RRGG.
KRRESHH
COME ON--I'M WAITING.
SO MUCH DARKNESS IN YOUR LIFE...

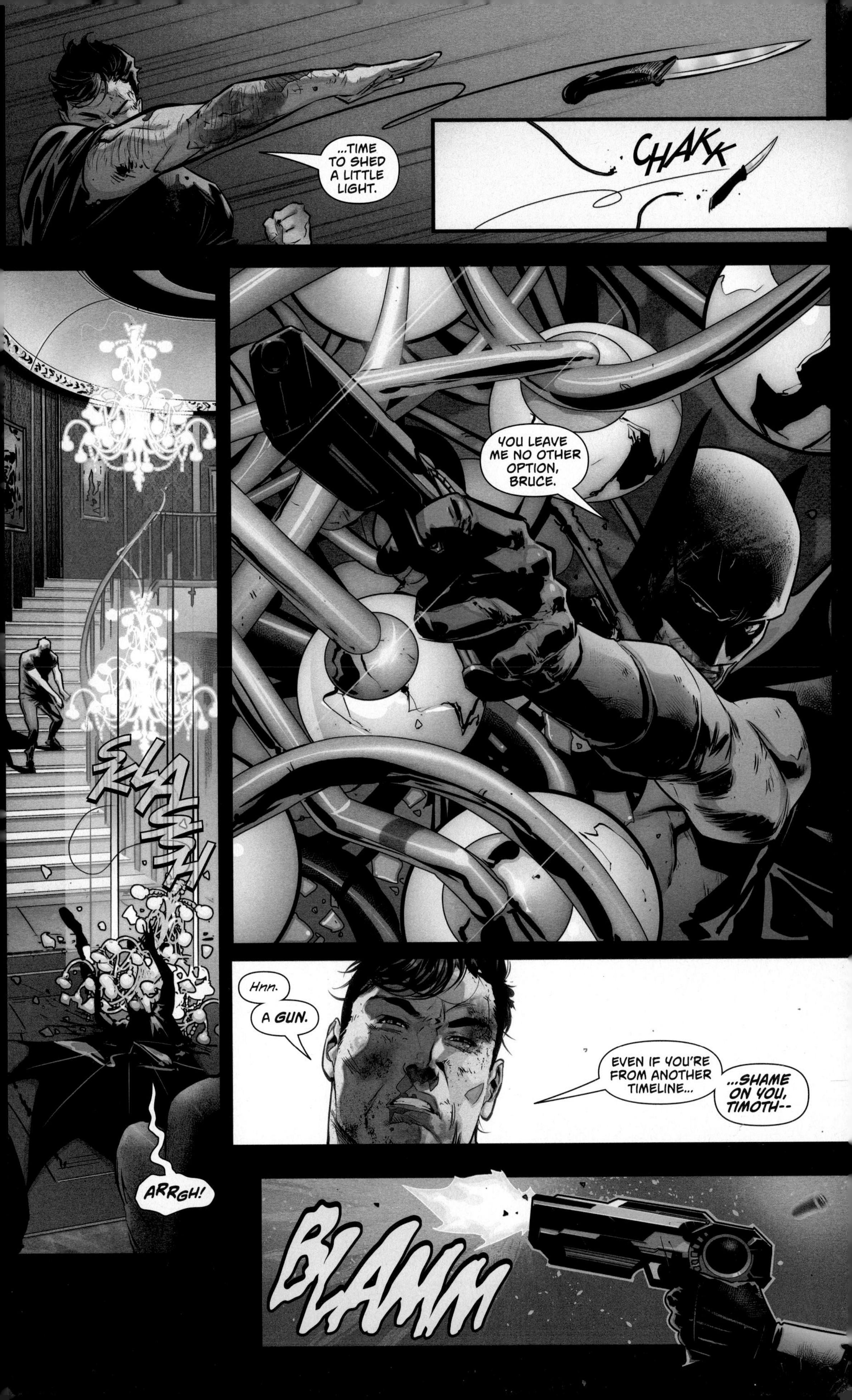
...TIME TO SHED A LITTLE LIGHT.
CHAKK
YOU LEAVE ME NO OTHER OPTION, BRUCE.
SHWUNN
ARRGH!
Hnn.
A GUN.
EVEN IF YOU'RE FROM ANOTHER TIMELINE...
...SHAME ON YOU, TIMOTH--
BLAMM

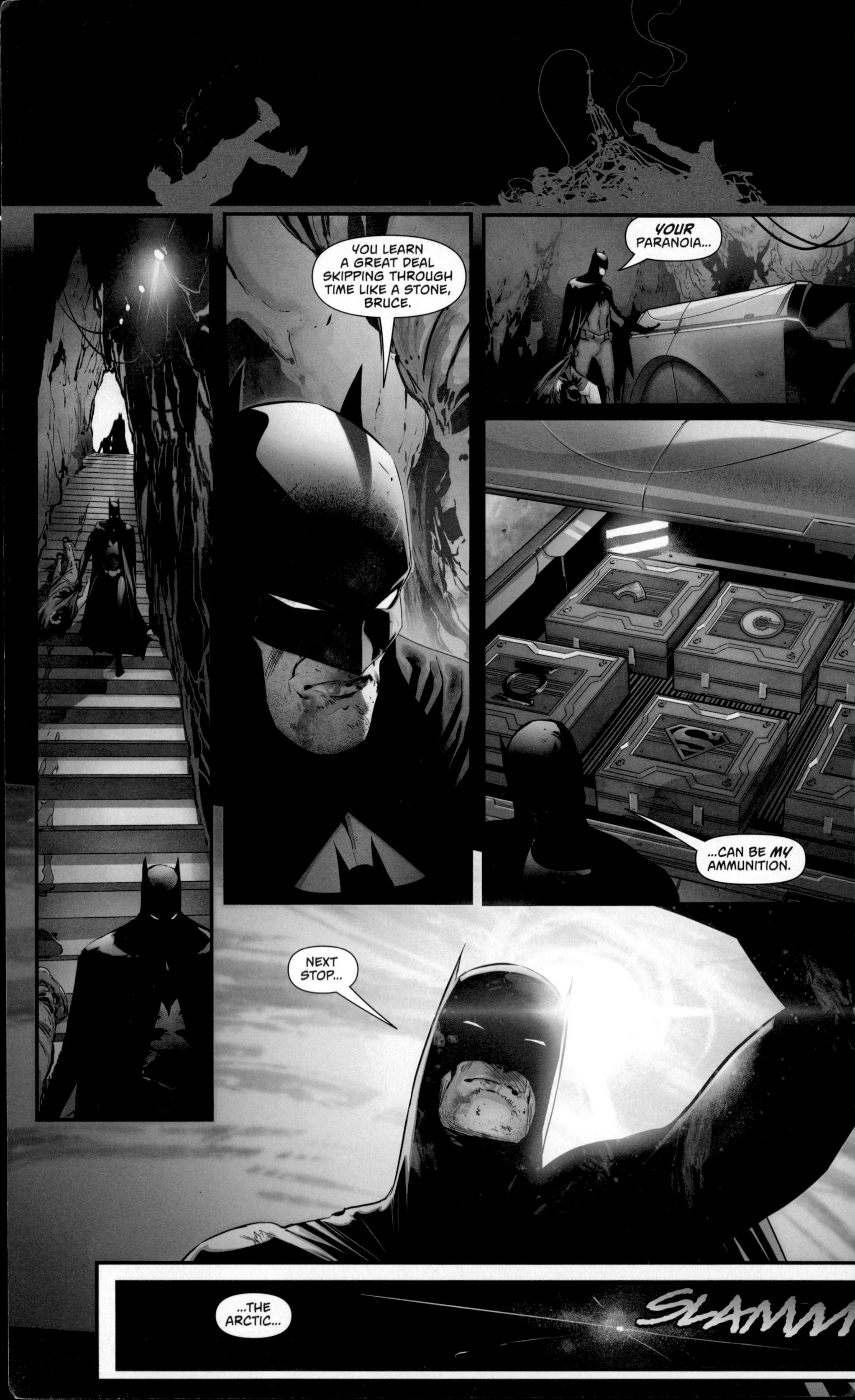
YOU LEARN A GREAT DEAL SKIPPING THROUGH TIME LIKE A STONE, BRUCE.
YOUR PARANOIA...
...CAN BE MY AMMUNITION.
NEXT STOP...
...THE ARCTIC...
SLAMM

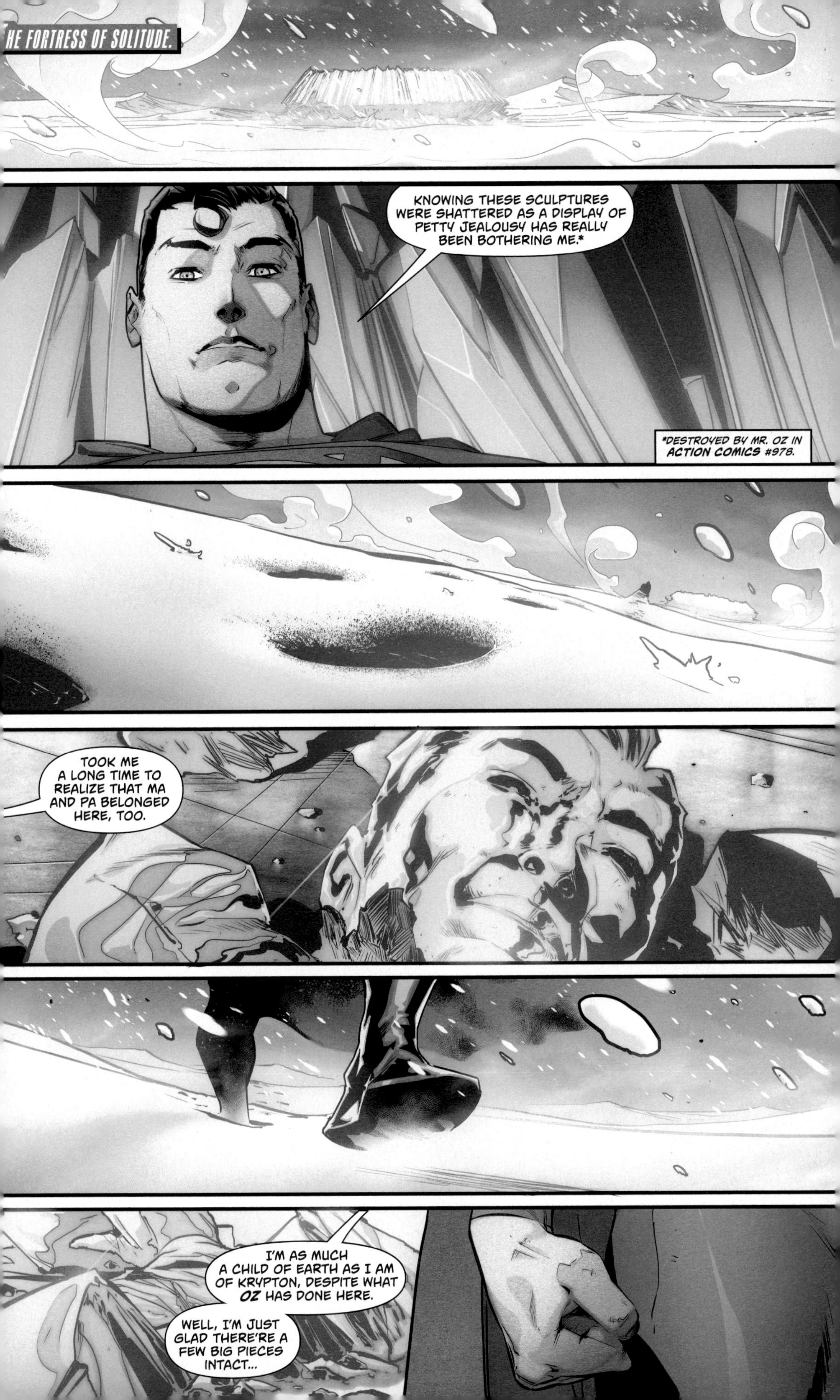
HE FORTRESS OF SOLITUDE.
KNOWING THESE SCULPTURES WERE SHATTERED AS A DISPLAY OF PETTY JEALOUSY HAS REALLY BEEN BOTHERING ME.*
*DESTROYED BY MR. OZ IN ACTION COMICS #978.
TOOK ME A LONG TIME TO REALIZE THAT MA AND PA BELONGED HERE, TOO.
I'M AS MUCH A CHILD OF EARTH AS I AM OF KRYPTON, DESPITE WHAT OZ HAS DONE HERE.
WELL, I'M JUST GLAD THERE'RE A FEW BIG PIECES INTACT...

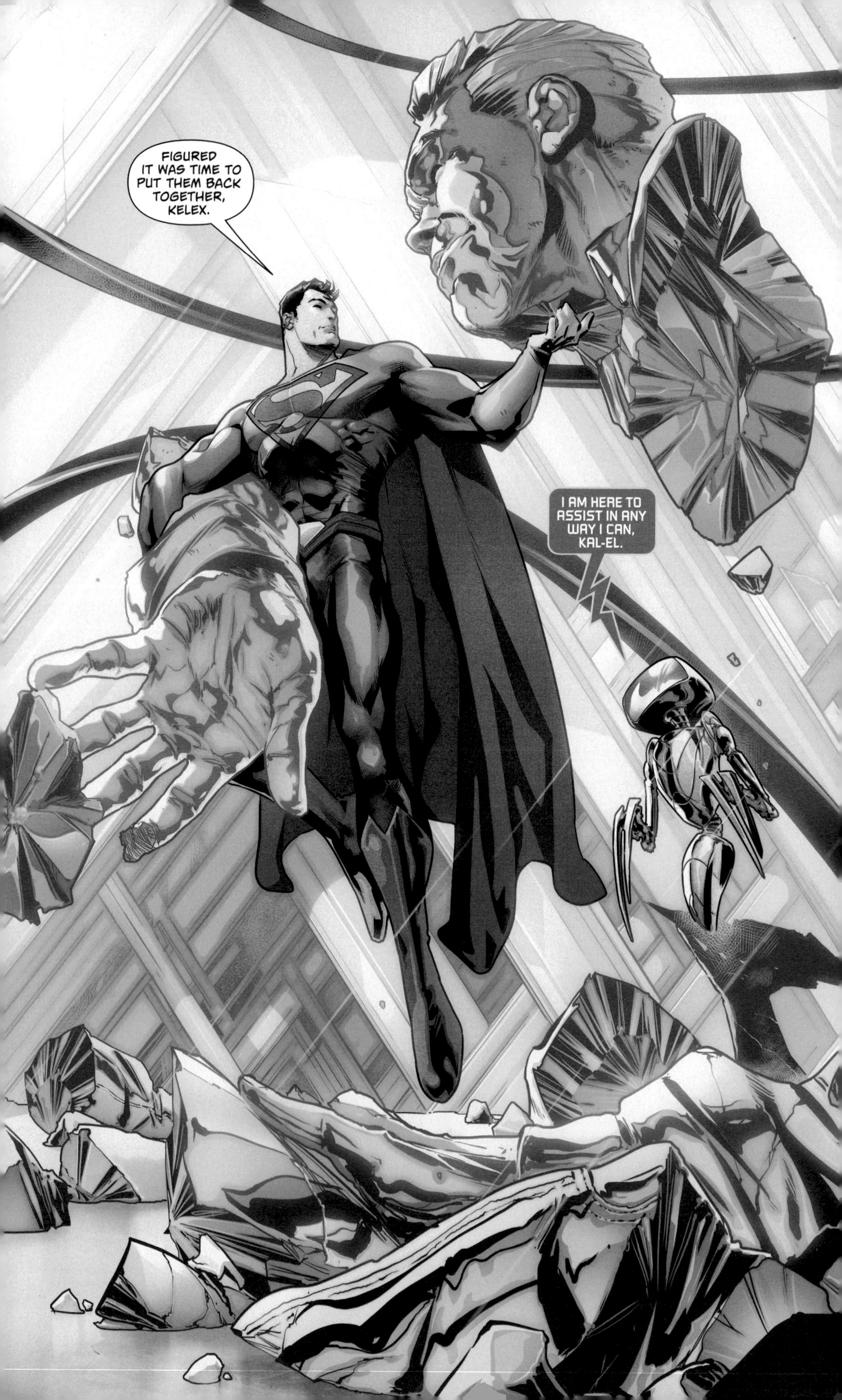
FIGURED IT WAS TIME TO PUT THEM BACK TOGETHER, KELEX.
I AM HERE TO ASSIST IN ANY WAY I CAN, KAL-EL.

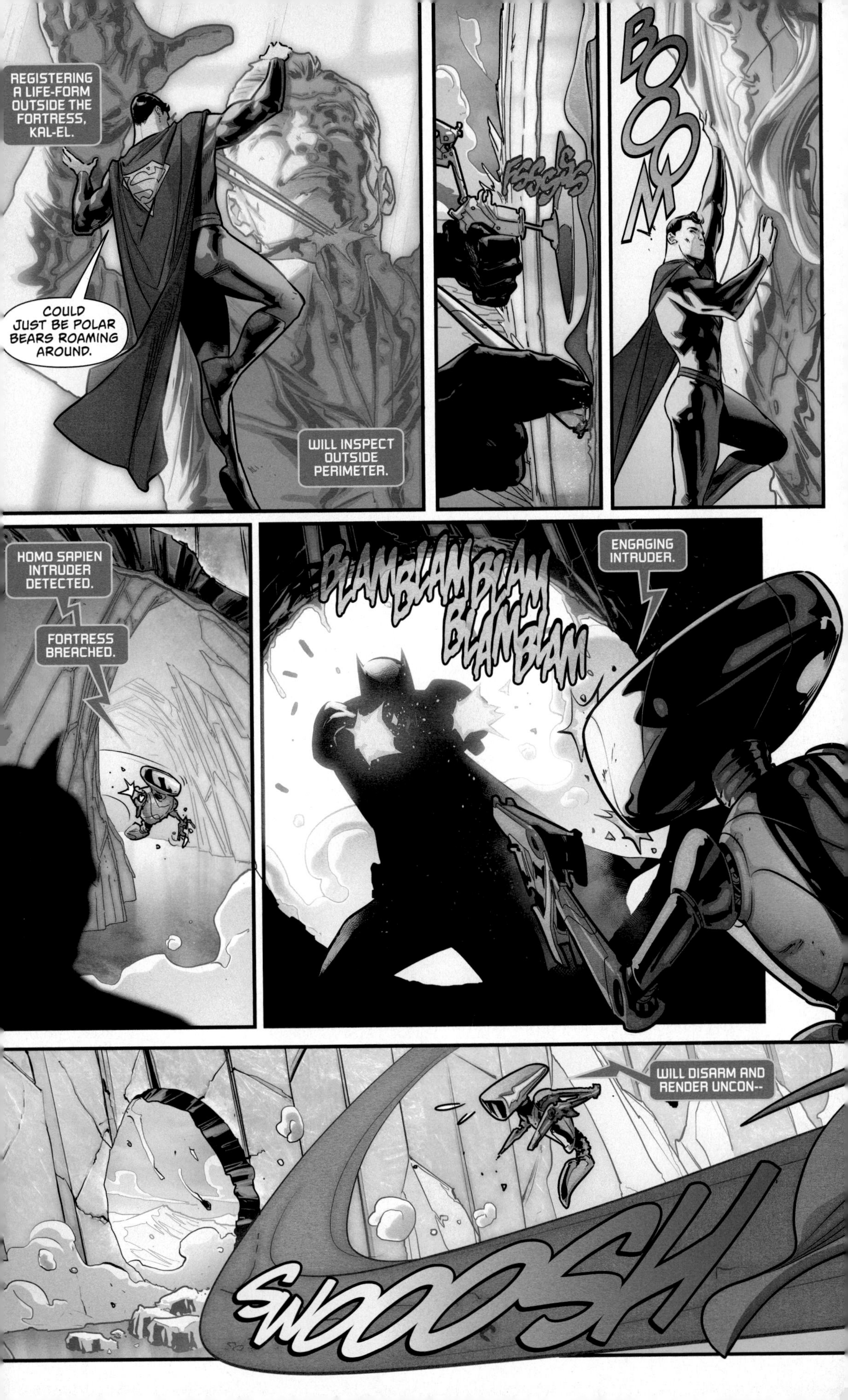
REGISTERING A LIFE-FORM OUTSIDE THE FORTRESS, KAL-EL.
COULD JUST BE POLAR BEARS ROAMING AROUND.
WILL INSPECT OUTSIDE PERIMETER.
FSSSSS
BOOM
HOMO SAPIEN INTRUDER DETECTED.
FORTRESS BREACHED.
ENGAGING INTRUDER.
BLAMBLAMBLAM BLAMBLAM
WILL DISARM AND RENDER UNCON--
SWOOSH

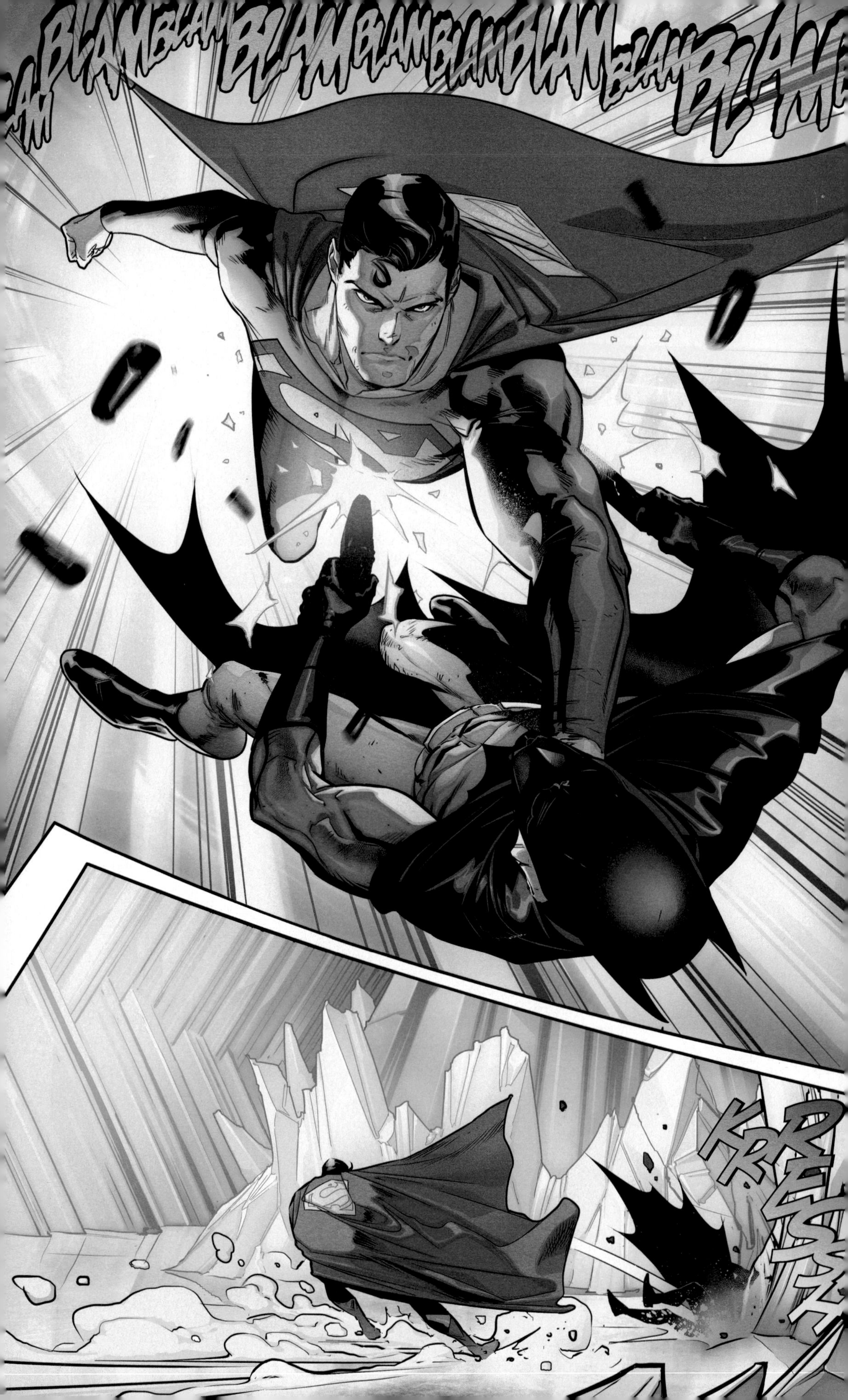
BLAM BLAM BLAM BLAM BLAM BLAM BLAM
KRRESSH

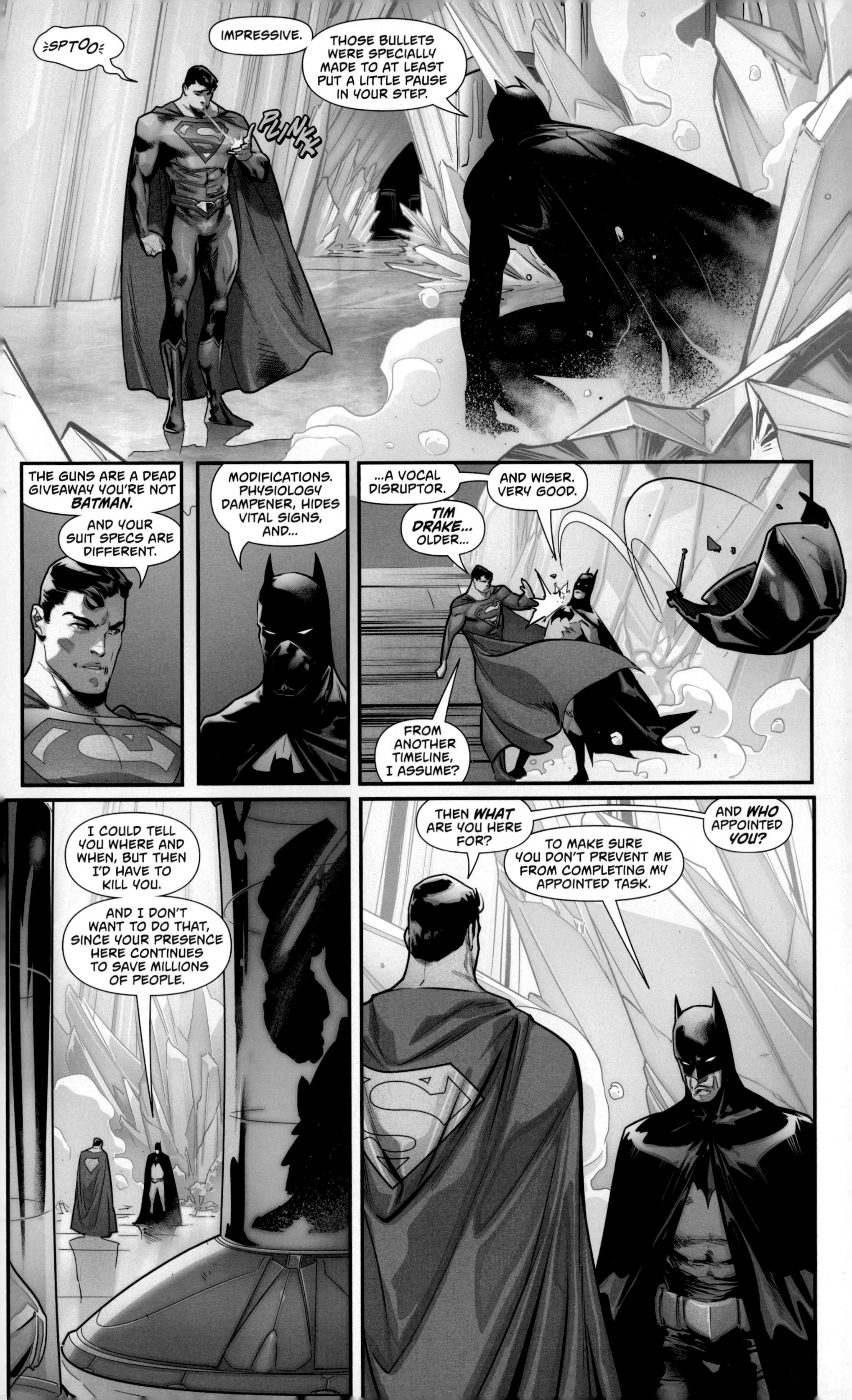
SPTOO
IMPRESSIVE.
THOSE BULLETS WERE SPECIALLY MADE TO AT LEAST PUT A LITTLE PAUSE IN YOUR STEP.
PLINK
THE GUNS ARE A DEAD GIVEAWAY YOU'RE NOT BATMAN.
AND YOUR SUIT SPECS ARE DIFFERENT.
MODIFICATIONS. PHYSIOLOGY DAMPENER, HIDES VITAL SIGNS, AND...
...A VOCAL DISRUPTOR.
TIM DRAKE... OLDER...
AND WISER. VERY GOOD.
FROM ANOTHER TIMELINE, I ASSUME?
I COULD TELL YOU WHERE AND WHEN, BUT THEN I'D HAVE TO KILL YOU.
AND I DON'T WANT TO DO THAT, SINCE YOUR PRESENCE HERE CONTINUES TO SAVE MILLIONS OF PEOPLE.
THEN WHAT ARE YOU HERE FOR?
TO MAKE SURE YOU DON'T PREVENT ME FROM COMPLETING MY APPOINTED TASK.
AND WHO APPOINTED YOU?

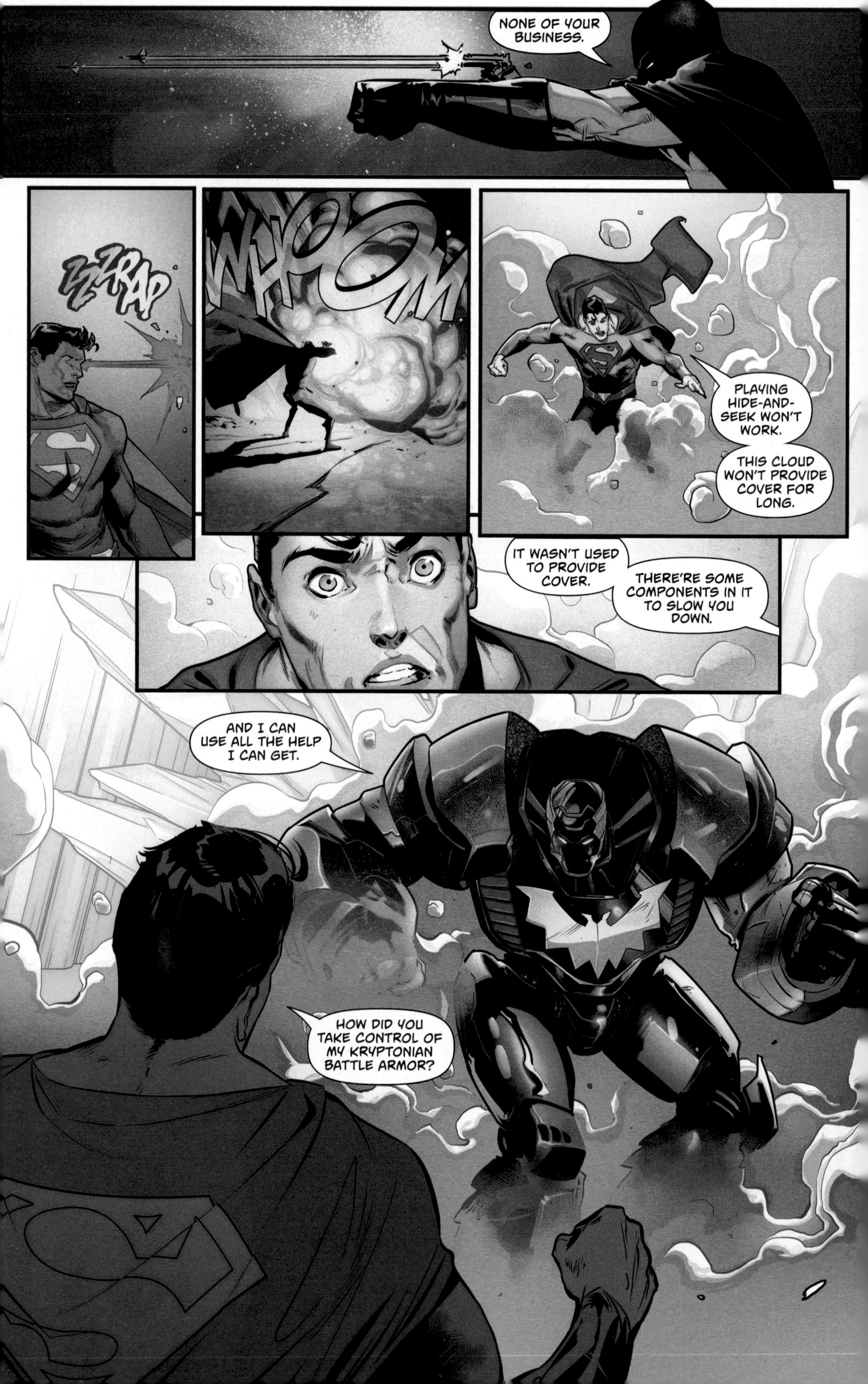
NONE OF YOUR BUSINESS.
WHOOM
PLAYING HIDE-AND-SEEK WON'T WORK.
THIS CLOUD WON'T PROVIDE COVER FOR LONG.
IT WASN'T USED TO PROVIDE COVER.
THERE'RE SOME COMPONENTS IN IT TO SLOW YOU DOWN.
AND I CAN USE ALL THE HELP I CAN GET.
HOW DID YOU TAKE CONTROL OF MY KRYPTONIAN BATTLE ARMOR?

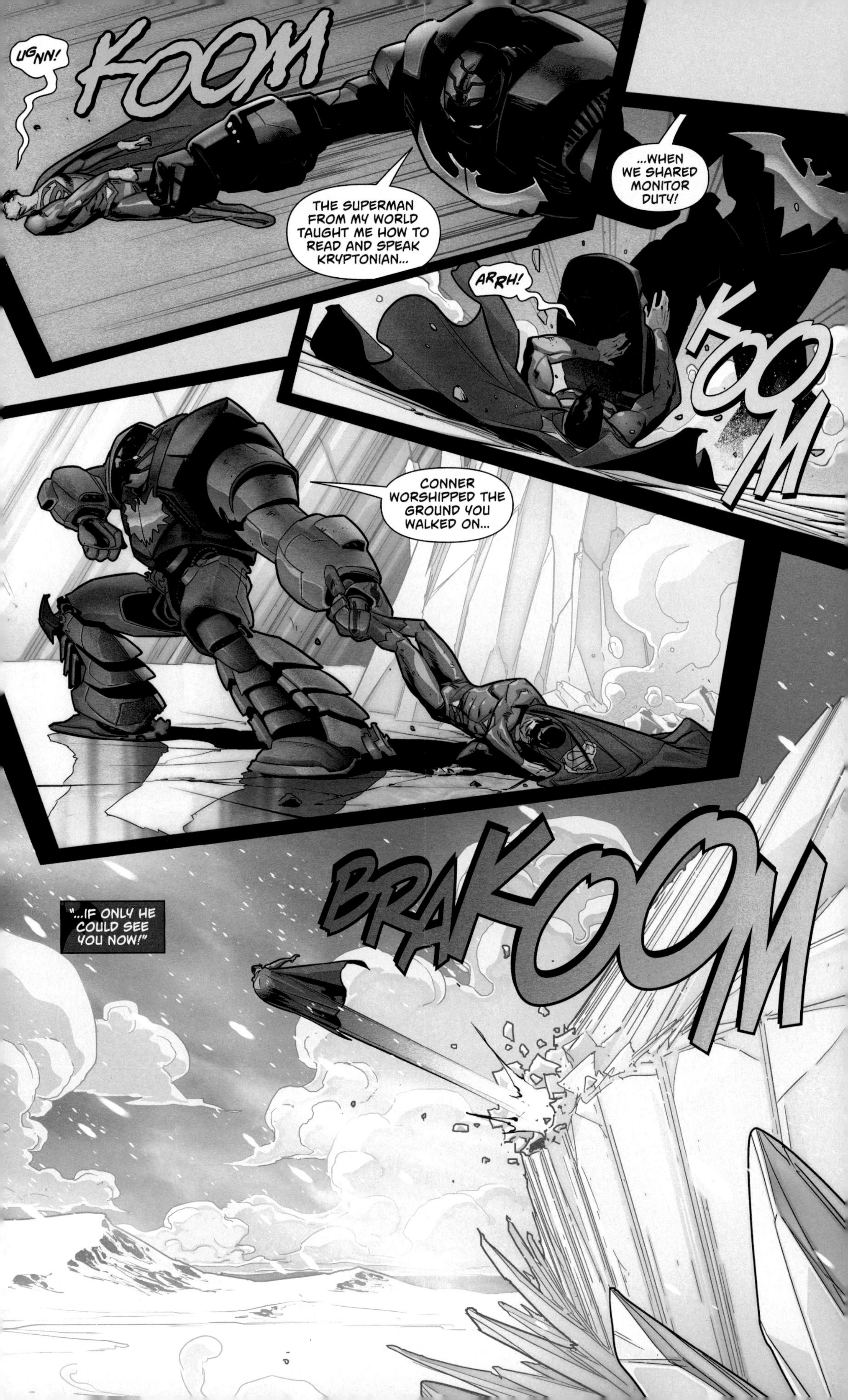
UGNN!
KOOM
THE SUPERMAN FROM MY WORLD TAUGHT ME HOW TO READ AND SPEAK KRYPTONIAN...
...WHEN WE SHARED MONITOR DUTY!
ARRH!
KOOM
CONNER WORSHIPPED THE GROUND YOU WALKED ON...
BRAKOOM
"...IF ONLY HE COULD SEE YOU NOW!"

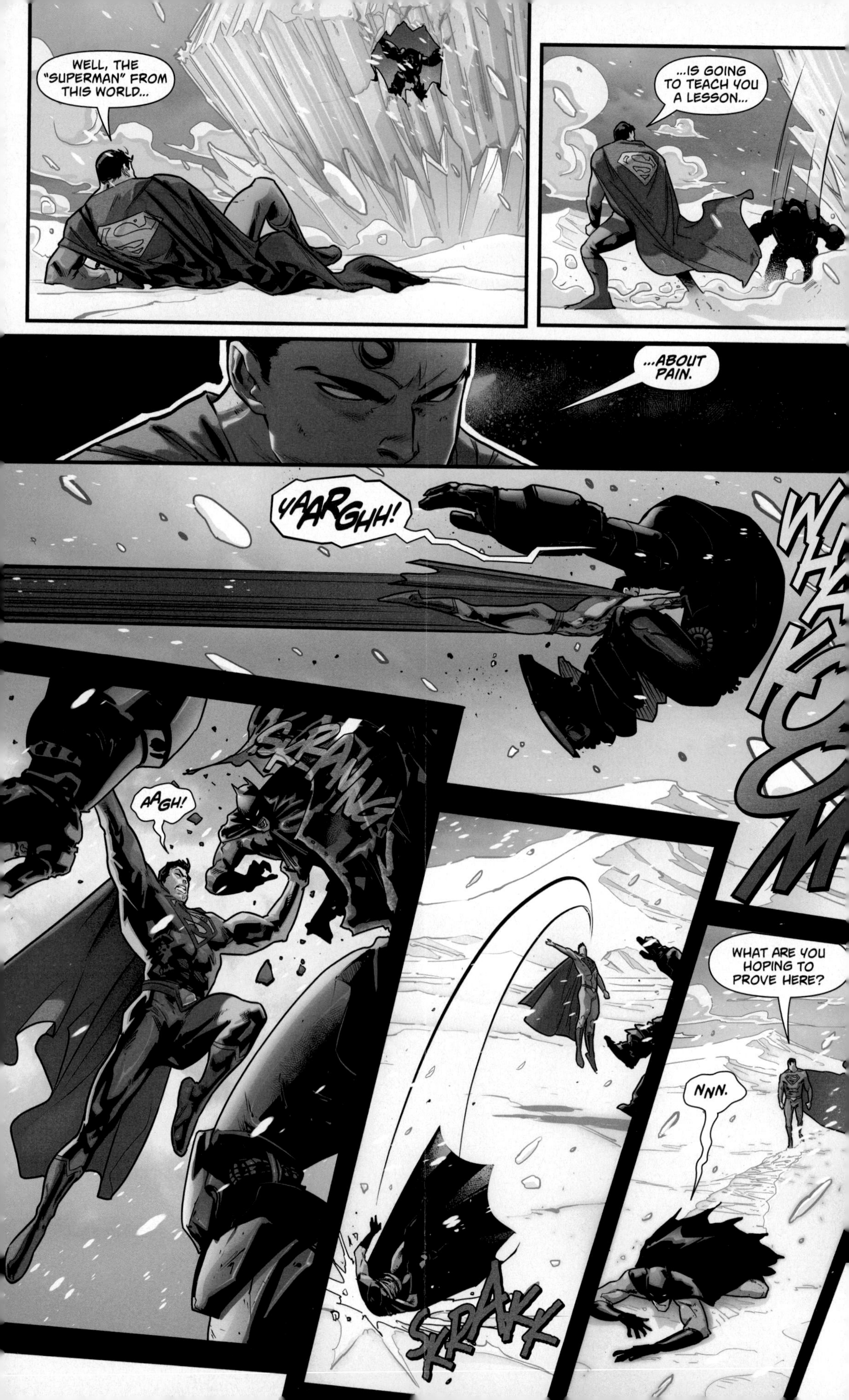
WELL, THE "SUPERMAN" FROM THIS WORLD...
...IS GOING TO TEACH YOU A LESSON...
...ABOUT PAIN.
YAARGHH!
WHAKOOM
AAGH!
SKRANNG!
SKRAKK
WHAT ARE YOU HOPING TO PROVE HERE?
NNN.

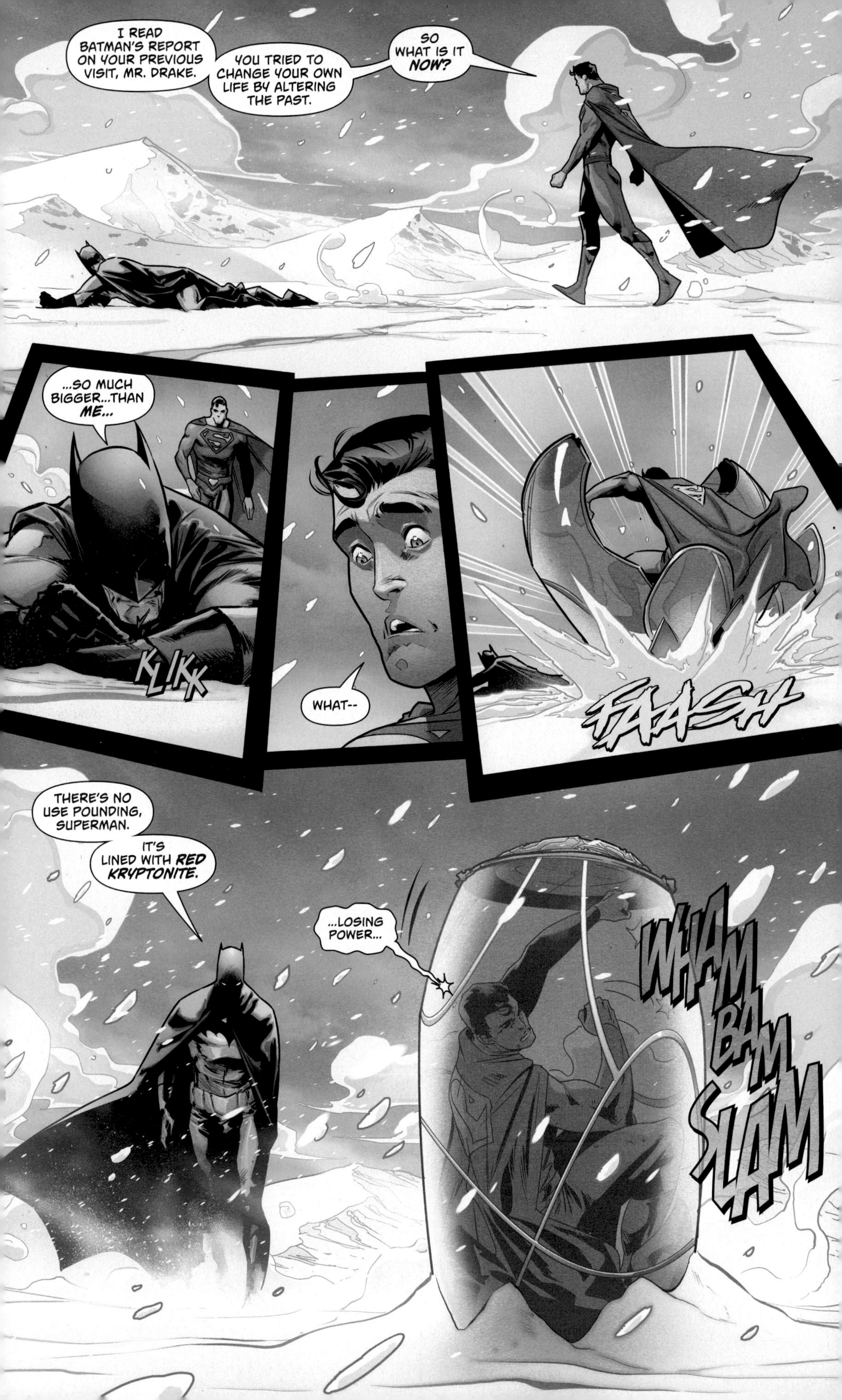
I READ BATMAN'S REPORT ON YOUR PREVIOUS VISIT, MR. DRAKE.
YOU TRIED TO CHANGE YOUR OWN LIFE BY ALTERING THE PAST.
SO WHAT IS IT NOW?
...SO MUCH BIGGER...THAN ME...
KLIKK
WHAT--
FAASH
THERE'S NO USE POUNDING, SUPERMAN.
IT'S LINED WITH RED KRYPTONITE.
...LOSING POWER...
WHAM
BAM
SLAM

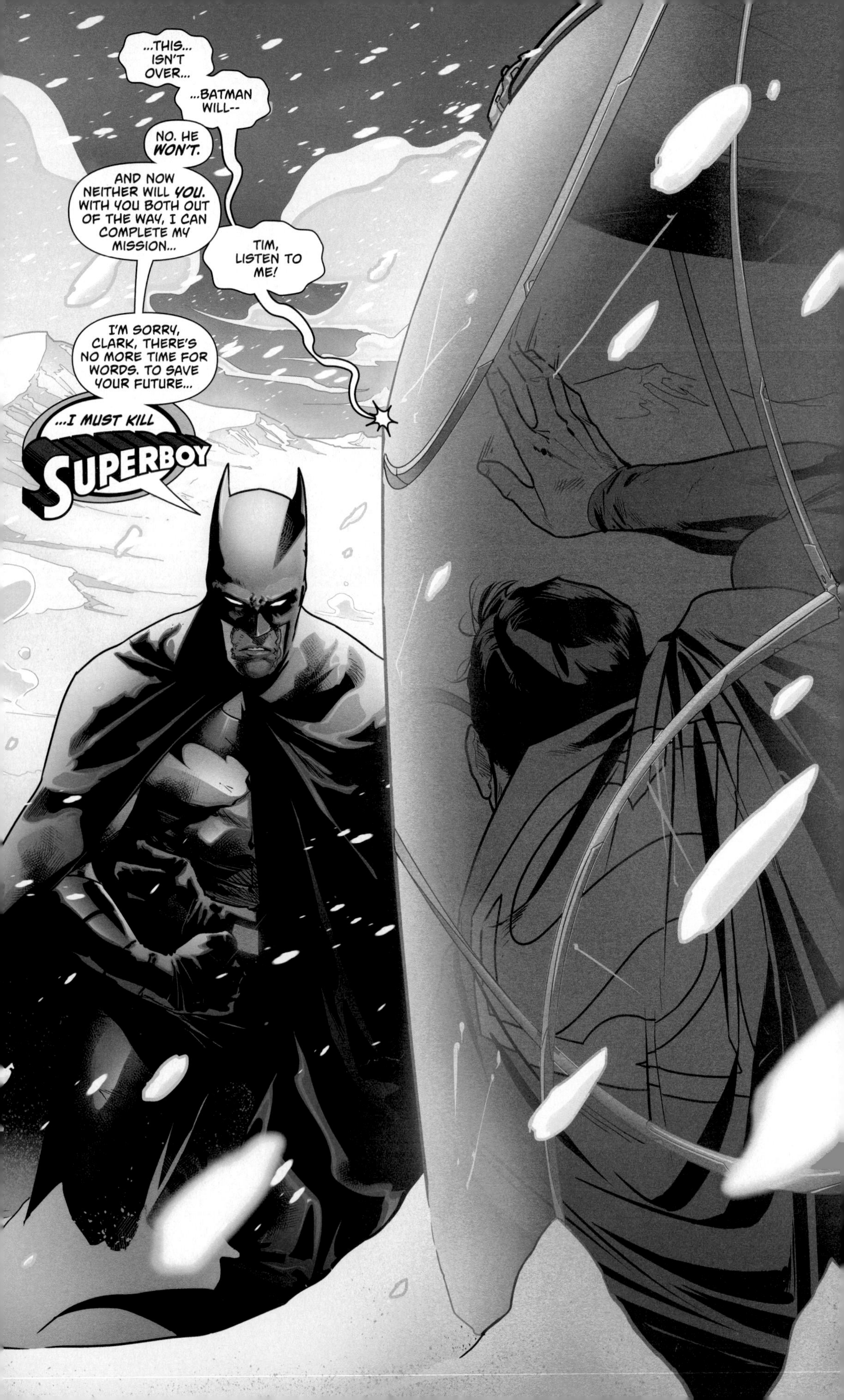
...THIS... ISN'T OVER...
...BATMAN WILL--
NO. HE WON'T.
AND NOW NEITHER WILL YOU. WITH YOU BOTH OUT OF THE WAY, I CAN COMPLETE MY MISSION...
TIM, LISTEN TO ME!
I'M SORRY, CLARK, THERE'S NO MORE TIME FOR WORDS. TO SAVE YOUR FUTURE...
...I MUST KILL SUPERBOY

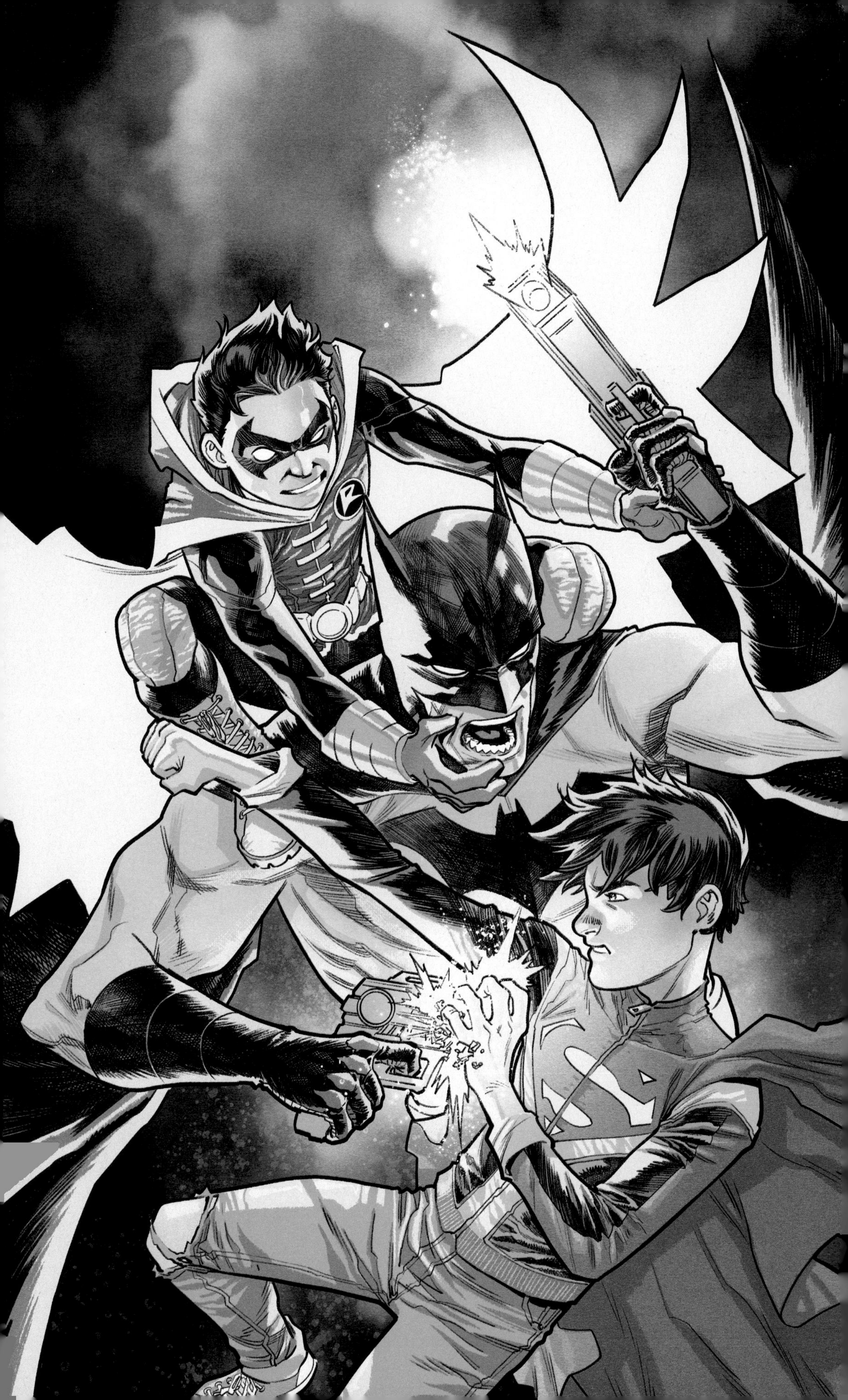

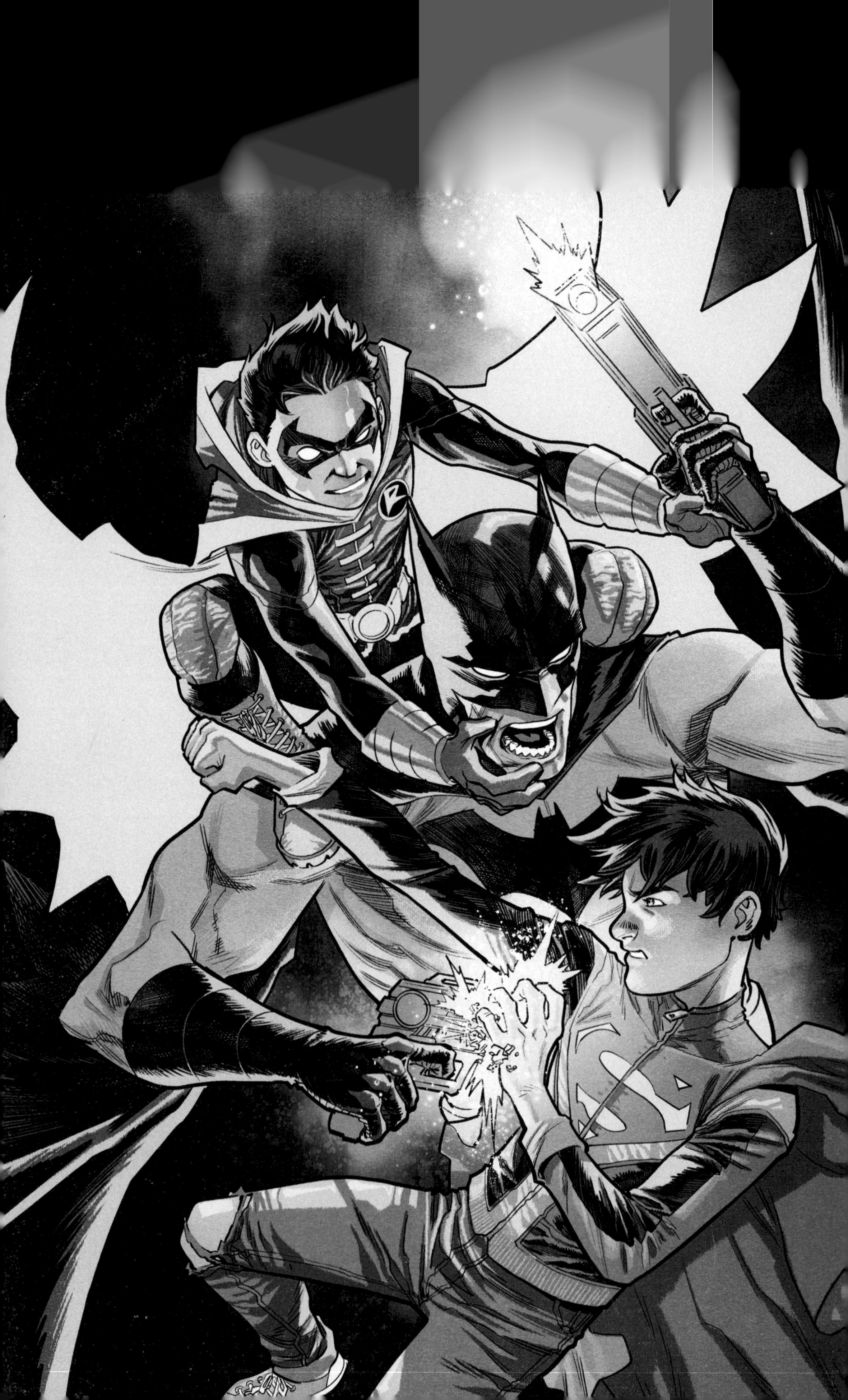

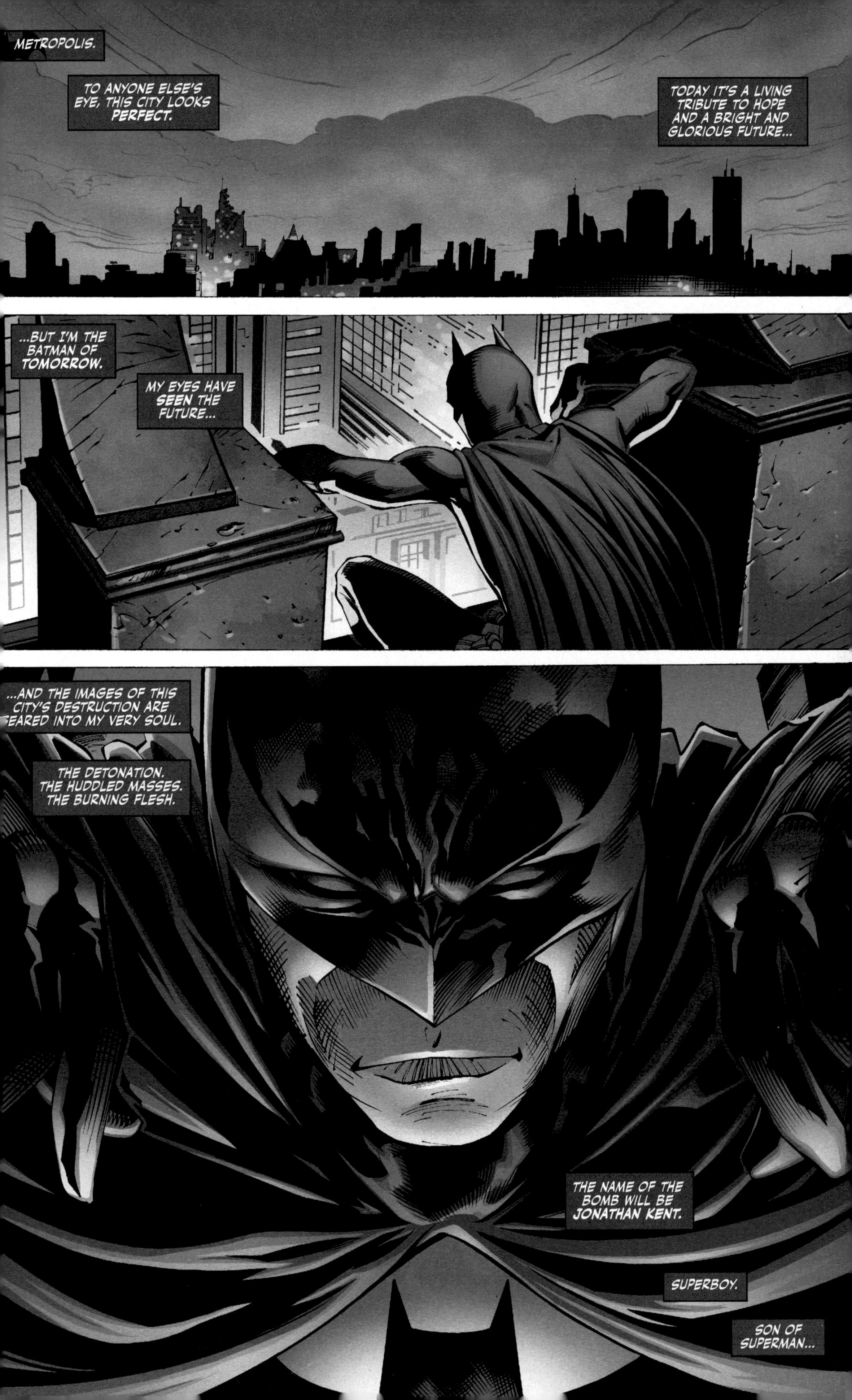
METROPOLIS.
TO ANYONE ELSE'S EYE, THIS CITY LOOKS PERFECT.
TODAY IT'S A LIVING TRIBUTE TO HOPE AND A BRIGHT AND GLORIOUS FUTURE...
...BUT I'M THE BATMAN OF TOMORROW.
MY EYES HAVE SEEN THE FUTURE...
...AND THE IMAGES OF THIS CITY'S DESTRUCTION ARE SEARED INTO MY VERY SOUL.
THE DETONATION. THE HUDDLED MASSES. THE BURNING FLESH.
THE NAME OF THE BOMB WILL BE JONATHAN KENT.
SUPERBOY.
SON OF SUPERMAN...

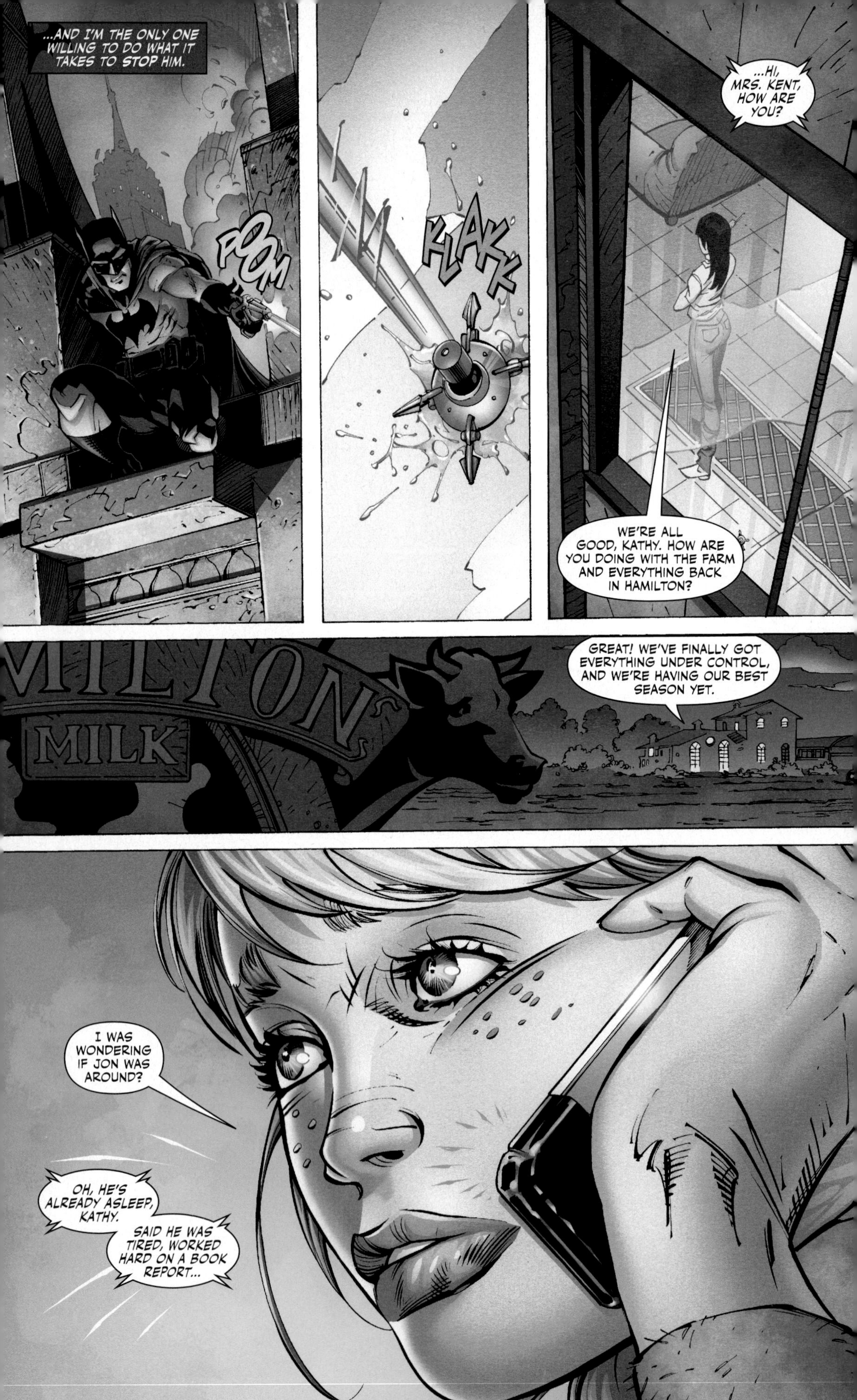
...AND I'M THE ONLY ONE WILLING TO DO WHAT IT TAKES TO STOP HIM.
POOM
KLAK
...HI, MRS. KENT, HOW ARE YOU?
WE'RE ALL GOOD, KATHY. HOW ARE YOU DOING WITH THE FARM AND EVERYTHING BACK IN HAMILTON?
MILTON
MILK
GREAT! WE'VE FINALLY GOT EVERYTHING UNDER CONTROL, AND WE'RE HAVING OUR BEST SEASON YET.
I WAS WONDERING IF JON WAS AROUND?
OH, HE'S ALREADY ASLEEP, KATHY.
SAID HE WAS TIRED, WORKED HARD ON A BOOK REPORT...

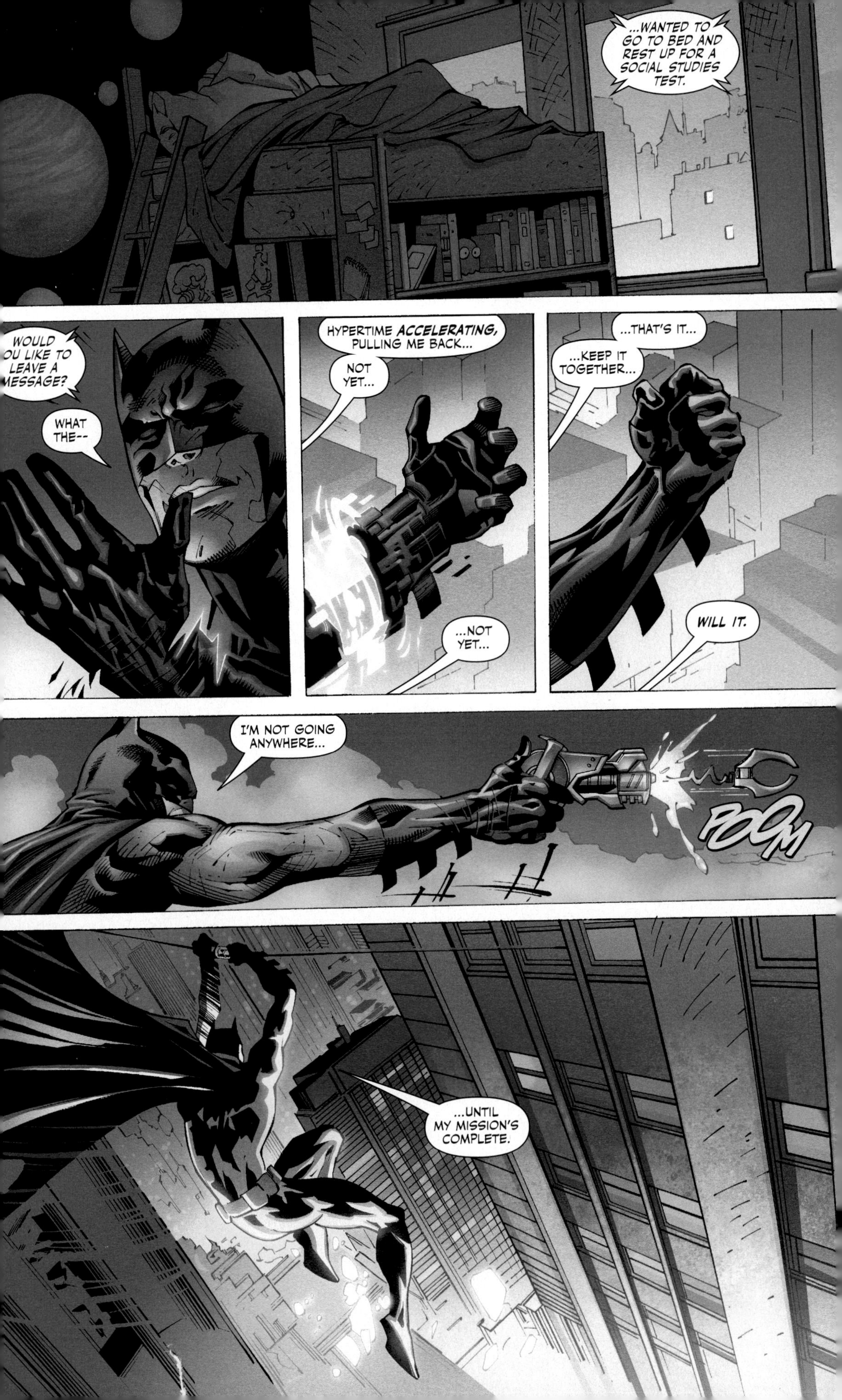
...WANTED TO GO TO BED AND REST UP FOR A SOCIAL STUDIES TEST.
WOULD OU LIKE TO LEAVE A MESSAGE?
WHAT THE--
HYPERTIME *ACCELERATING,* PULLING ME BACK...
NOT YET...
...NOT YET...
...THAT'S IT...
...KEEP IT TOGETHER...
WILL IT.
I'M NOT GOING ANYWHERE...
POOM
...UNTIL MY MISSION'S COMPLETE.

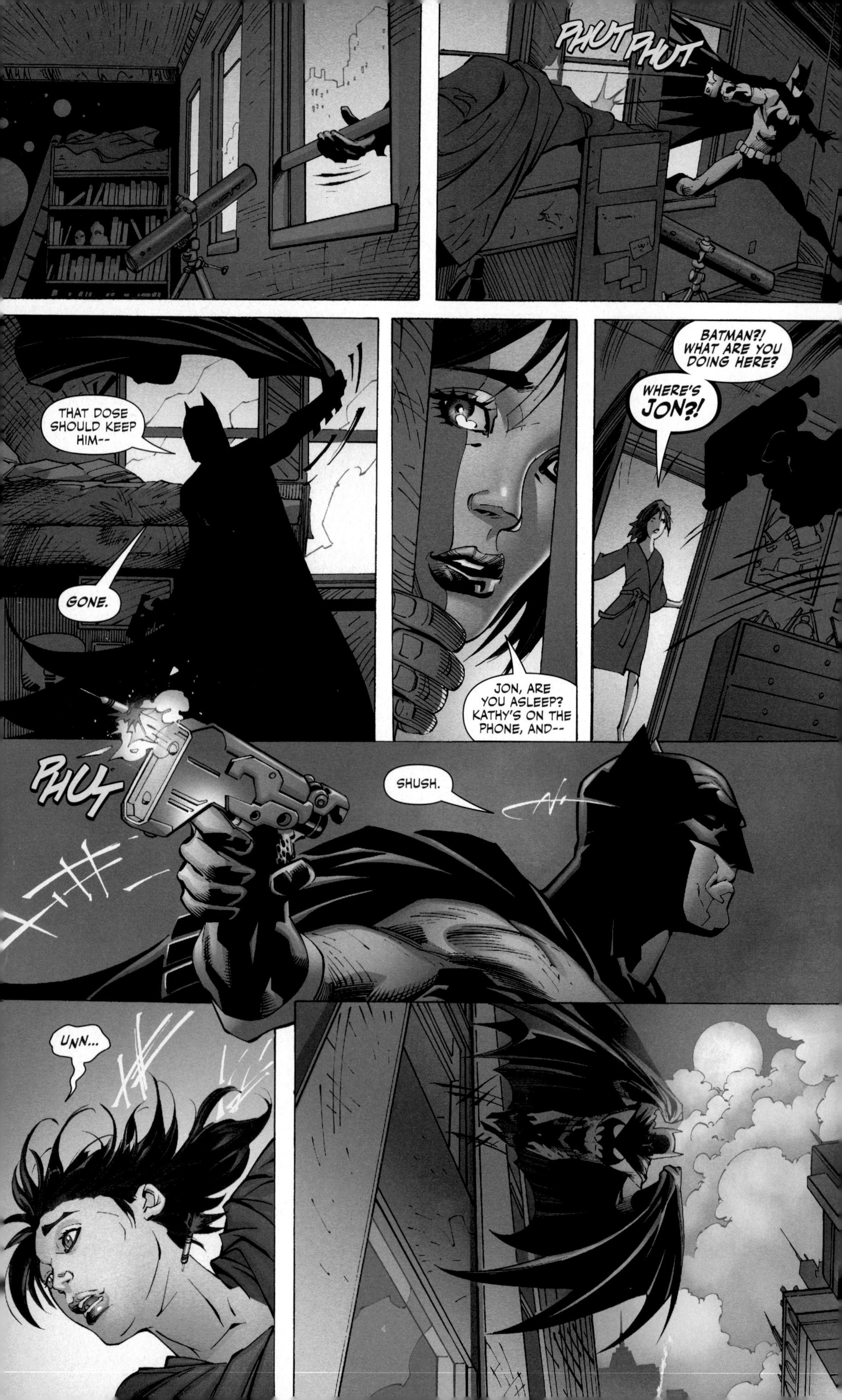
PHUT PHUT
THAT DOSE SHOULD KEEP HIM--
GONE.
JON, ARE YOU ASLEEP? KATHY'S ON THE PHONE, AND--
BATMAN?! WHAT ARE YOU DOING HERE?
WHERE'S JON?!
PHUT
SHUSH.
UNN...

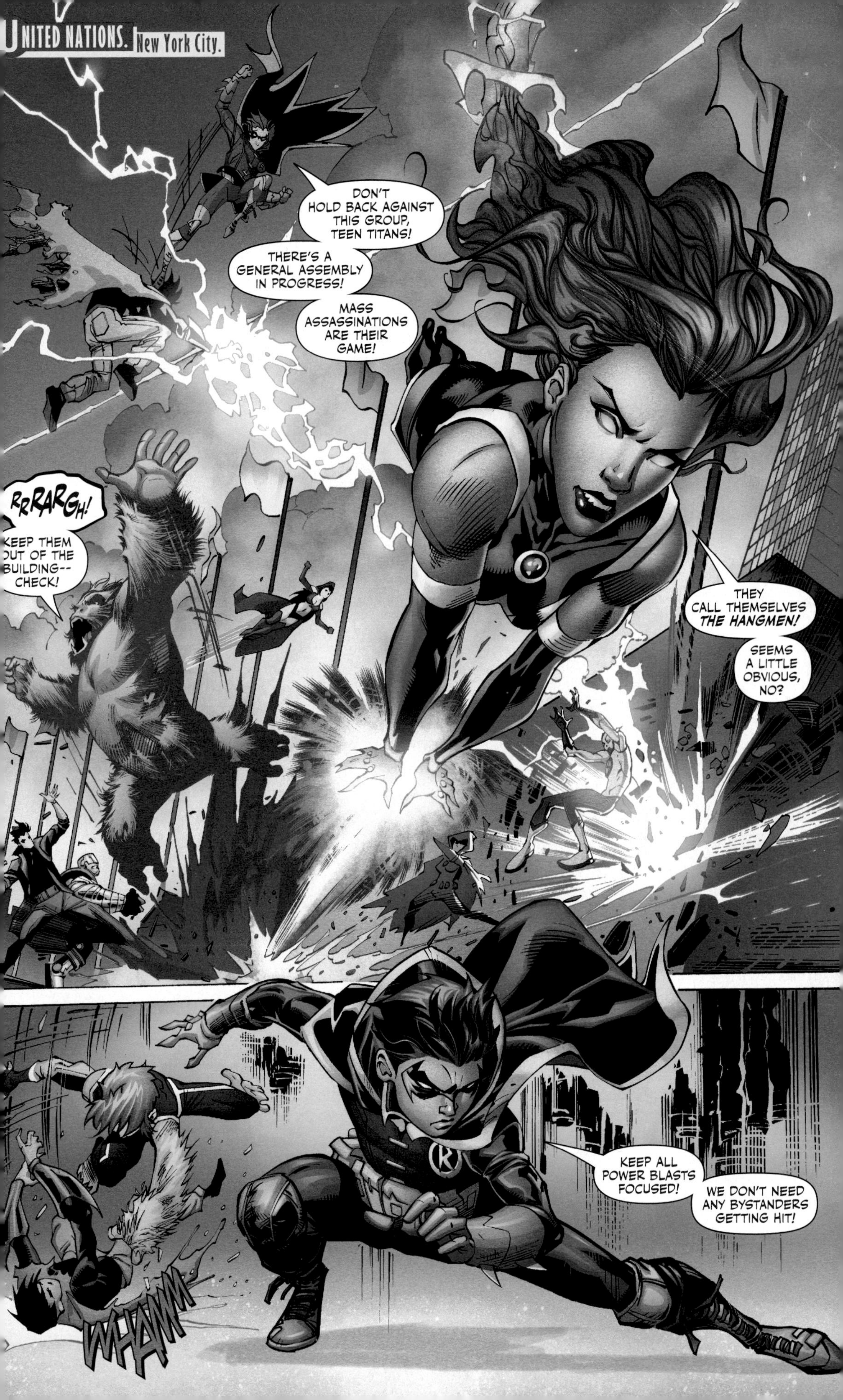
UNITED NATIONS. New York City.
DON'T HOLD BACK AGAINST THIS GROUP, TEEN TITANS!
THERE'S A GENERAL ASSEMBLY IN PROGRESS!
MASS ASSASSINATIONS ARE THEIR GAME!
RRRARGH!
KEEP THEM OUT OF THE BUILDING-- CHECK!
THEY CALL THEMSELVES THE HANGMEN!
SEEMS A LITTLE OBVIOUS, NO?
KEEP ALL POWER BLASTS FOCUSED!
WE DON'T NEED ANY BYSTANDERS GETTING HIT!
WHAMM

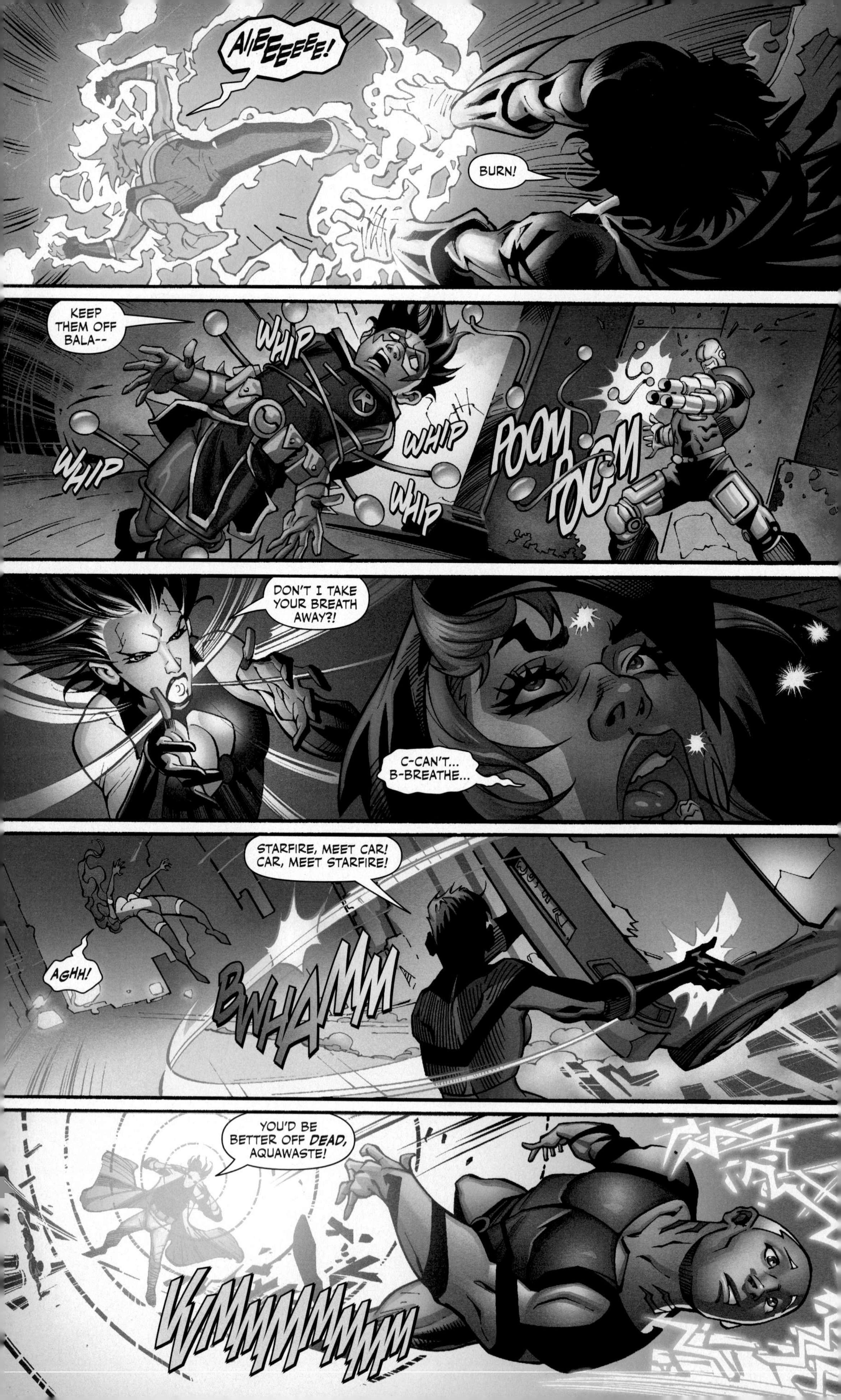
AIIEEEEEEE!
BURN!
KEEP THEM OFF BALA--
WHIP
WHIP
WHIP
WHIP
POOM
POOM
DON'T I TAKE YOUR BREATH AWAY?!
C-CAN'T... B-BREATHE...
STARFIRE, MEET CAR! CAR, MEET STARFIRE!
AGHH!
BWHAMMM
YOU'D BE BETTER OFF DEAD, AQUAWASTE!
VVMMMMMMMMM

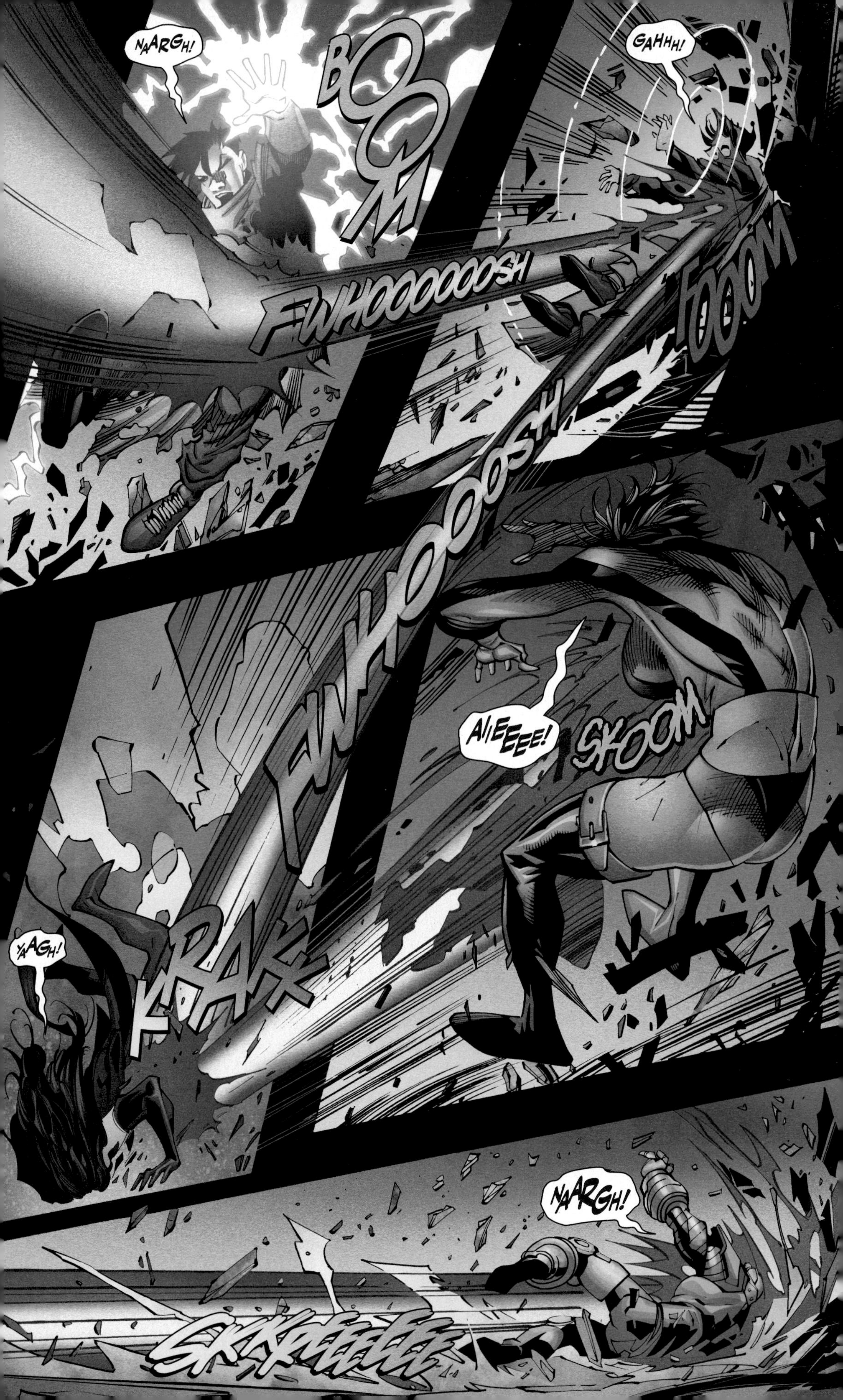
NAARGH!
BOOM
GAHHH!
FWHOOOOOOSH
FOOOM
FWHOOOOOSH
AIIEEEEE!
SKOOM
YAAGH!
KRAK
NAARGH!
SKRREEEEE

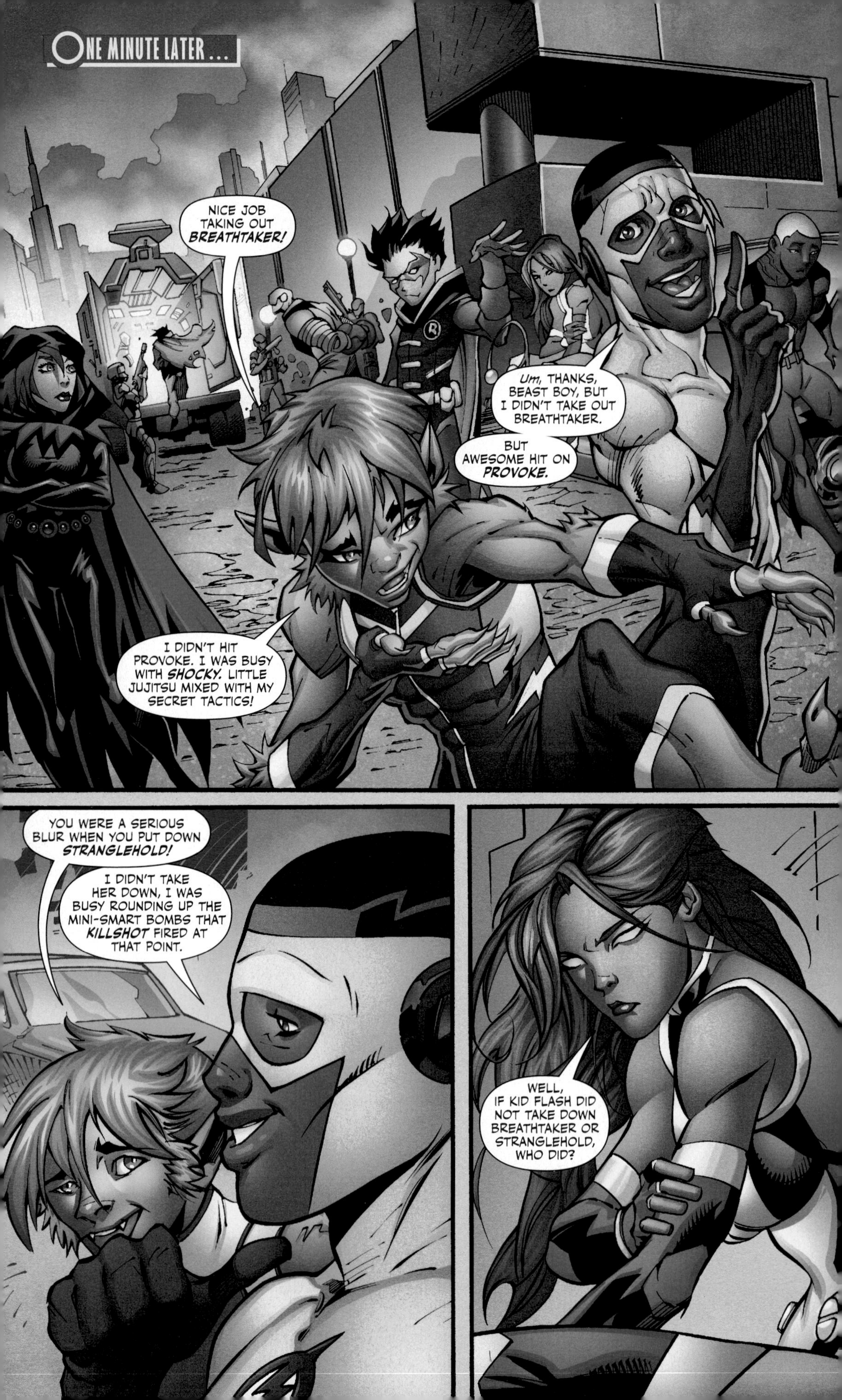
ONE MINUTE LATER . . .
NICE JOB TAKING OUT BREATHTAKER!
Um, THANKS, BEAST BOY, BUT I DIDN'T TAKE OUT BREATHTAKER.
BUT AWESOME HIT ON PROVOKE.
I DIDN'T HIT PROVOKE. I WAS BUSY WITH SHOCKY. LITTLE JUJITSU MIXED WITH MY SECRET TACTICS!
YOU WERE A SERIOUS BLUR WHEN YOU PUT DOWN STRANGLEHOLD!
I DIDN'T TAKE HER DOWN, I WAS BUSY ROUNDING UP THE MINI-SMART BOMBS THAT KILLSHOT FIRED AT THAT POINT.
WELL, IF KID FLASH DID NOT TAKE DOWN BREATHTAKER OR STRANGLEHOLD, WHO DID?

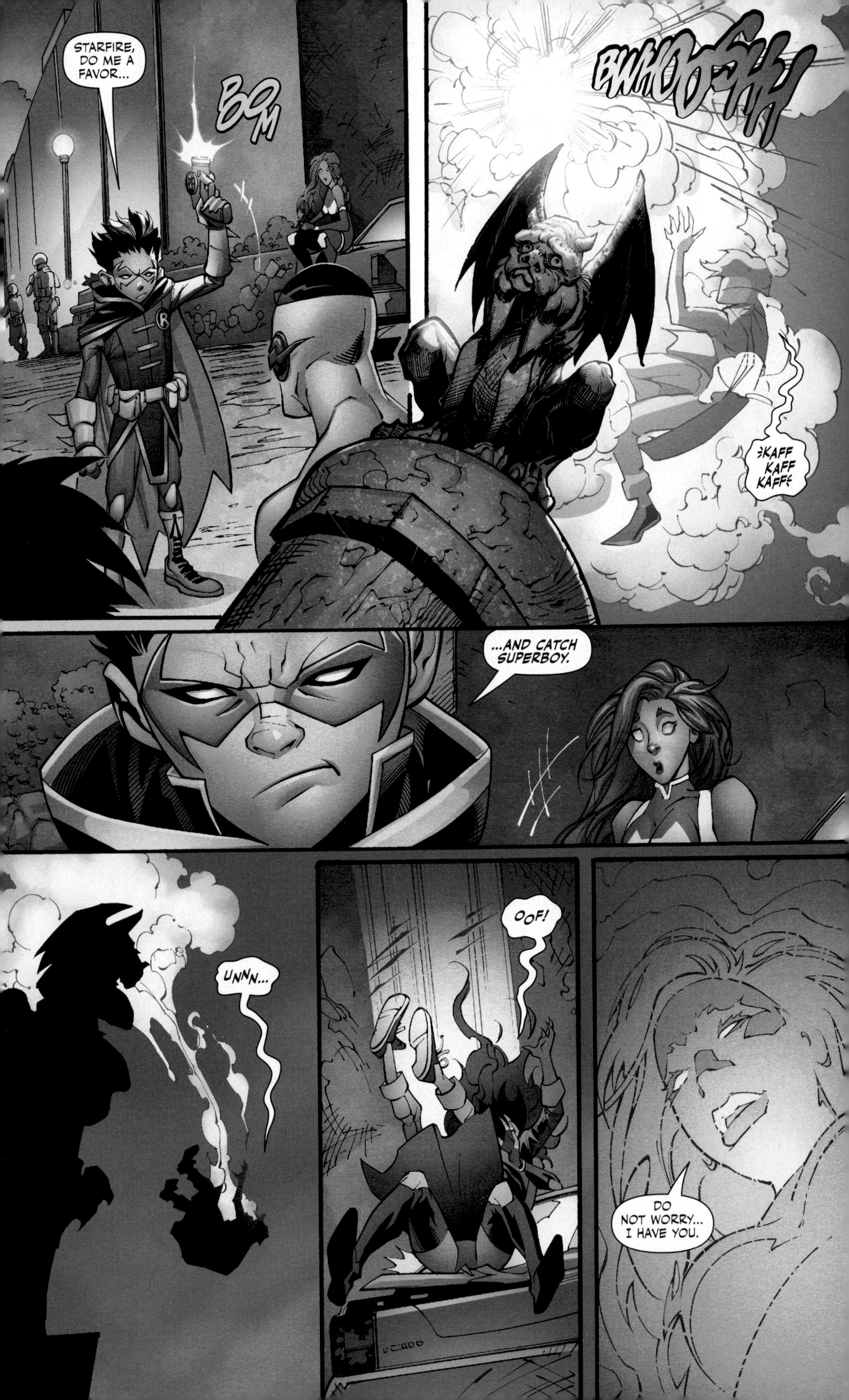
STARFIRE, DO ME A FAVOR...
BOOM
BWHOOSHH
KAFF KAFF KAFF
...AND CATCH SUPERBOY.
UNNN...
OOF!
DO NOT WORRY... I HAVE YOU.

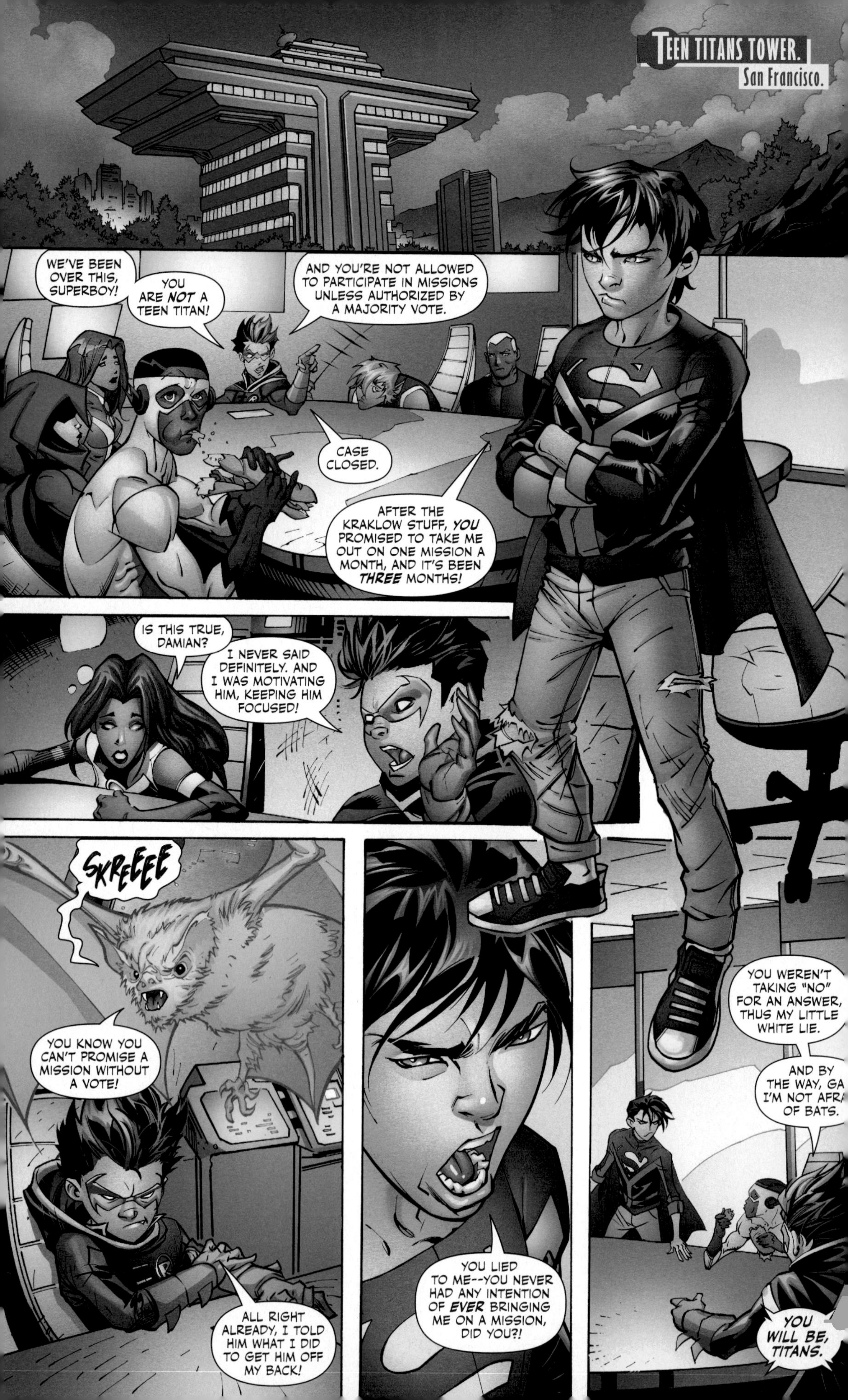
TEEN TITANS TOWER.
San Francisco.
WE'VE BEEN OVER THIS, SUPERBOY!
YOU ARE NOT A TEEN TITAN!
AND YOU'RE NOT ALLOWED TO PARTICIPATE IN MISSIONS UNLESS AUTHORIZED BY A MAJORITY VOTE.
CASE CLOSED.
AFTER THE KRAKLOW STUFF, YOU PROMISED TO TAKE ME OUT ON ONE MISSION A MONTH, AND IT'S BEEN THREE MONTHS!
IS THIS TRUE, DAMIAN?
I NEVER SAID DEFINITELY. AND I WAS MOTIVATING HIM, KEEPING HIM FOCUSED!
SKREEEE
YOU KNOW YOU CAN'T PROMISE A MISSION WITHOUT A VOTE!
ALL RIGHT ALREADY, I TOLD HIM WHAT I DID TO GET HIM OFF MY BACK!
YOU LIED TO ME--YOU NEVER HAD ANY INTENTION OF EVER BRINGING ME ON A MISSION, DID YOU?!
YOU WEREN'T TAKING "NO" FOR AN ANSWER, THUS MY LITTLE WHITE LIE.
YOU WILL BE, TITANS.

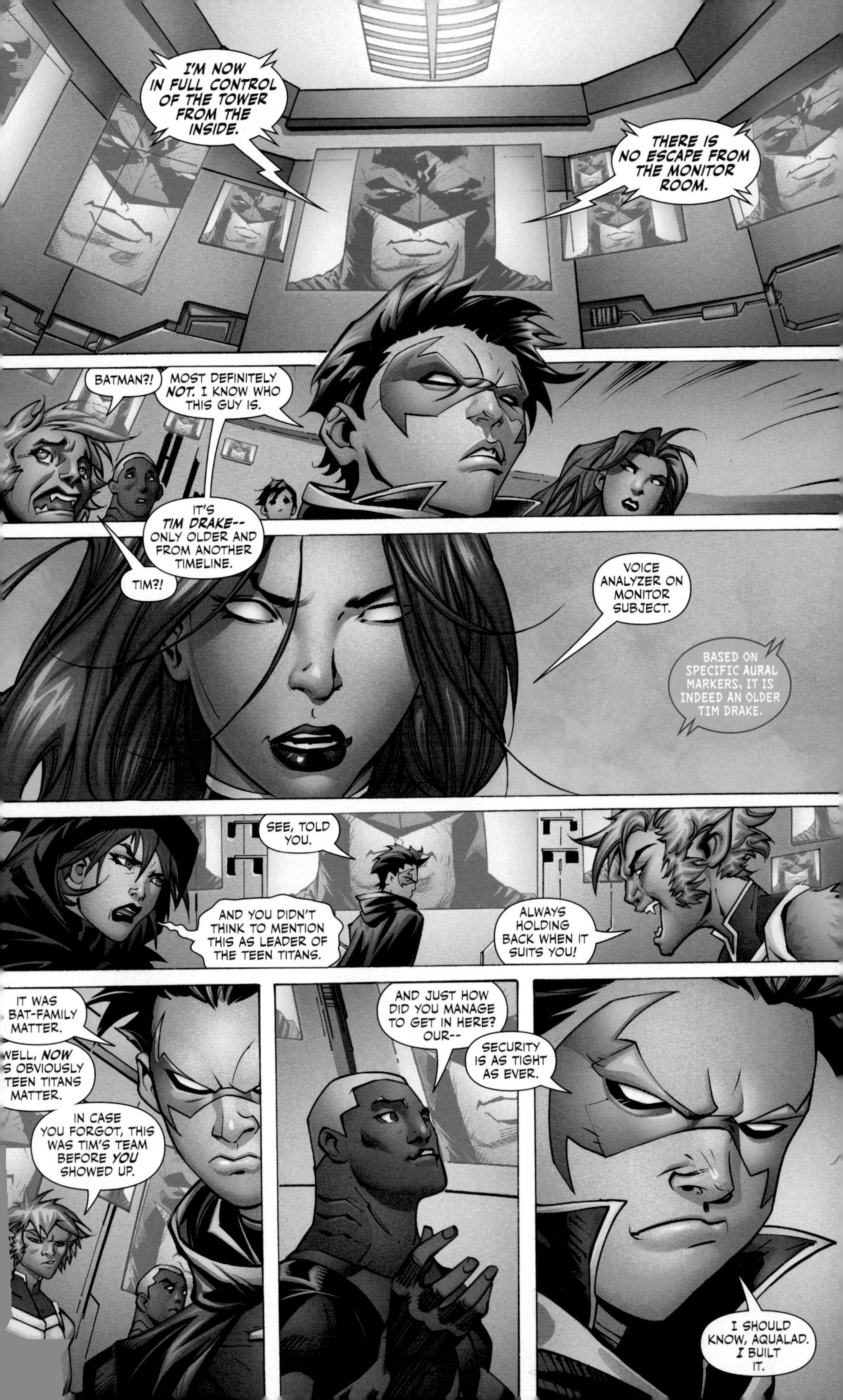
I'M NOW IN FULL CONTROL OF THE TOWER FROM THE INSIDE.
THERE IS NO ESCAPE FROM THE MONITOR ROOM.
BATMAN?!
MOST DEFINITELY NOT. I KNOW WHO THIS GUY IS.
IT'S TIM DRAKE-- ONLY OLDER AND FROM ANOTHER TIMELINE.
TIM?!
VOICE ANALYZER ON MONITOR SUBJECT.
BASED ON SPECIFIC AURAL MARKERS, IT IS INDEED AN OLDER TIM DRAKE.
SEE, TOLD YOU.
AND YOU DIDN'T THINK TO MENTION THIS AS LEADER OF THE TEEN TITANS.
ALWAYS HOLDING BACK WHEN IT SUITS YOU!
IT WAS BAT-FAMILY MATTER.
WELL, NOW S OBVIOUSLY TEEN TITANS MATTER.
IN CASE YOU FORGOT, THIS WAS TIM'S TEAM BEFORE YOU SHOWED UP.
AND JUST HOW DID YOU MANAGE TO GET IN HERE? OUR--
SECURITY IS AS TIGHT AS EVER.
I SHOULD KNOW, AQUALAD. I BUILT IT.

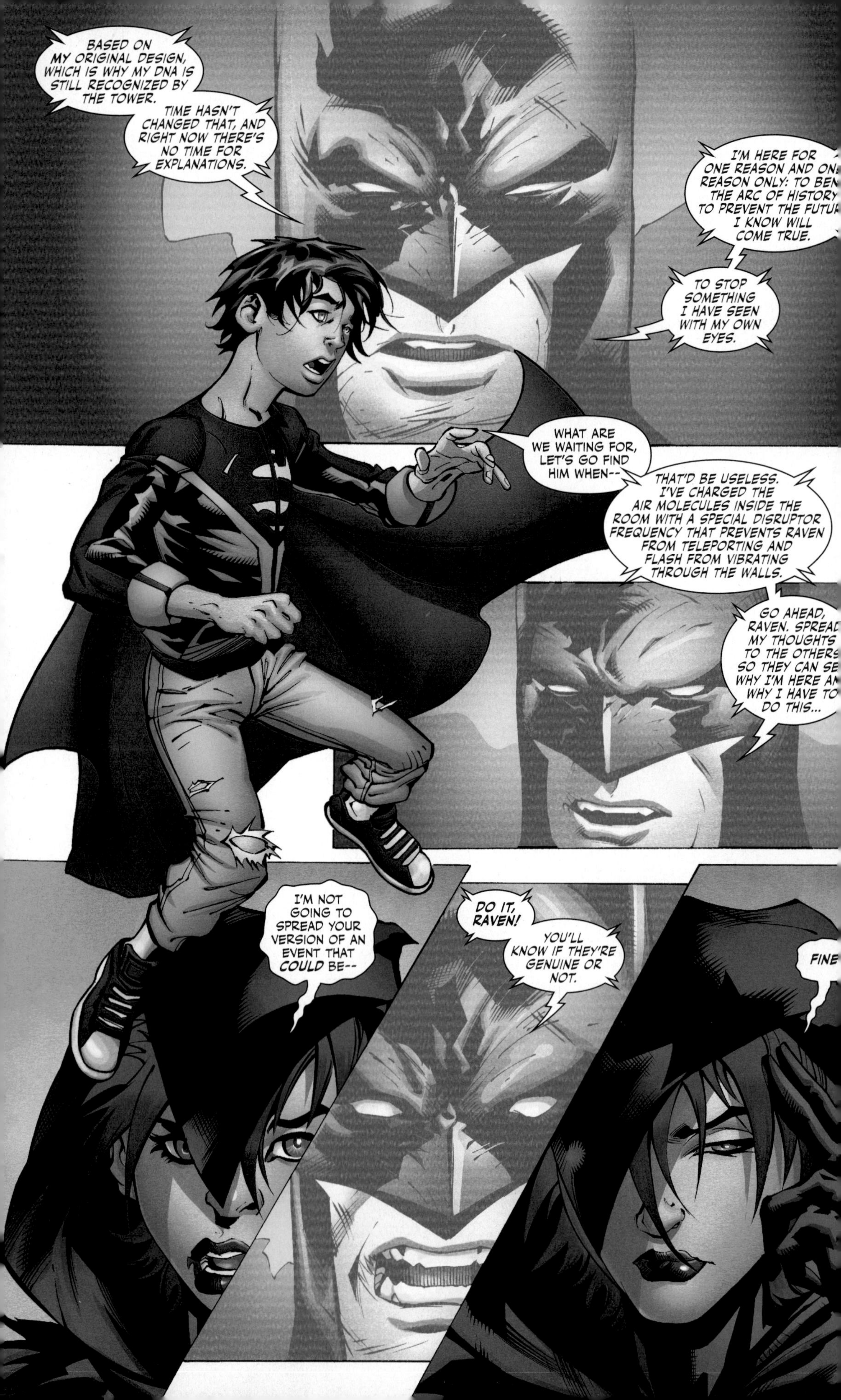
BASED ON MY ORIGINAL DESIGN, WHICH IS WHY MY DNA IS STILL RECOGNIZED BY THE TOWER.
TIME HASN'T CHANGED THAT, AND RIGHT NOW THERE'S NO TIME FOR EXPLANATIONS.
I'M HERE FOR ONE REASON AND ON REASON ONLY: TO BEN THE ARC OF HISTORY TO PREVENT THE FUTU I KNOW WILL COME TRUE.
TO STOP SOMETHING I HAVE SEEN WITH MY OWN EYES.
WHAT ARE WE WAITING FOR, LET'S GO FIND HIM WHEN--
THAT'D BE USELESS. I'VE CHARGED THE AIR MOLECULES INSIDE THE ROOM WITH A SPECIAL DISRUPTOR FREQUENCY THAT PREVENTS RAVEN FROM TELEPORTING AND FLASH FROM VIBRATING THROUGH THE WALLS.
GO AHEAD, RAVEN. SPREAD MY THOUGHTS TO THE OTHERS SO THEY CAN SE WHY I'M HERE A WHY I HAVE T DO THIS...
I'M NOT GOING TO SPREAD YOUR VERSION OF AN EVENT THAT COULD BE--
DO IT, RAVEN!
YOU'LL KNOW IF THEY'RE GENUINE OR NOT.
FINE

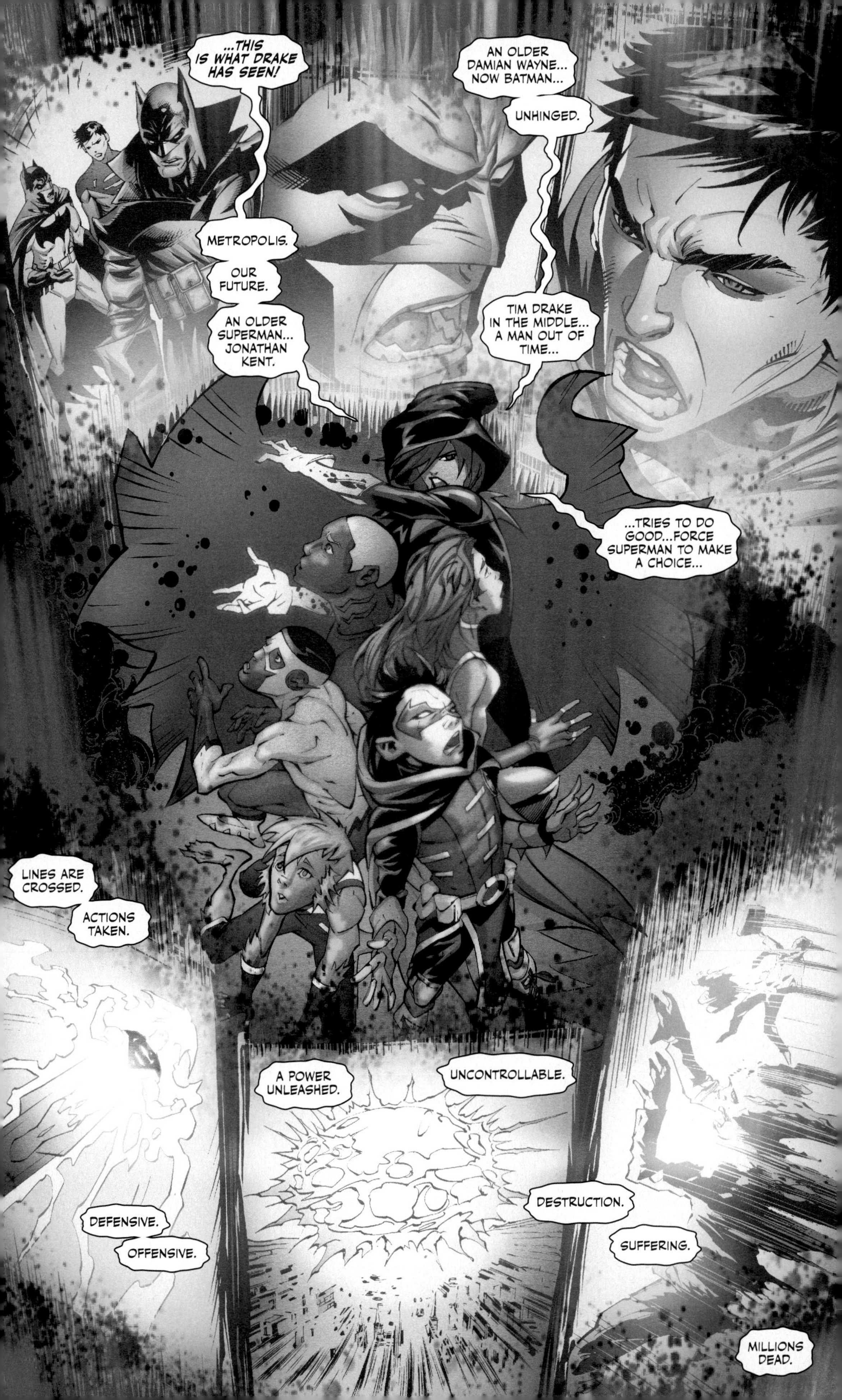
...THIS IS WHAT DRAKE HAS SEEN!
METROPOLIS.
OUR FUTURE.
AN OLDER SUPERMAN... JONATHAN KENT.
AN OLDER DAMIAN WAYNE... NOW BATMAN...
UNHINGED.
TIM DRAKE IN THE MIDDLE... A MAN OUT OF TIME...
...TRIES TO DO GOOD...FORCE SUPERMAN TO MAKE A CHOICE...
LINES ARE CROSSED.
ACTIONS TAKEN.
DEFENSIVE.
OFFENSIVE.
A POWER UNLEASHED.
UNCONTROLLABLE.
DESTRUCTION.
SUFFERING.
MILLIONS DEAD.

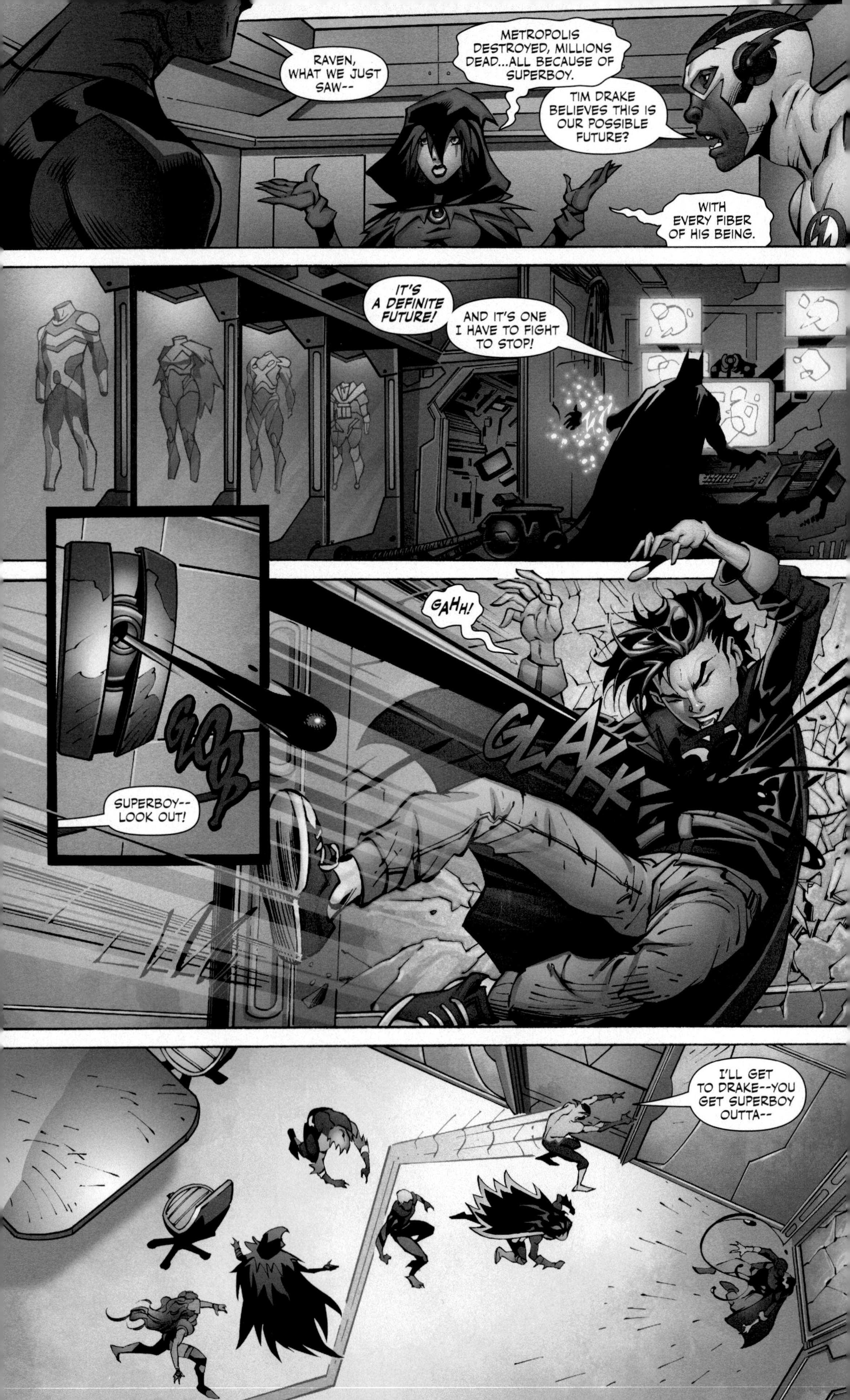
RAVEN, WHAT WE JUST SAW--
METROPOLIS DESTROYED, MILLIONS DEAD...ALL BECAUSE OF SUPERBOY.
TIM DRAKE BELIEVES THIS IS OUR POSSIBLE FUTURE?
WITH EVERY FIBER OF HIS BEING.
IT'S A DEFINITE FUTURE!
AND IT'S ONE I HAVE TO FIGHT TO STOP!
GAHH!
GLOOP
SUPERBOY-- LOOK OUT!
GLAKK
I'LL GET TO DRAKE--YOU GET SUPERBOY OUTTA--

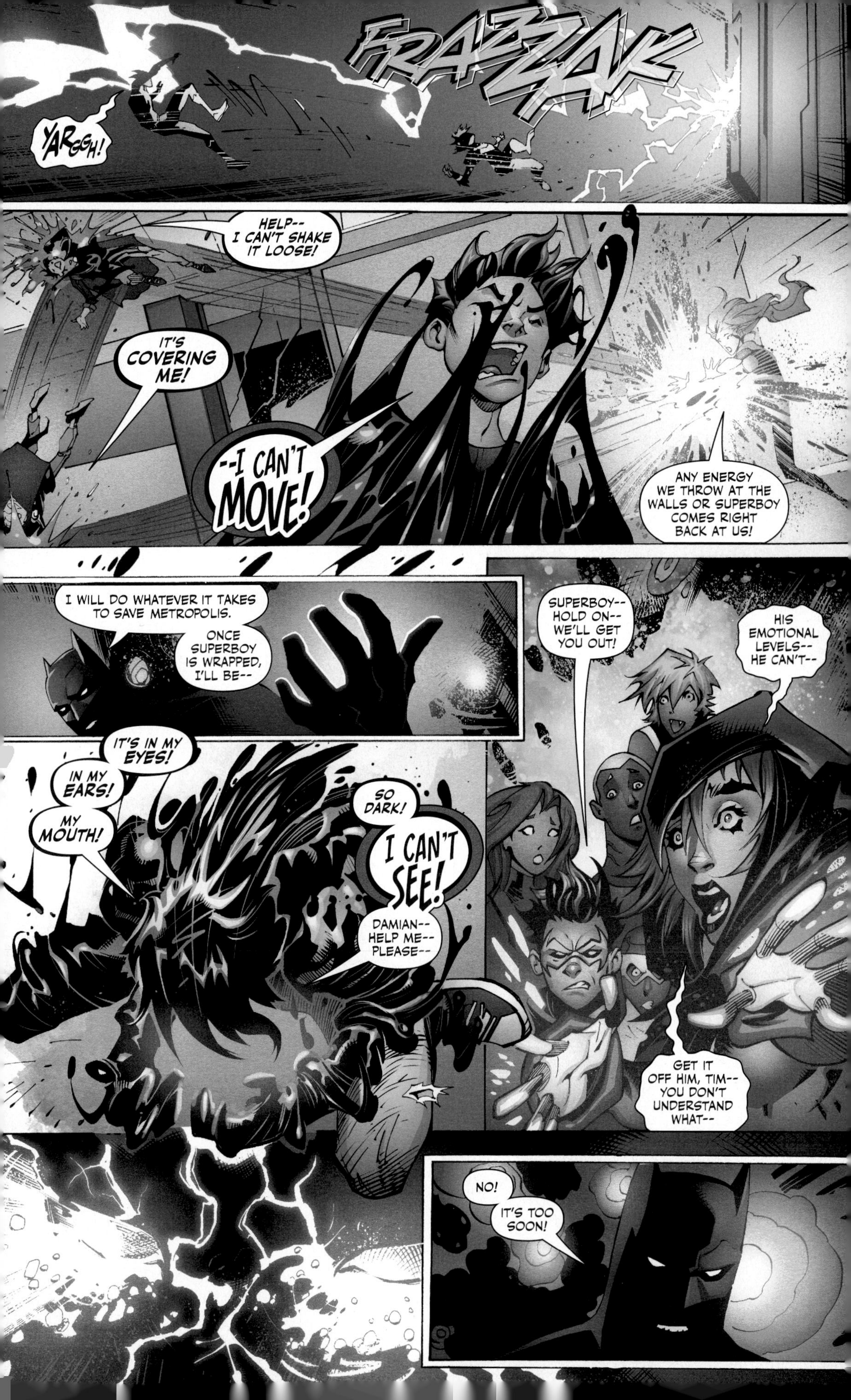
FRAZZAK
YARGGH!
HELP-- I CAN'T SHAKE IT LOOSE!
IT'S COVERING ME!
--I CAN'T MOVE!
ANY ENERGY WE THROW AT THE WALLS OR SUPERBOY COMES RIGHT BACK AT US!
I WILL DO WHATEVER IT TAKES TO SAVE METROPOLIS.
ONCE SUPERBOY IS WRAPPED, I'LL BE--
SUPERBOY-- HOLD ON-- WE'LL GET YOU OUT!
HIS EMOTIONAL LEVELS-- HE CAN'T--
IT'S IN MY EYES!
IN MY EARS!
MY MOUTH!
SO DARK!
I CAN'T SEE!
DAMIAN-- HELP ME-- PLEASE--
GET IT OFF HIM, TIM-- YOU DON'T UNDERSTAND WHAT--
NO!
IT'S TOO SOON!

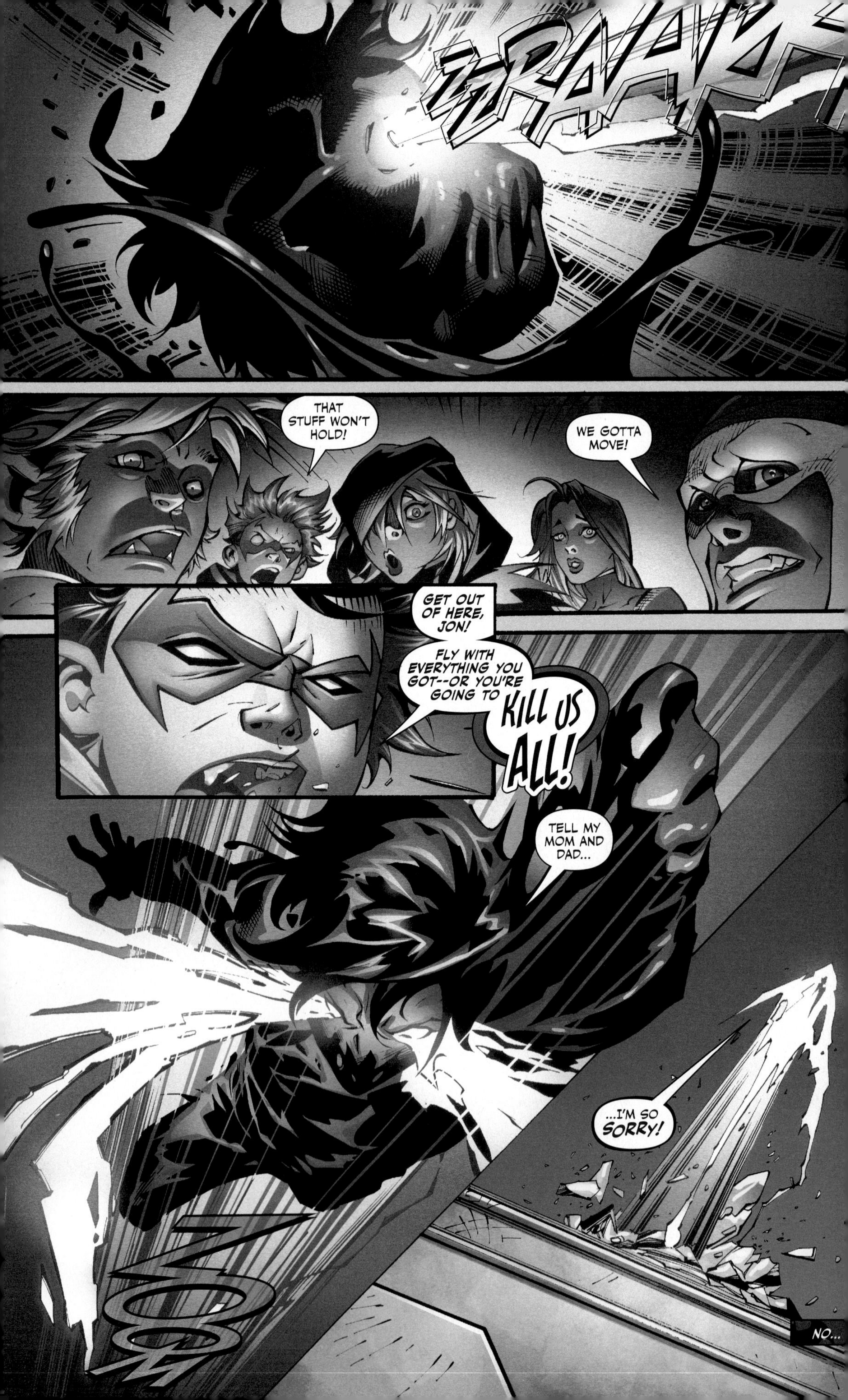

THAT STUFF WON'T HOLD!
WE GOTTA MOVE!
GET OUT OF HERE, JON!
FLY WITH EVERYTHING YOU GOT--OR YOU'RE GOING TO KILL US ALL!
TELL MY MOM AND DAD...
...I'M SO SORRY!
NO...

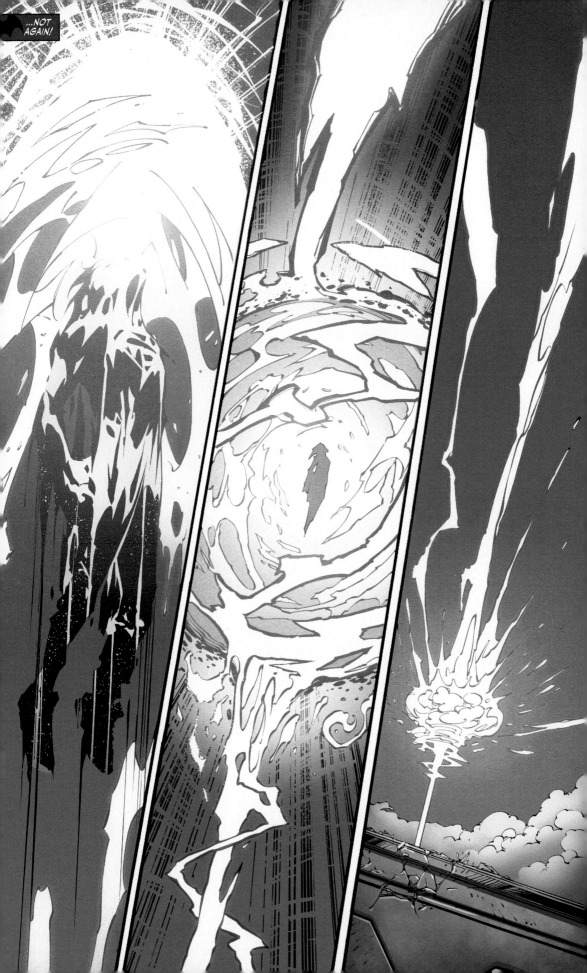

...NOT AGAIN!

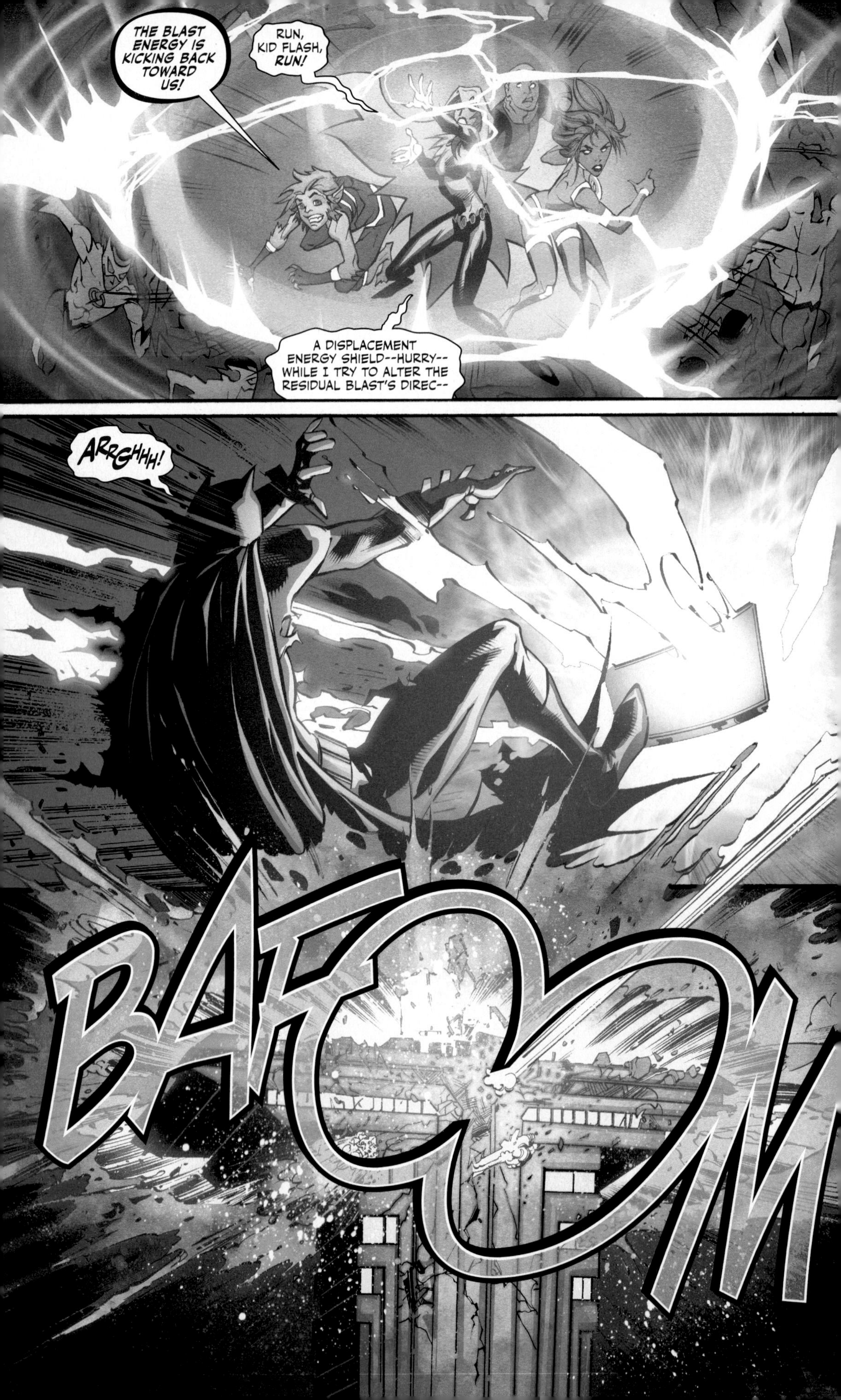
THE BLAST ENERGY IS KICKING BACK TOWARD US!
RUN, KID FLASH, RUN!
A DISPLACEMENT ENERGY SHIELD--HURRY--WHILE I TRY TO ALTER THE RESIDUAL BLAST'S DIREC--
ARRGHHH!
BATOOM

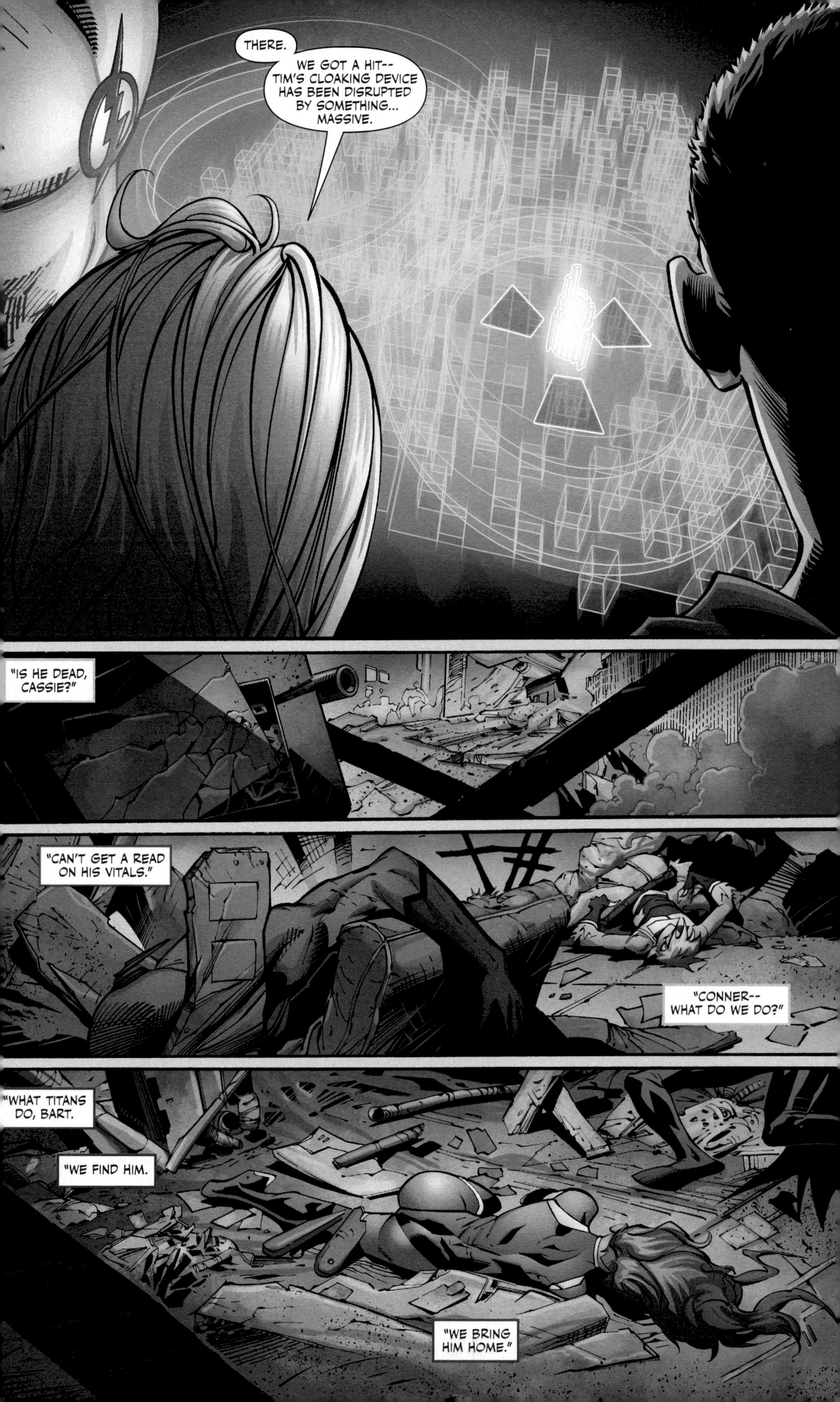
THERE.
WE GOT A HIT--
TIM'S CLOAKING DEVICE HAS BEEN DISRUPTED BY SOMETHING... MASSIVE.
"IS HE DEAD, CASSIE?"
"CAN'T GET A READ ON HIS VITALS."
"CONNER-- WHAT DO WE DO?"
"WHAT TITANS DO, BART.
"WE FIND HIM.
"WE BRING HIM HOME."

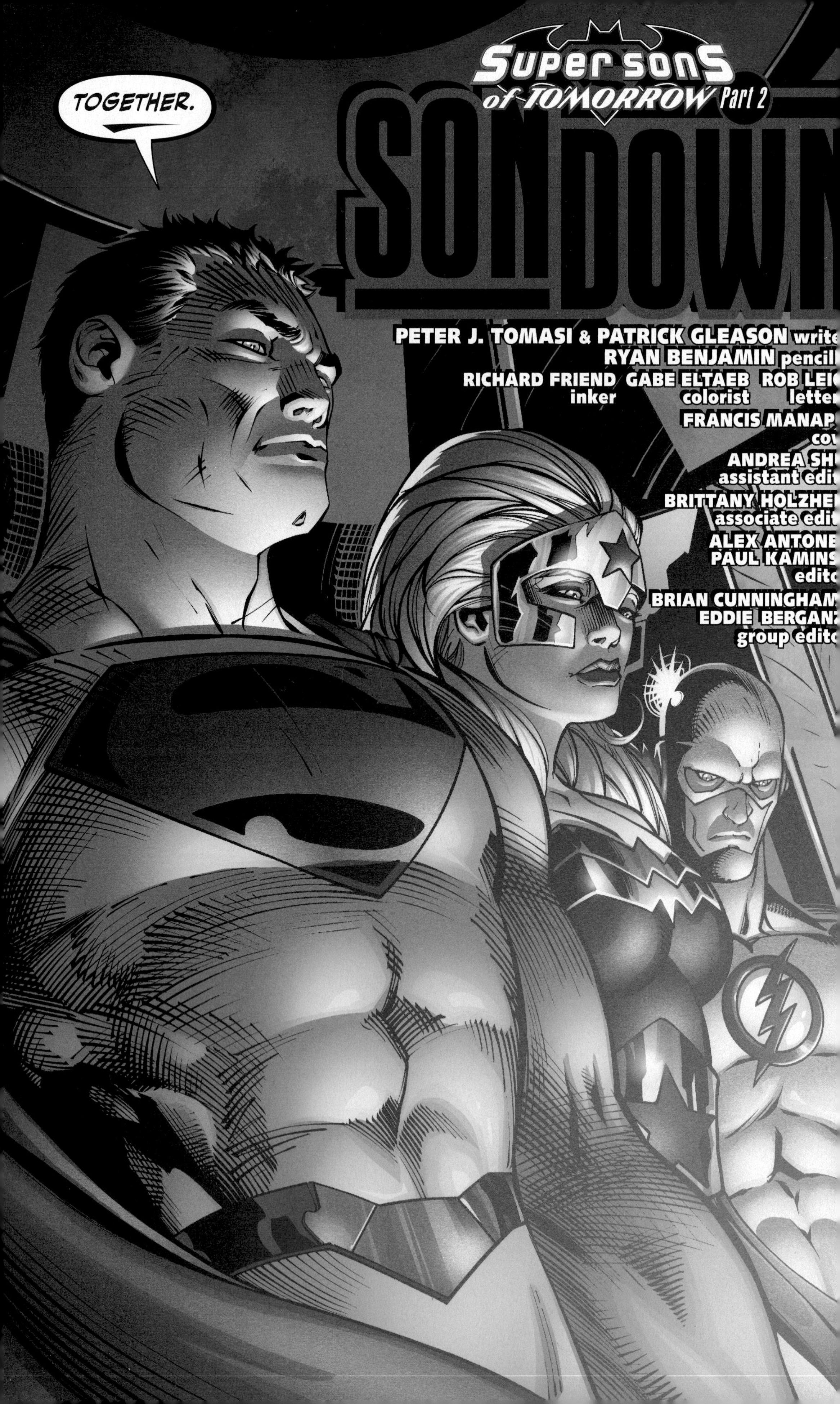
TOGETHER.
Super sons of TOMORROW Part 2
SONDOWN
PETER J. TOMASI & PATRICK GLEASON write
RYAN BENJAMIN pencil
RICHARD FRIEND inker
GABE ELTAEB colorist
ROB LEI lette
FRANCIS MANAP cov
ANDREA SH assistant edi
BRITTANY HOLZHE associate edi
ALEX ANTONE
PAUL KAMINS edito
BRIAN CUNNINGHAM
EDDIE BERGAN group edito

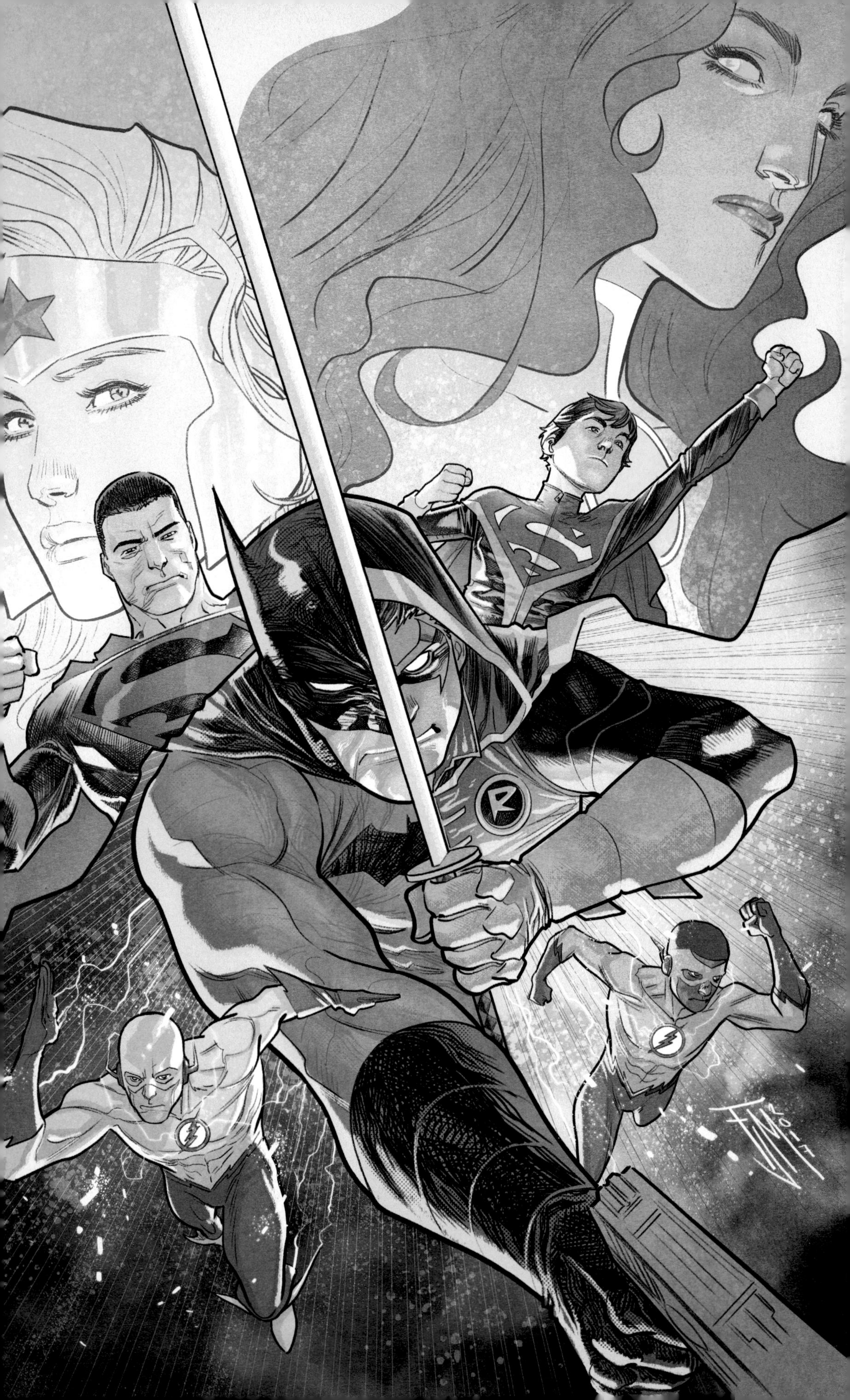

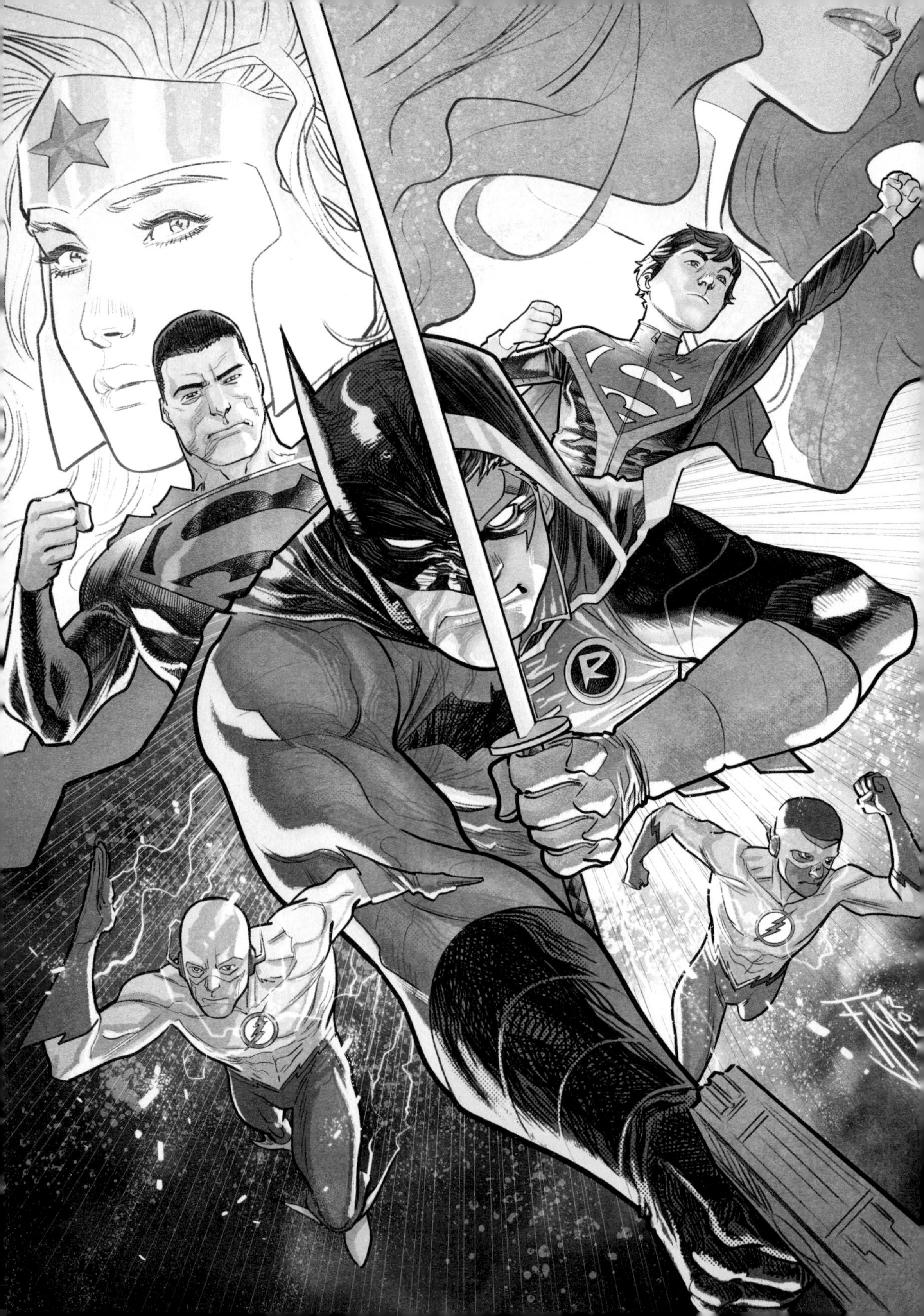

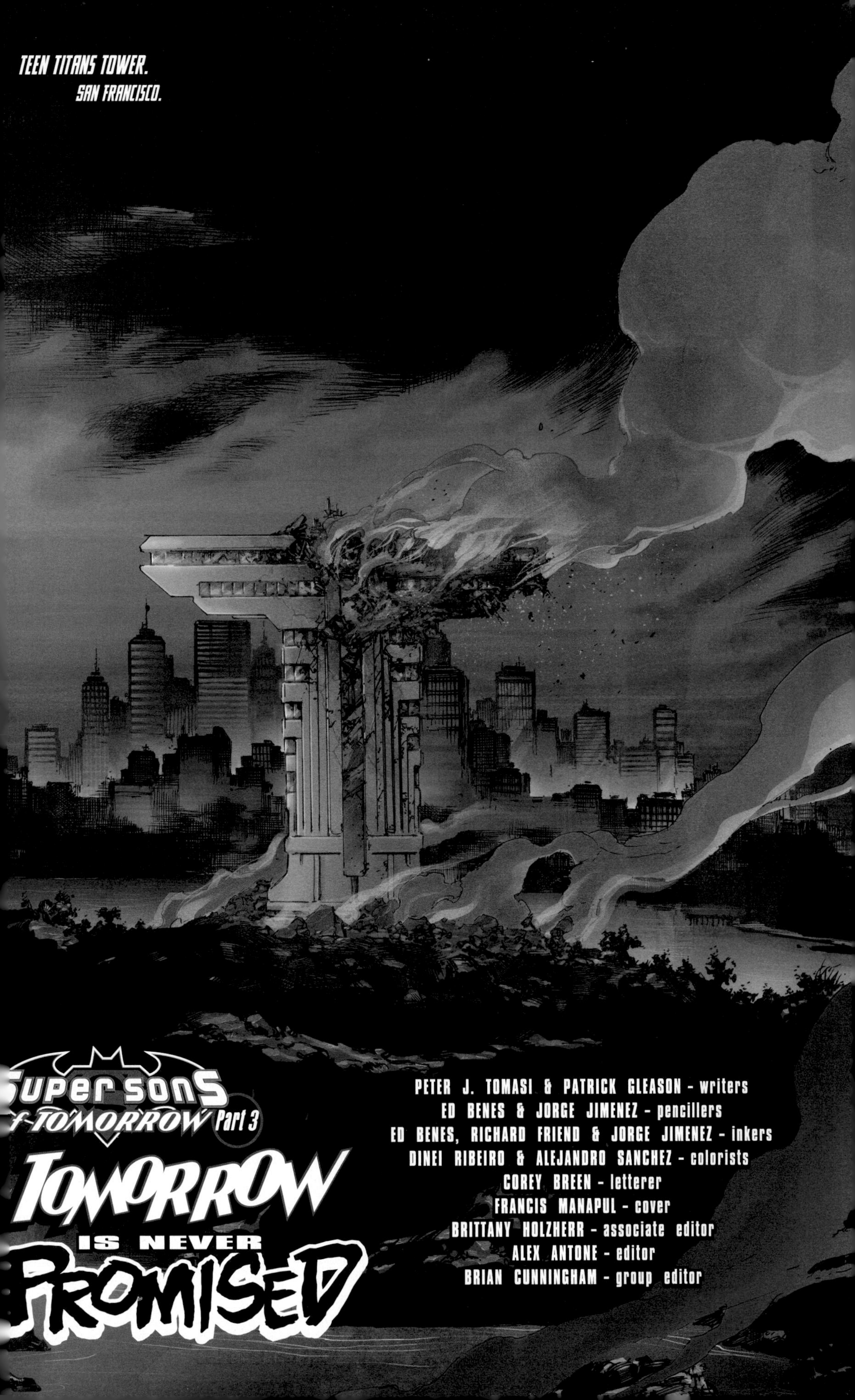

TEEN TITANS TOWER.
SAN FRANCISCO.
Super Sons
TOMORROW Part 3
TOMORROW IS NEVER PROMISED
PETER J. TOMASI & PATRICK GLEASON - writers
ED BENES & JORGE JIMENEZ - pencillers
ED BENES, RICHARD FRIEND & JORGE JIMENEZ - inkers
DINEI RIBEIRO & ALEJANDRO SANCHEZ - colorists
COREY BREEN - letterer
FRANCIS MANAPUL - cover
BRITTANY HOLZHERR - associate editor
ALEX ANTONE - editor
BRIAN CUNNINGHAM - group editor

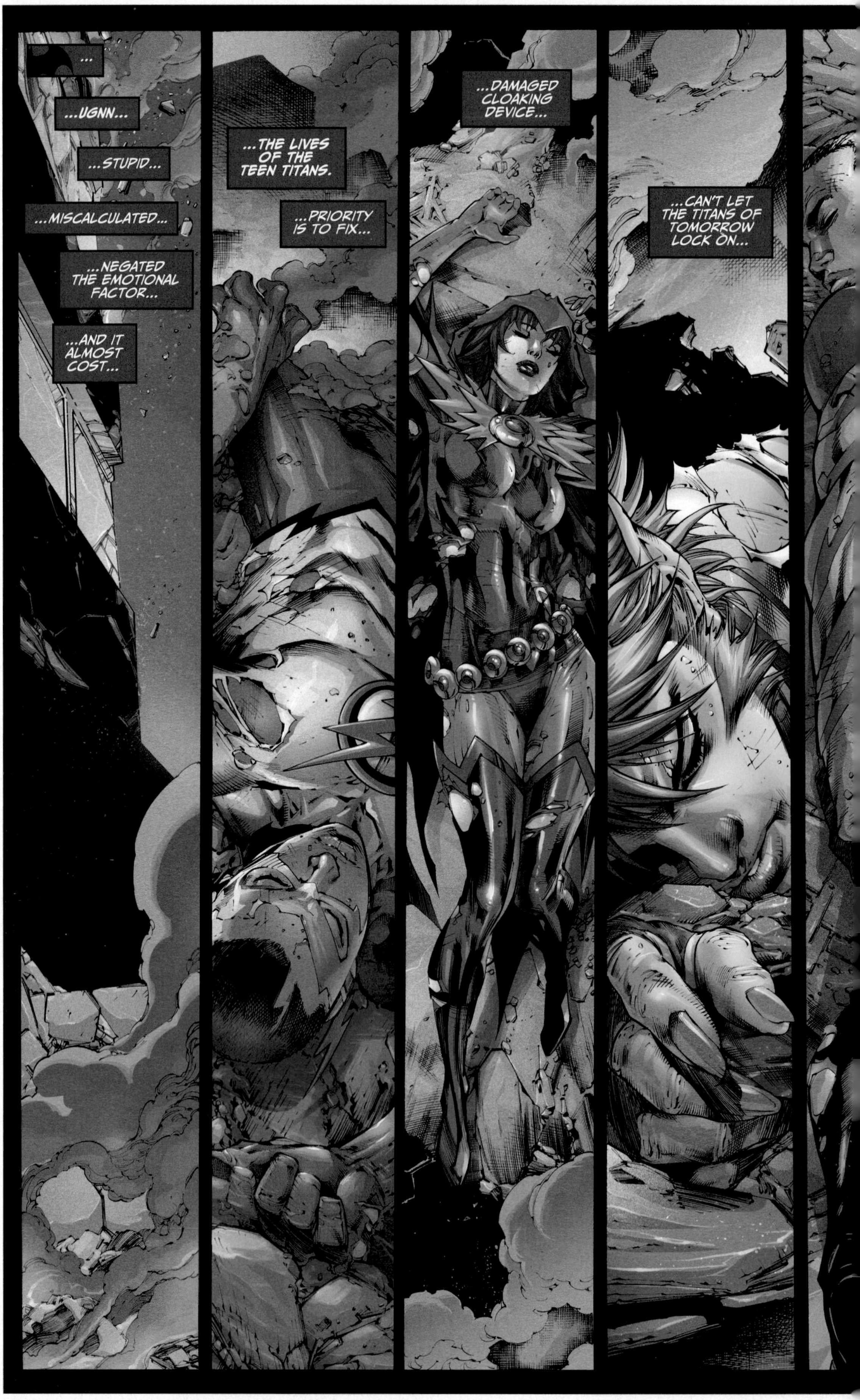
...
...UGNN...
...STUPID...
...MISCALCULATED...
...NEGATED THE EMOTIONAL FACTOR...
...AND IT ALMOST COST...
...THE LIVES OF THE TEEN TITANS.
...PRIORITY IS TO FIX...
...DAMAGED CLOAKING DEVICE...
...CAN'T LET THE TITANS OF TOMORROW LOCK ON...

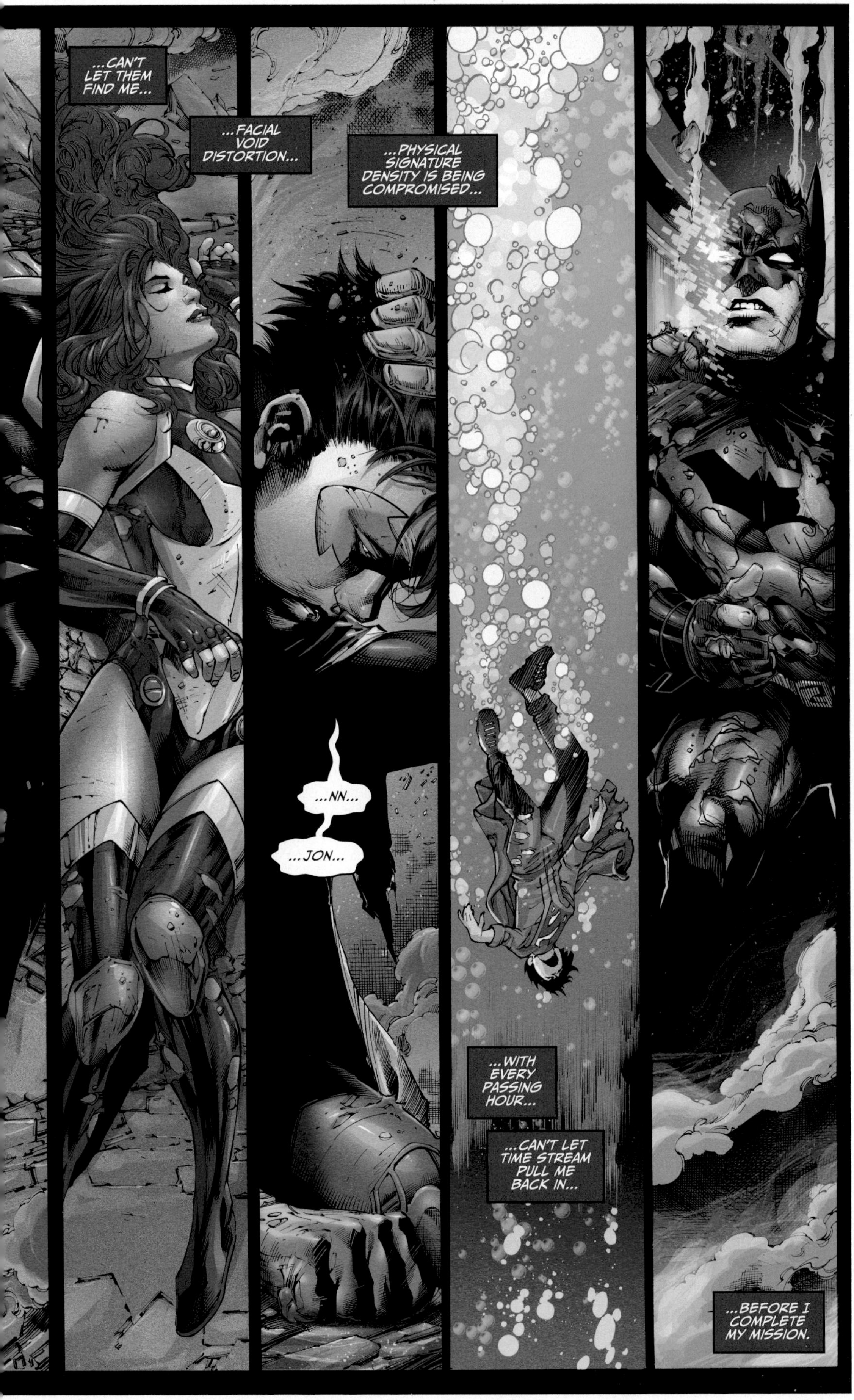
...CAN'T LET THEM FIND ME...
...FACIAL VOID DISTORTION...
...PHYSICAL SIGNATURE DENSITY IS BEING COMPROMISED...
...NN...
...JON...
...WITH EVERY PASSING HOUR...
...CAN'T LET TIME STREAM PULL ME BACK IN...
...BEFORE I COMPLETE MY MISSION.

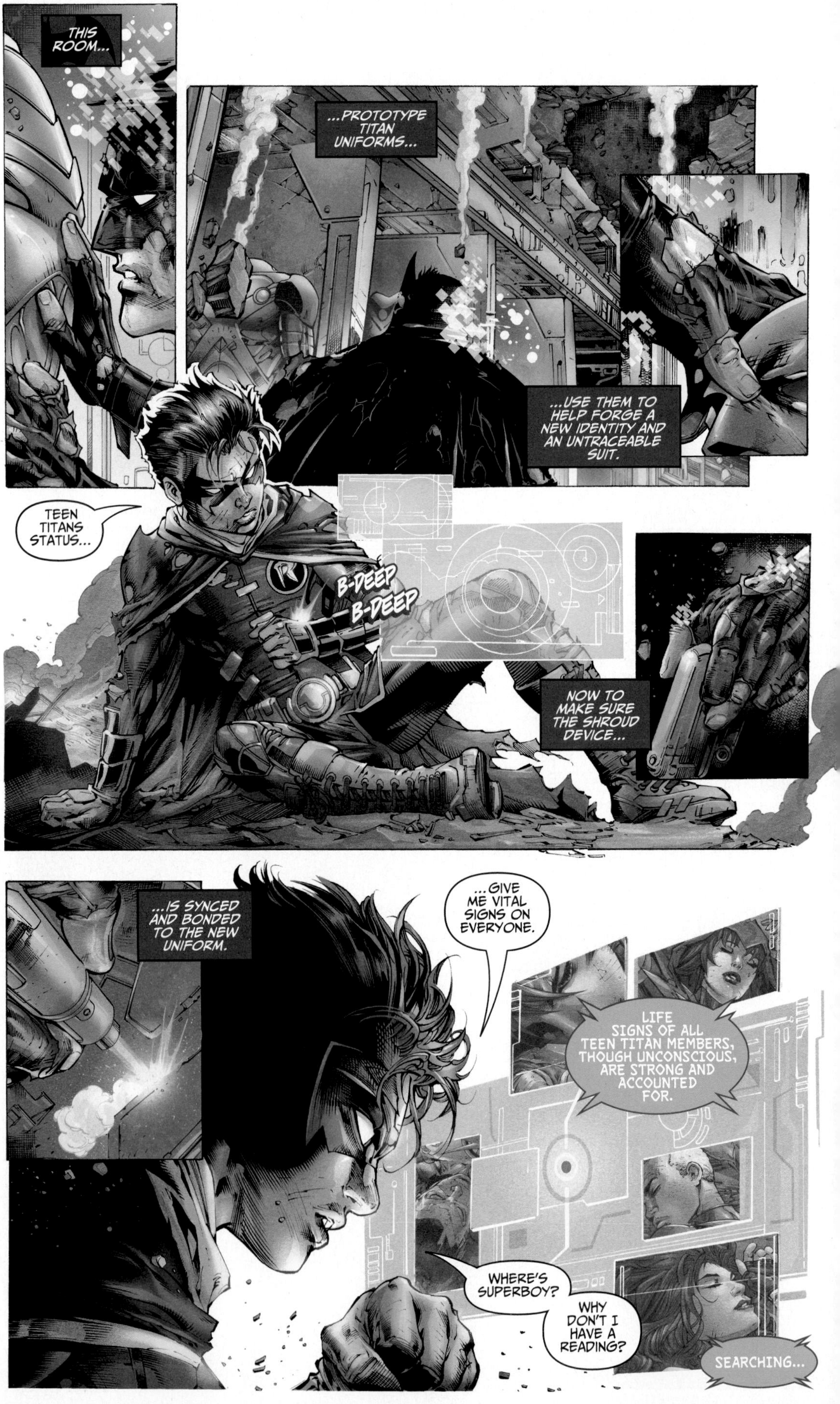
THIS ROOM...
...PROTOTYPE TITAN UNIFORMS...
...USE THEM TO HELP FORGE A NEW IDENTITY AND AN UNTRACEABLE SUIT.
TEEN TITANS STATUS...
B-DEEP
B-DEEP
NOW TO MAKE SURE THE SHROUD DEVICE...
...IS SYNCED AND BONDED TO THE NEW UNIFORM.
...GIVE ME VITAL SIGNS ON EVERYONE.
LIFE SIGNS OF ALL TEEN TITAN MEMBERS, THOUGH UNCONSCIOUS, ARE STRONG AND ACCOUNTED FOR.
WHERE'S SUPERBOY?
WHY DON'T I HAVE A READING?
SEARCHING...

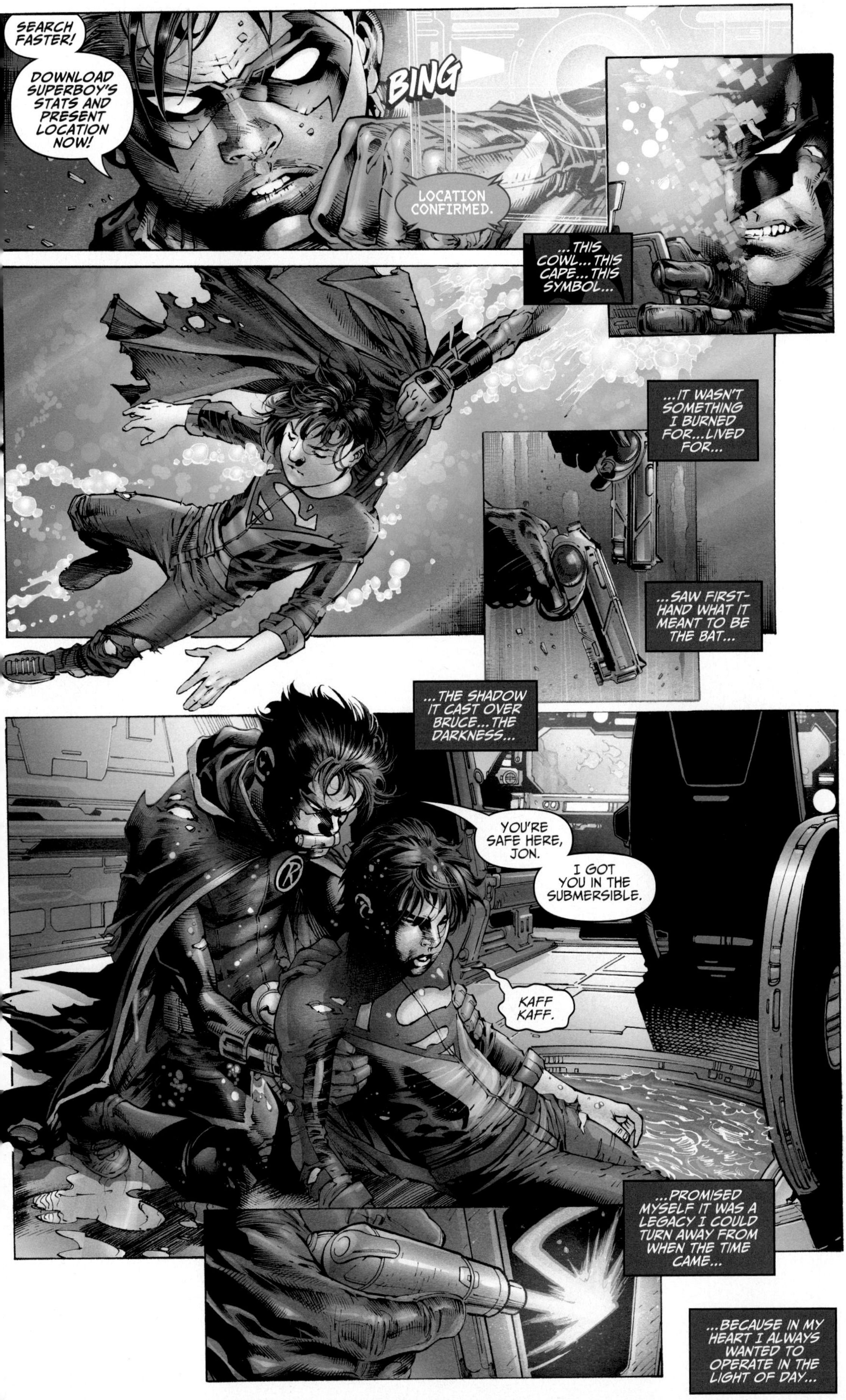

SEARCH FASTER!
DOWNLOAD SUPERBOY'S STATS AND PRESENT LOCATION NOW!
BING
LOCATION CONFIRMED.
...THIS COWL...THIS CAPE...THIS SYMBOL...
...IT WASN'T SOMETHING I BURNED FOR...LIVED FOR...
...SAW FIRST-HAND WHAT IT MEANT TO BE THE BAT...
...THE SHADOW IT CAST OVER BRUCE...THE DARKNESS...
YOU'RE SAFE HERE, JON.
I GOT YOU IN THE SUBMERSIBLE.
KAFF KAFF.
...PROMISED MYSELF IT WAS A LEGACY I COULD TURN AWAY FROM WHEN THE TIME CAME...
...BECAUSE IN MY HEART I ALWAYS WANTED TO OPERATE IN THE LIGHT OF DAY...

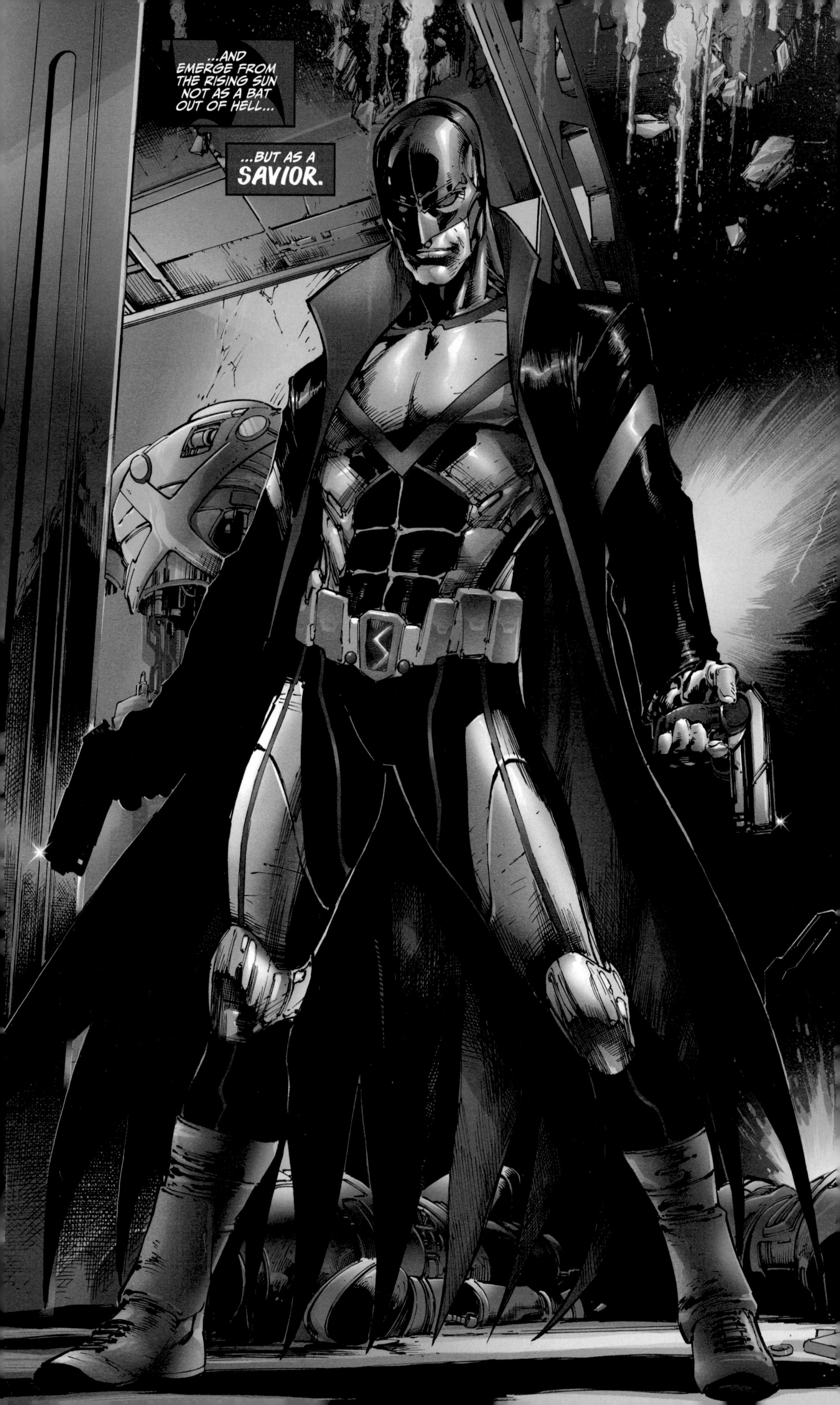
...AND EMERGE FROM THE RISING SUN NOT AS A BAT OUT OF HELL...
...BUT AS A SAVIOR.

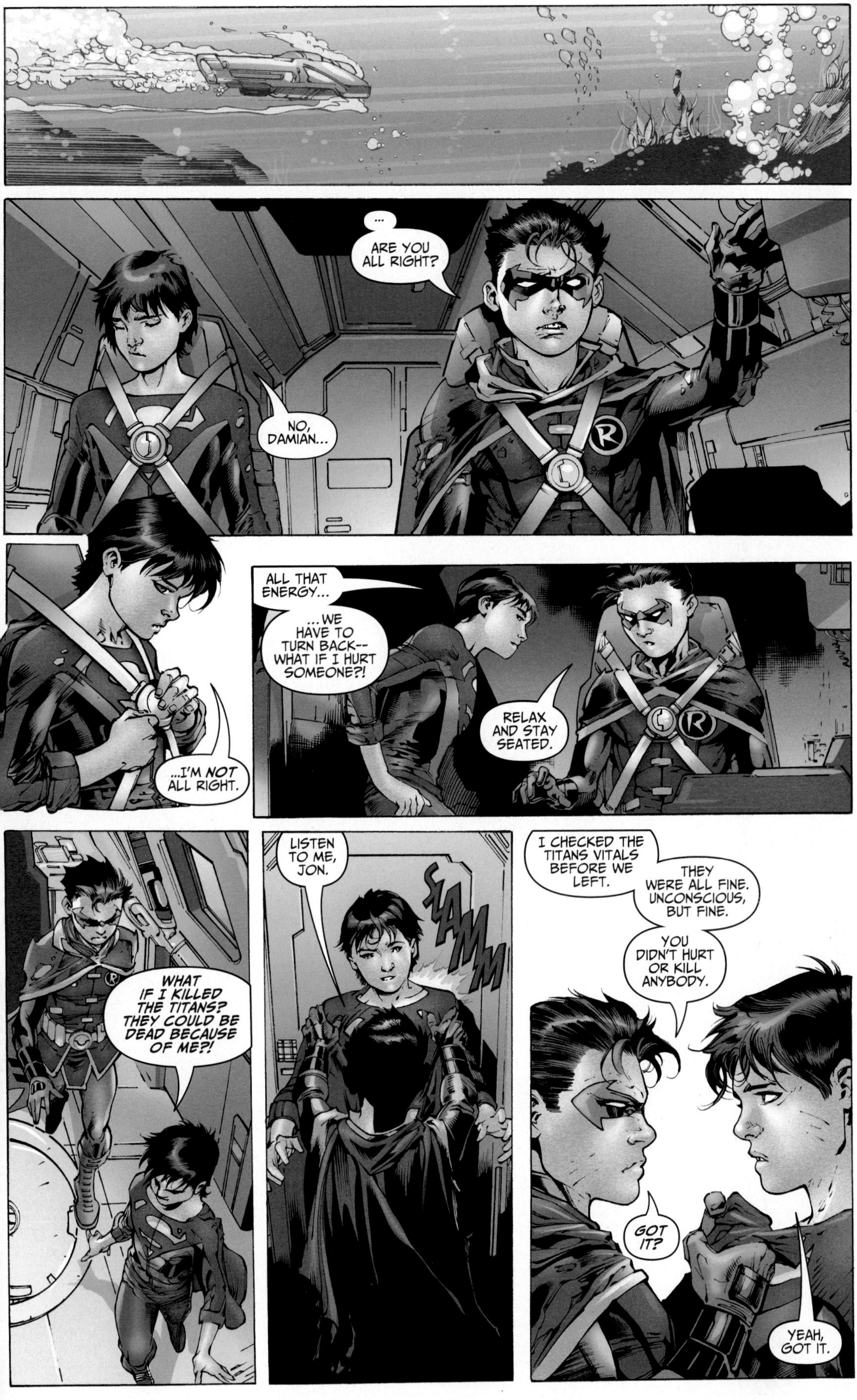
...
ARE YOU ALL RIGHT?
NO, DAMIAN...
...I'M NOT ALL RIGHT.
ALL THAT ENERGY...
...WE HAVE TO TURN BACK-- WHAT IF I HURT SOMEONE?!
RELAX AND STAY SEATED.
WHAT IF I KILLED THE TITANS? THEY COULD BE DEAD BECAUSE OF ME?!
LISTEN TO ME, JON.
SLAMM
I CHECKED THE TITANS VITALS BEFORE WE LEFT.
THEY WERE ALL FINE. UNCONSCIOUS, BUT FINE.
YOU DIDN'T HURT OR KILL ANYBODY.
GOT IT?
YEAH, GOT IT.

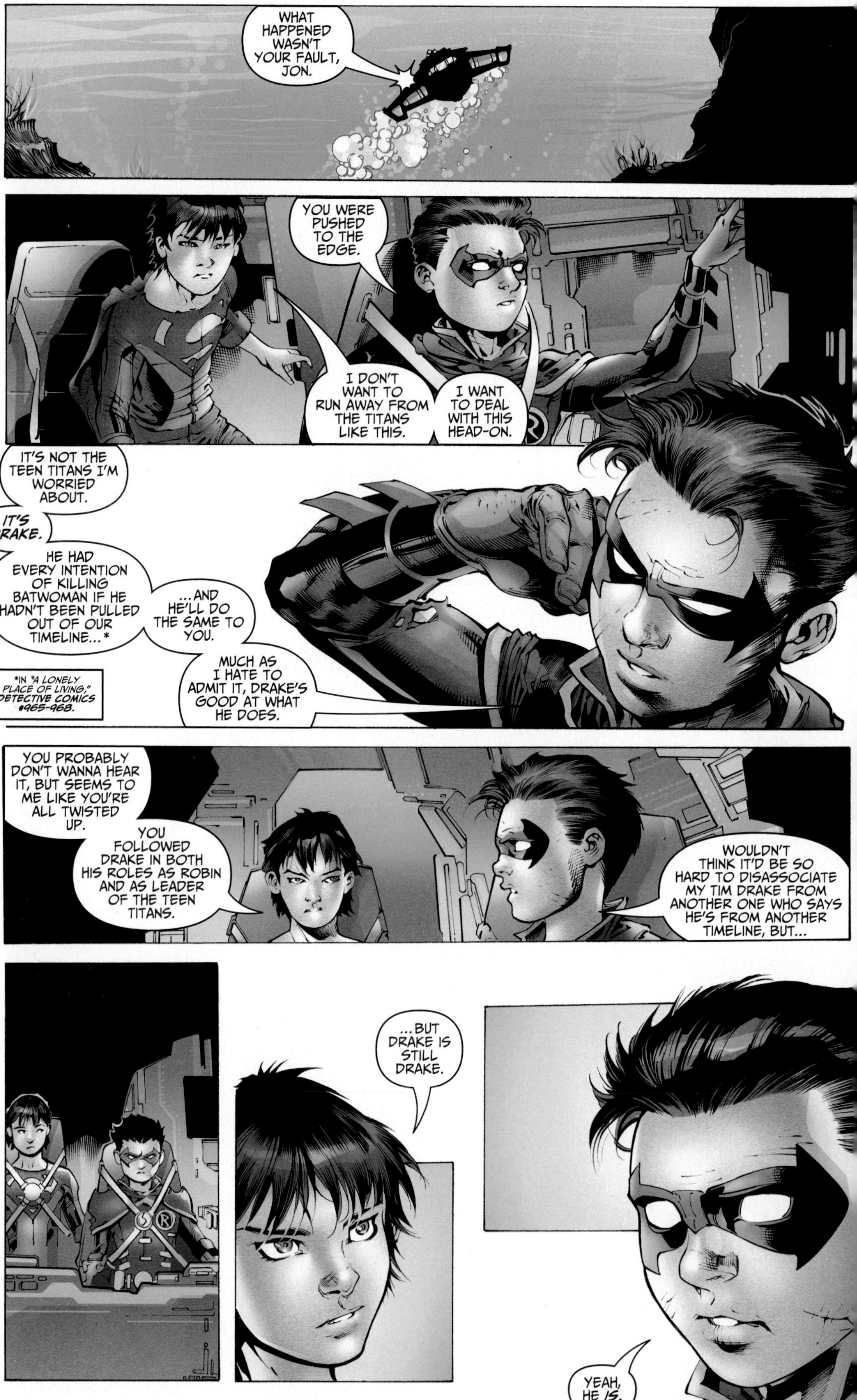
WHAT HAPPENED WASN'T YOUR FAULT, JON.
YOU WERE PUSHED TO THE EDGE.
I DON'T WANT TO RUN AWAY FROM THE TITANS LIKE THIS.
I WANT TO DEAL WITH THIS HEAD-ON.
IT'S NOT THE TEEN TITANS I'M WORRIED ABOUT.
IT'S DRAKE.
HE HAD EVERY INTENTION OF KILLING BATWOMAN IF HE HADN'T BEEN PULLED OUT OF OUR TIMELINE...*
...AND HE'LL DO THE SAME TO YOU.
MUCH AS I HATE TO ADMIT IT, DRAKE'S GOOD AT WHAT HE DOES.
*IN "A LONELY PLACE OF LIVING," DETECTIVE COMICS #965-968.
YOU PROBABLY DON'T WANNA HEAR IT, BUT SEEMS TO ME LIKE YOU'RE ALL TWISTED UP.
YOU FOLLOWED DRAKE IN BOTH HIS ROLES AS ROBIN AND AS LEADER OF THE TEEN TITANS.
WOULDN'T THINK IT'D BE SO HARD TO DISASSOCIATE MY TIM DRAKE FROM ANOTHER ONE WHO SAYS HE'S FROM ANOTHER TIMELINE, BUT...
...BUT DRAKE IS STILL DRAKE.
YEAH, HE IS.

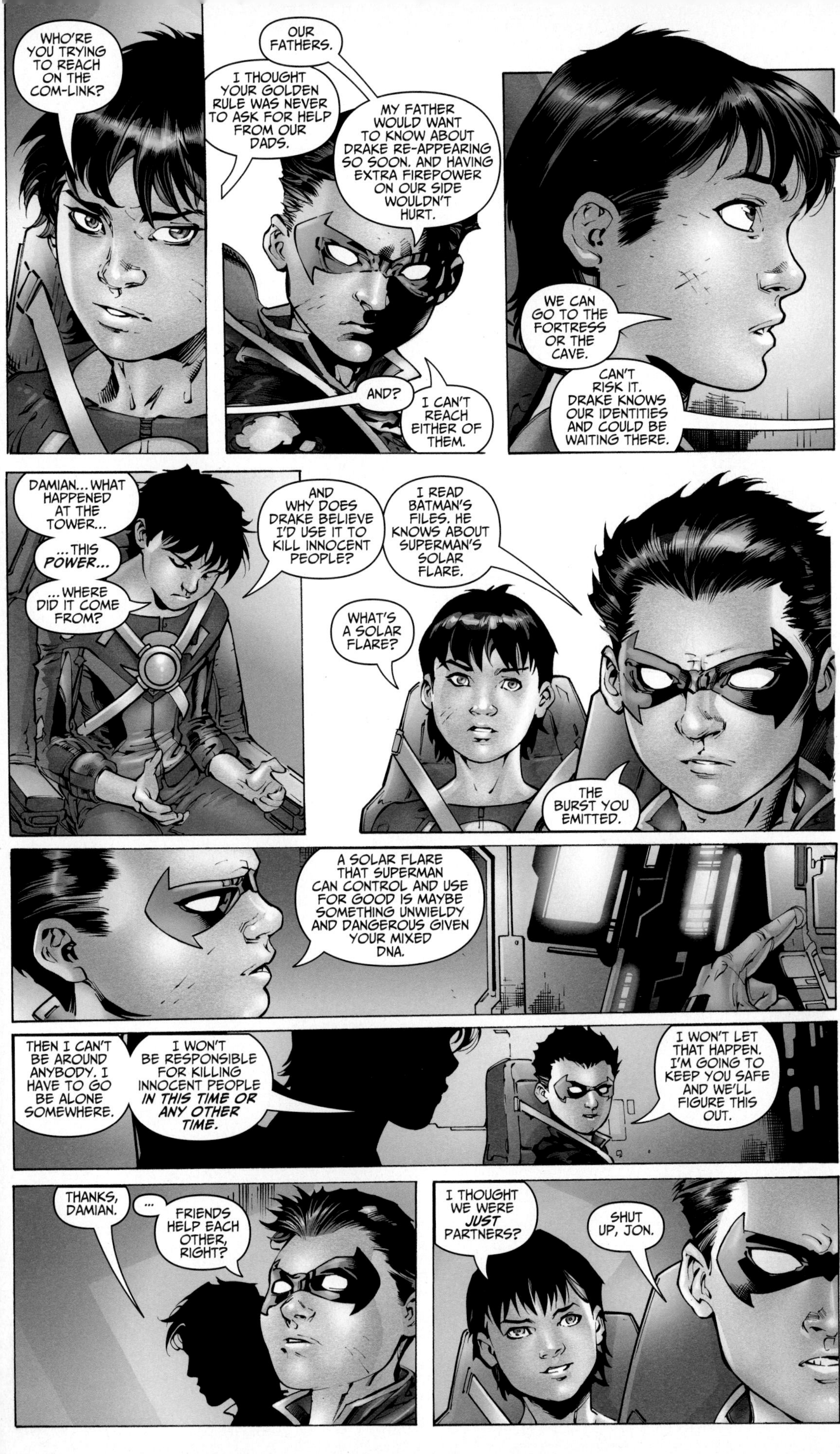
WHO'RE YOU TRYING TO REACH ON THE COM-LINK?
OUR FATHERS.
I THOUGHT YOUR GOLDEN RULE WAS NEVER TO ASK FOR HELP FROM OUR DADS.
MY FATHER WOULD WANT TO KNOW ABOUT DRAKE RE-APPEARING SO SOON. AND HAVING EXTRA FIREPOWER ON OUR SIDE WOULDN'T HURT.
AND?
I CAN'T REACH EITHER OF THEM.
WE CAN GO TO THE FORTRESS OR THE CAVE.
CAN'T RISK IT. DRAKE KNOWS OUR IDENTITIES AND COULD BE WAITING THERE.
DAMIAN... WHAT HAPPENED AT THE TOWER...
...THIS *POWER...*
...WHERE DID IT COME FROM?
AND WHY DOES DRAKE BELIEVE I'D USE IT TO KILL INNOCENT PEOPLE?
I READ BATMAN'S FILES. HE KNOWS ABOUT SUPERMAN'S SOLAR FLARE.
WHAT'S A SOLAR FLARE?
THE BURST YOU EMITTED.
A SOLAR FLARE THAT SUPERMAN CAN CONTROL AND USE FOR GOOD IS MAYBE SOMETHING UNWIELDY AND DANGEROUS GIVEN YOUR MIXED DNA.
THEN I CAN'T BE AROUND ANYBODY. I HAVE TO GO BE ALONE SOMEWHERE.
I WON'T BE RESPONSIBLE FOR KILLING INNOCENT PEOPLE ***IN THIS TIME OR ANY OTHER TIME.***
I WON'T LET THAT HAPPEN. I'M GOING TO KEEP YOU SAFE AND WE'LL FIGURE THIS OUT.
THANKS, DAMIAN.
...
FRIENDS HELP EACH OTHER, RIGHT?
I THOUGHT WE WERE *JUST* PARTNERS?
SHUT UP, JON.

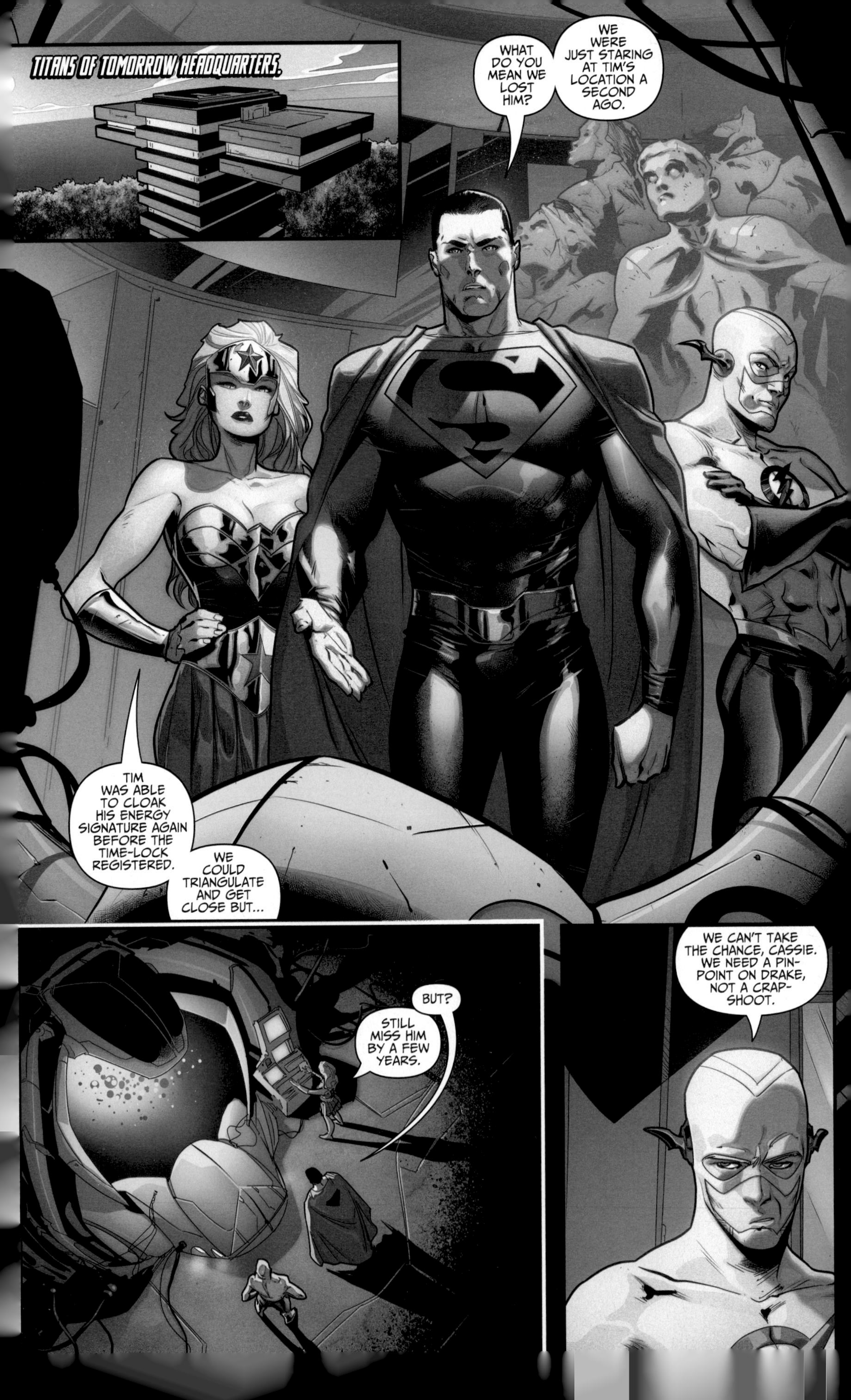
TITANS OF TOMORROW HEADQUARTERS.
WHAT DO YOU MEAN WE LOST HIM?
WE WERE JUST STARING AT TIM'S LOCATION A SECOND AGO.
TIM WAS ABLE TO CLOAK HIS ENERGY SIGNATURE AGAIN BEFORE THE TIME-LOCK REGISTERED.
WE COULD TRIANGULATE AND GET CLOSE BUT...
BUT?
STILL MISS HIM BY A FEW YEARS.
WE CAN'T TAKE THE CHANCE, CASSIE. WE NEED A PIN-POINT ON DRAKE, NOT A CRAP-SHOOT.

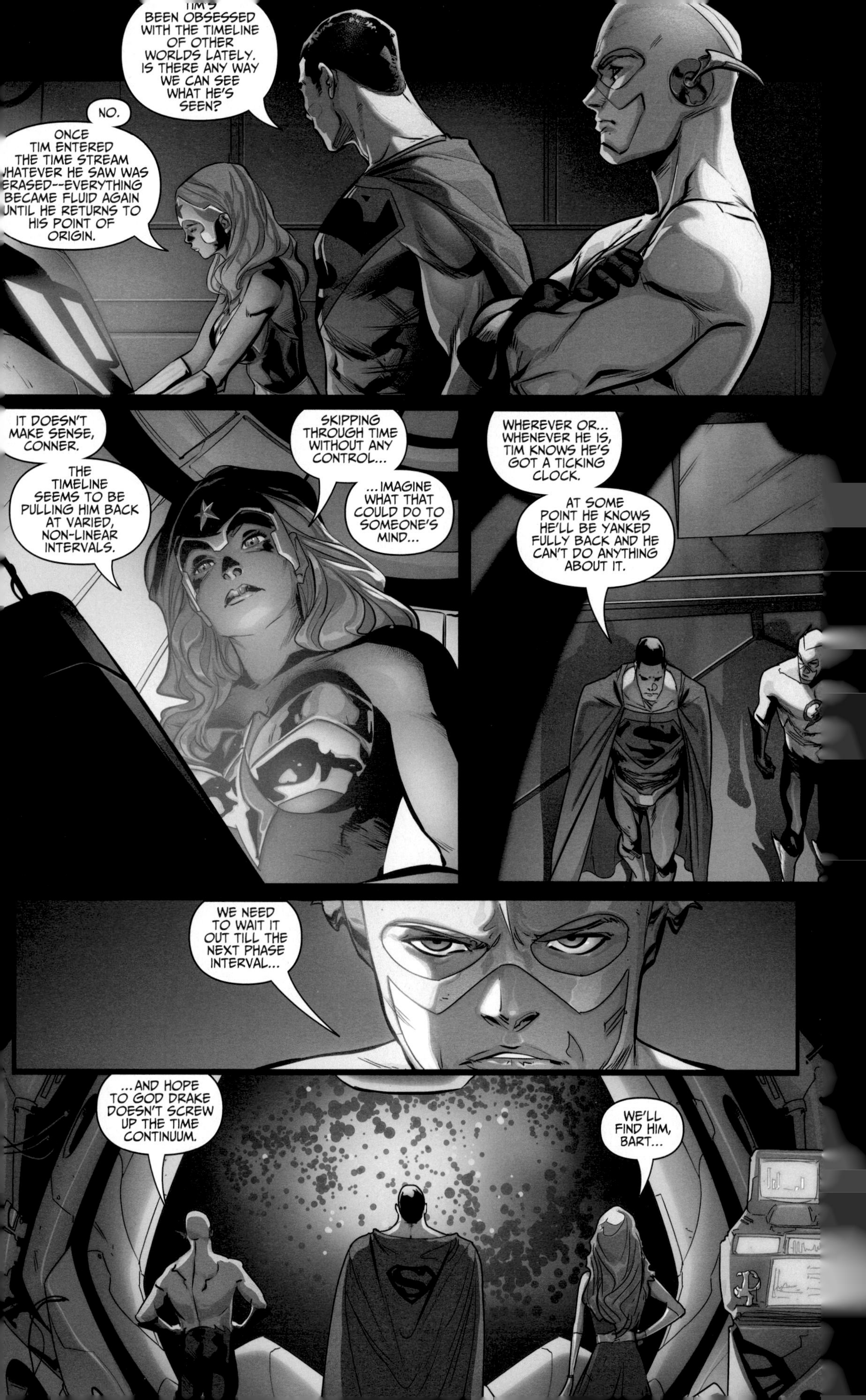
TIM'S BEEN OBSESSED WITH THE TIMELINE OF OTHER WORLDS LATELY. IS THERE ANY WAY WE CAN SEE WHAT HE'S SEEN?
NO.
ONCE TIM ENTERED THE TIME STREAM WHATEVER HE SAW WAS ERASED--EVERYTHING BECAME FLUID AGAIN UNTIL HE RETURNS TO HIS POINT OF ORIGIN.
IT DOESN'T MAKE SENSE, CONNER.
THE TIMELINE SEEMS TO BE PULLING HIM BACK AT VARIED, NON-LINEAR INTERVALS.
SKIPPING THROUGH TIME WITHOUT ANY CONTROL...
...IMAGINE WHAT THAT COULD DO TO SOMEONE'S MIND...
WHEREVER OR... WHENEVER HE IS, TIM KNOWS HE'S GOT A TICKING CLOCK.
AT SOME POINT HE KNOWS HE'LL BE YANKED FULLY BACK AND HE CAN'T DO ANYTHING ABOUT IT.
WE NEED TO WAIT IT OUT TILL THE NEXT PHASE INTERVAL...
...AND HOPE TO GOD DRAKE DOESN'T SCREW UP THE TIME CONTINUUM.
WE'LL FIND HIM, BART...

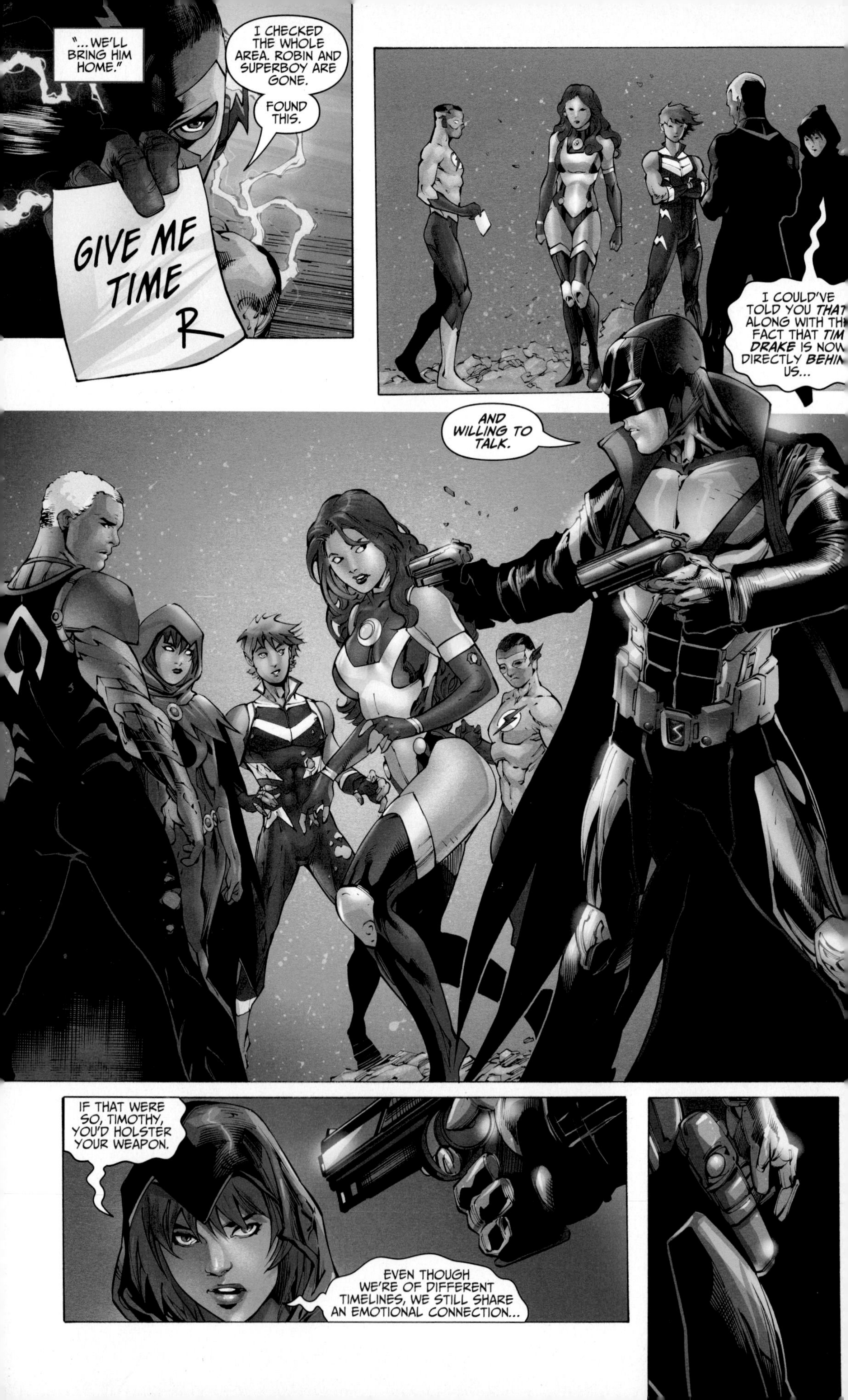
"...WE'LL BRING HIM HOME."
I CHECKED THE WHOLE AREA. ROBIN AND SUPERBOY ARE GONE.
FOUND THIS.
GIVE ME TIME
R
I COULD'VE TOLD YOU THAT ALONG WITH TH FACT THAT TIM DRAKE IS NOW DIRECTLY BEHIN US...
AND WILLING TO TALK.
IF THAT WERE SO, TIMOTHY, YOU'D HOLSTER YOUR WEAPON.
EVEN THOUGH WE'RE OF DIFFERENT TIMELINES, WE STILL SHARE AN EMOTIONAL CONNECTION...

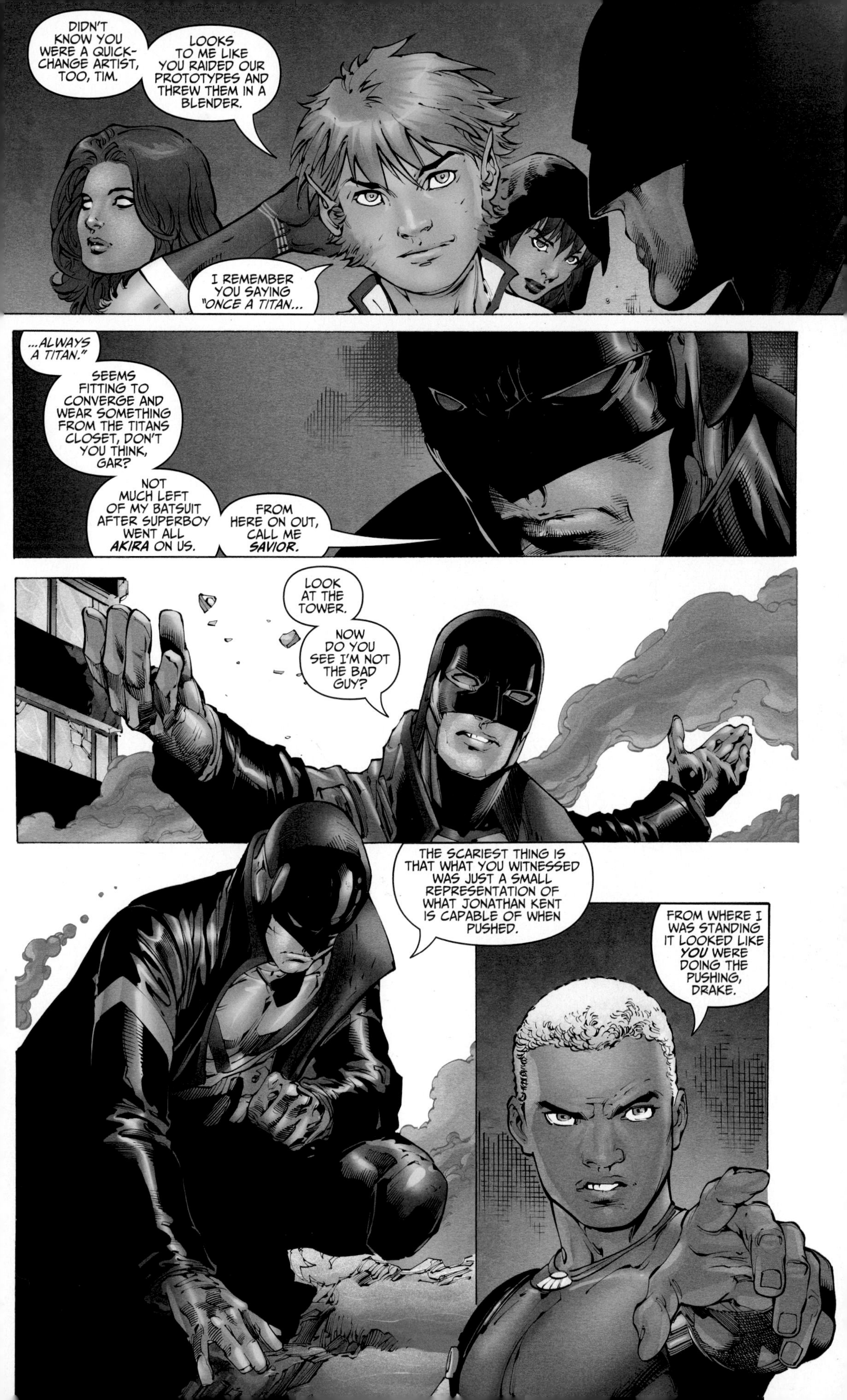
DIDN'T KNOW YOU WERE A QUICK-CHANGE ARTIST, TOO, TIM.
LOOKS TO ME LIKE YOU RAIDED OUR PROTOTYPES AND THREW THEM IN A BLENDER.
I REMEMBER YOU SAYING "ONCE A TITAN...
...ALWAYS A TITAN."
SEEMS FITTING TO CONVERGE AND WEAR SOMETHING FROM THE TITANS CLOSET, DON'T YOU THINK, GAR?
NOT MUCH LEFT OF MY BATSUIT AFTER SUPERBOY WENT ALL AKIRA ON US.
FROM HERE ON OUT, CALL ME SAVIOR.
LOOK AT THE TOWER.
NOW DO YOU SEE I'M NOT THE BAD GUY?
THE SCARIEST THING IS THAT WHAT YOU WITNESSED WAS JUST A SMALL REPRESENTATION OF WHAT JONATHAN KENT IS CAPABLE OF WHEN PUSHED.
FROM WHERE I WAS STANDING IT LOOKED LIKE YOU WERE DOING THE PUSHING, DRAKE.

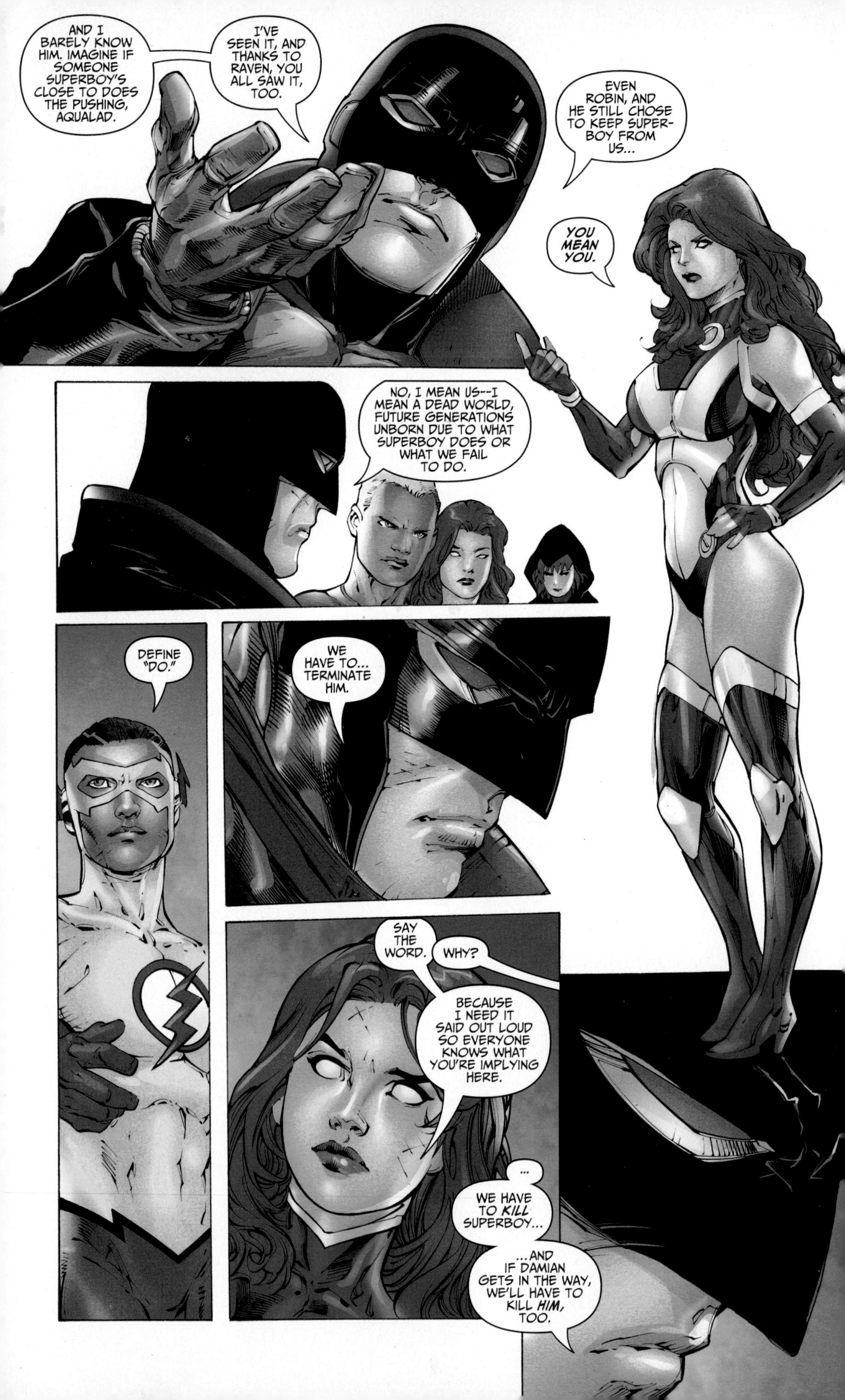
AND I BARELY KNOW HIM. IMAGINE IF SOMEONE SUPERBOY'S CLOSE TO DOES THE PUSHING, AQUALAD.
I'VE SEEN IT, AND THANKS TO RAVEN, YOU ALL SAW IT, TOO.
EVEN ROBIN, AND HE STILL CHOSE TO KEEP SUPER-BOY FROM US...
YOU MEAN YOU.
NO, I MEAN US--I MEAN A DEAD WORLD, FUTURE GENERATIONS UNBORN DUE TO WHAT SUPERBOY DOES OR WHAT WE FAIL TO DO.
DEFINE "DO."
WE HAVE TO... TERMINATE HIM.
SAY THE WORD.
WHY?
BECAUSE I NEED IT SAID OUT LOUD SO EVERYONE KNOWS WHAT YOU'RE IMPLYING HERE.
...
WE HAVE TO KILL SUPERBOY...
...AND IF DAMIAN GETS IN THE WAY, WE'LL HAVE TO KILL HIM, TOO.

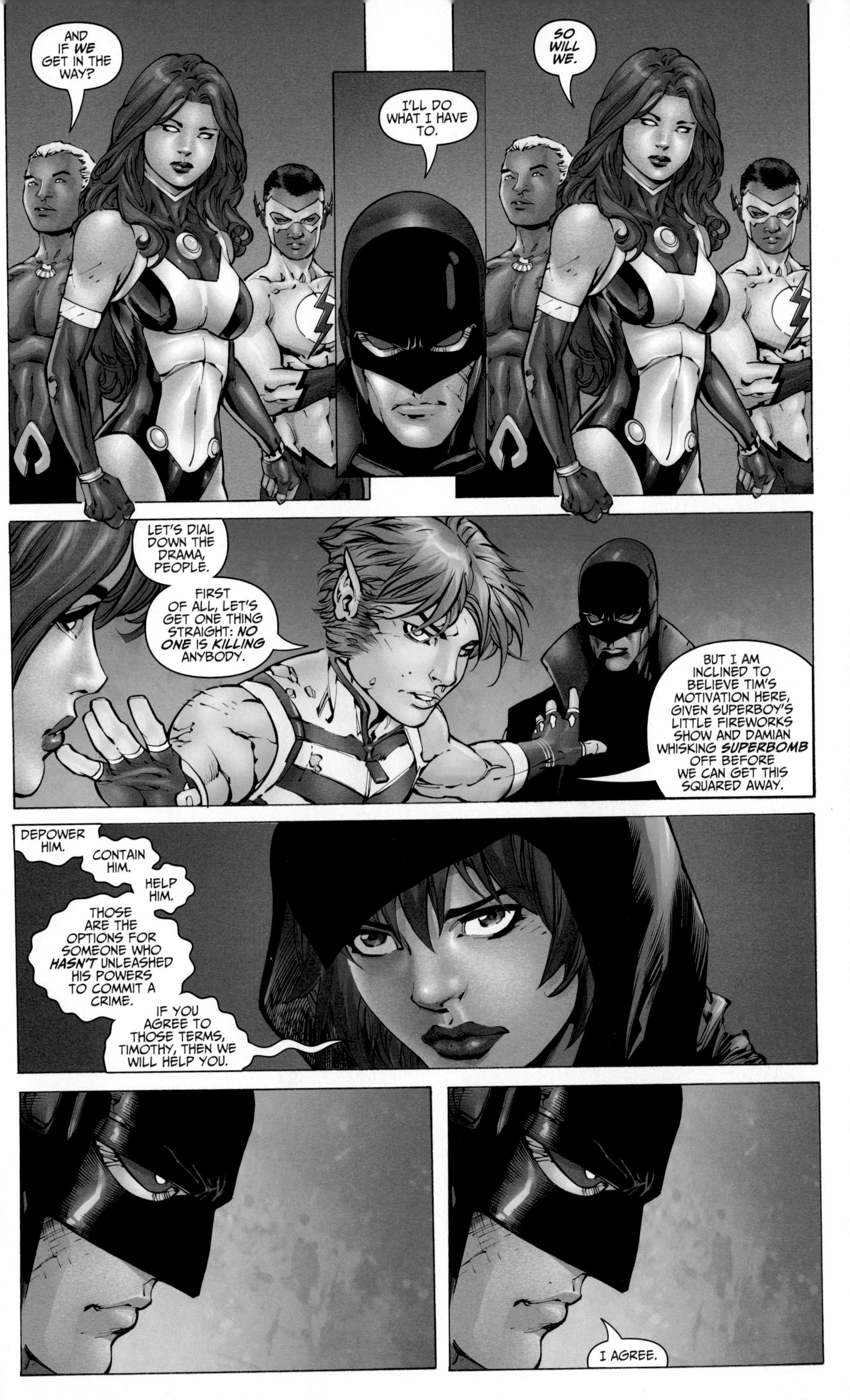
AND IF WE GET IN THE WAY?
I'LL DO WHAT I HAVE TO.
SO WILL WE.
LET'S DIAL DOWN THE DRAMA, PEOPLE.
FIRST OF ALL, LET'S GET ONE THING STRAIGHT: NO ONE IS KILLING ANYBODY.
BUT I AM INCLINED TO BELIEVE TIM'S MOTIVATION HERE, GIVEN SUPERBOY'S LITTLE FIREWORKS SHOW AND DAMIAN WHISKING SUPERBOMB OFF BEFORE WE CAN GET THIS SQUARED AWAY.
DEPOWER HIM.
CONTAIN HIM.
HELP HIM.
THOSE ARE THE OPTIONS FOR SOMEONE WHO HASN'T UNLEASHED HIS POWERS TO COMMIT A CRIME.
IF YOU AGREE TO THOSE TERMS, TIMOTHY, THEN WE WILL HELP YOU.
I AGREE.

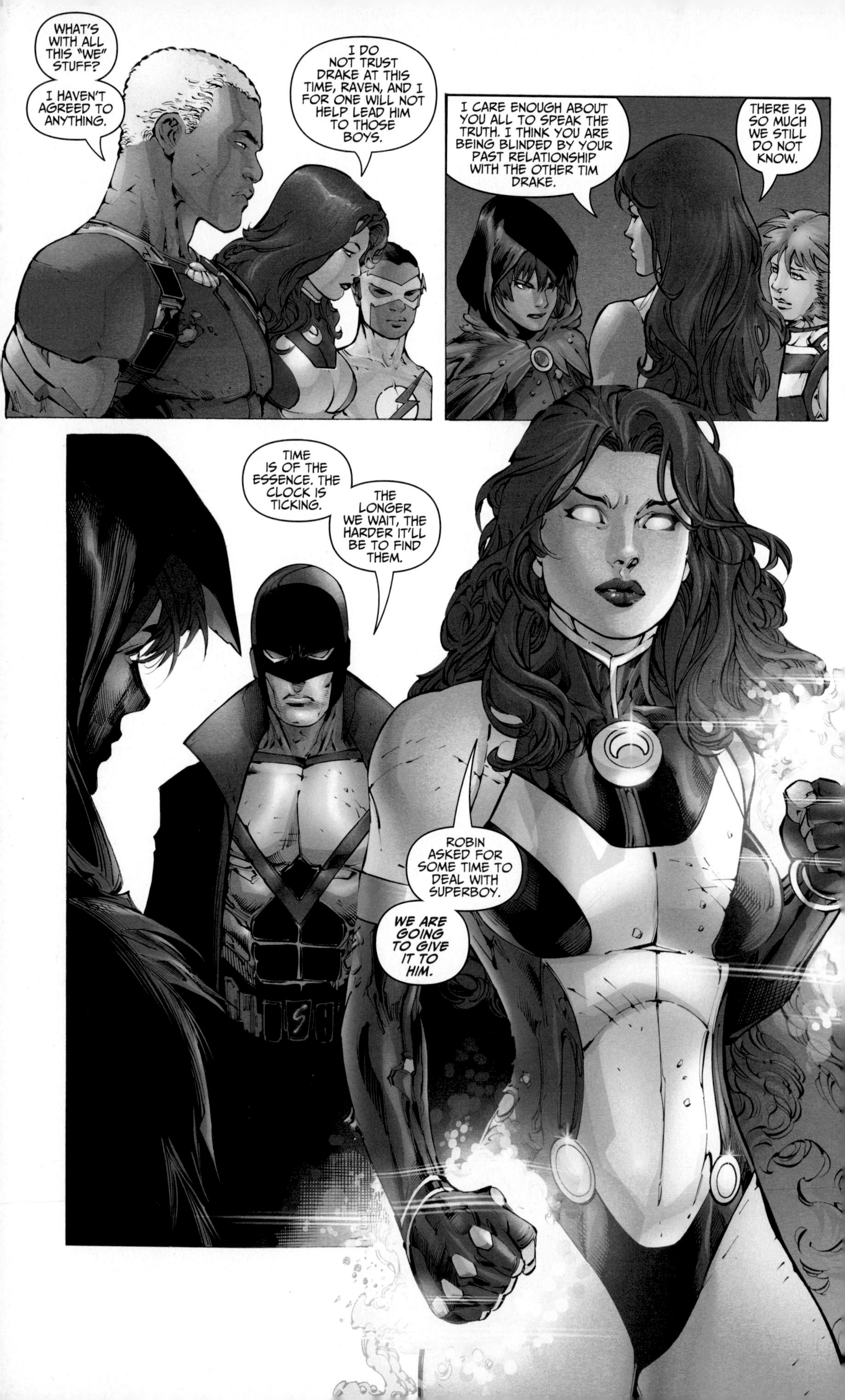
WHAT'S WITH ALL THIS "WE" STUFF?
I HAVEN'T AGREED TO ANYTHING.
I DO NOT TRUST DRAKE AT THIS TIME, RAVEN, AND I FOR ONE WILL NOT HELP LEAD HIM TO THOSE BOYS.
I CARE ENOUGH ABOUT YOU ALL TO SPEAK THE TRUTH. I THINK YOU ARE BEING BLINDED BY YOUR PAST RELATIONSHIP WITH THE OTHER TIM DRAKE.
THERE IS SO MUCH WE STILL DO NOT KNOW.
TIME IS OF THE ESSENCE. THE CLOCK IS TICKING.
THE LONGER WE WAIT, THE HARDER IT'LL BE TO FIND THEM.
ROBIN ASKED FOR SOME TIME TO DEAL WITH SUPERBOY.
WE ARE GOING TO GIVE IT TO HIM.

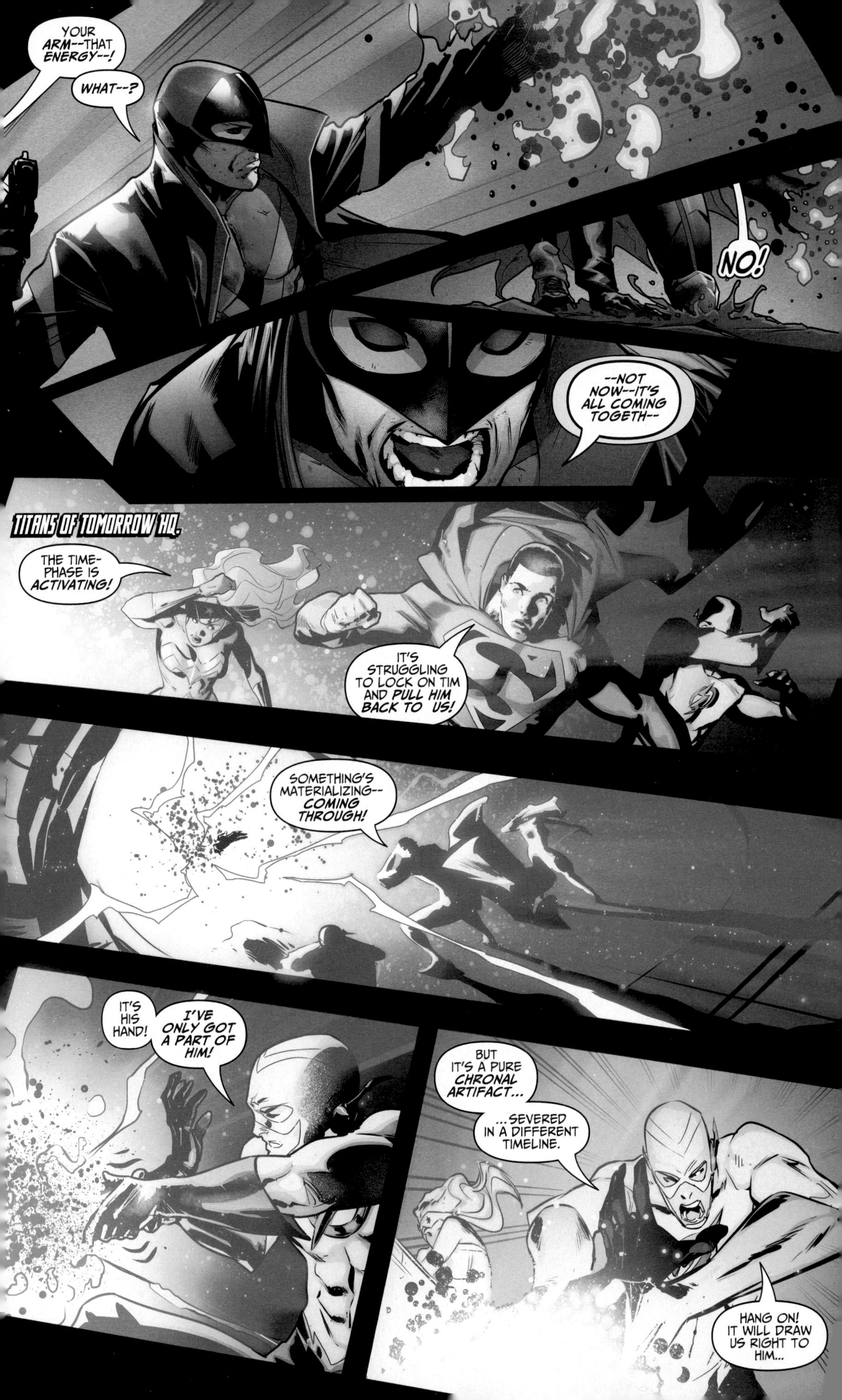

YOUR ARM--THAT ENERGY--!
WHAT--?
NO!
--NOT NOW--IT'S ALL COMING TOGETH--
TITANS OF TOMORROW HQ.
THE TIME-PHASE IS ACTIVATING!
IT'S STRUGGLING TO LOCK ON TIM AND PULL HIM BACK TO US!
SOMETHING'S MATERIALIZING--COMING THROUGH!
IT'S HIS HAND!
I'VE ONLY GOT A PART OF HIM!
BUT IT'S A PURE CHRONAL ARTIFACT...
...SEVERED IN A DIFFERENT TIMELINE.
HANG ON! IT WILL DRAW US RIGHT TO HIM...

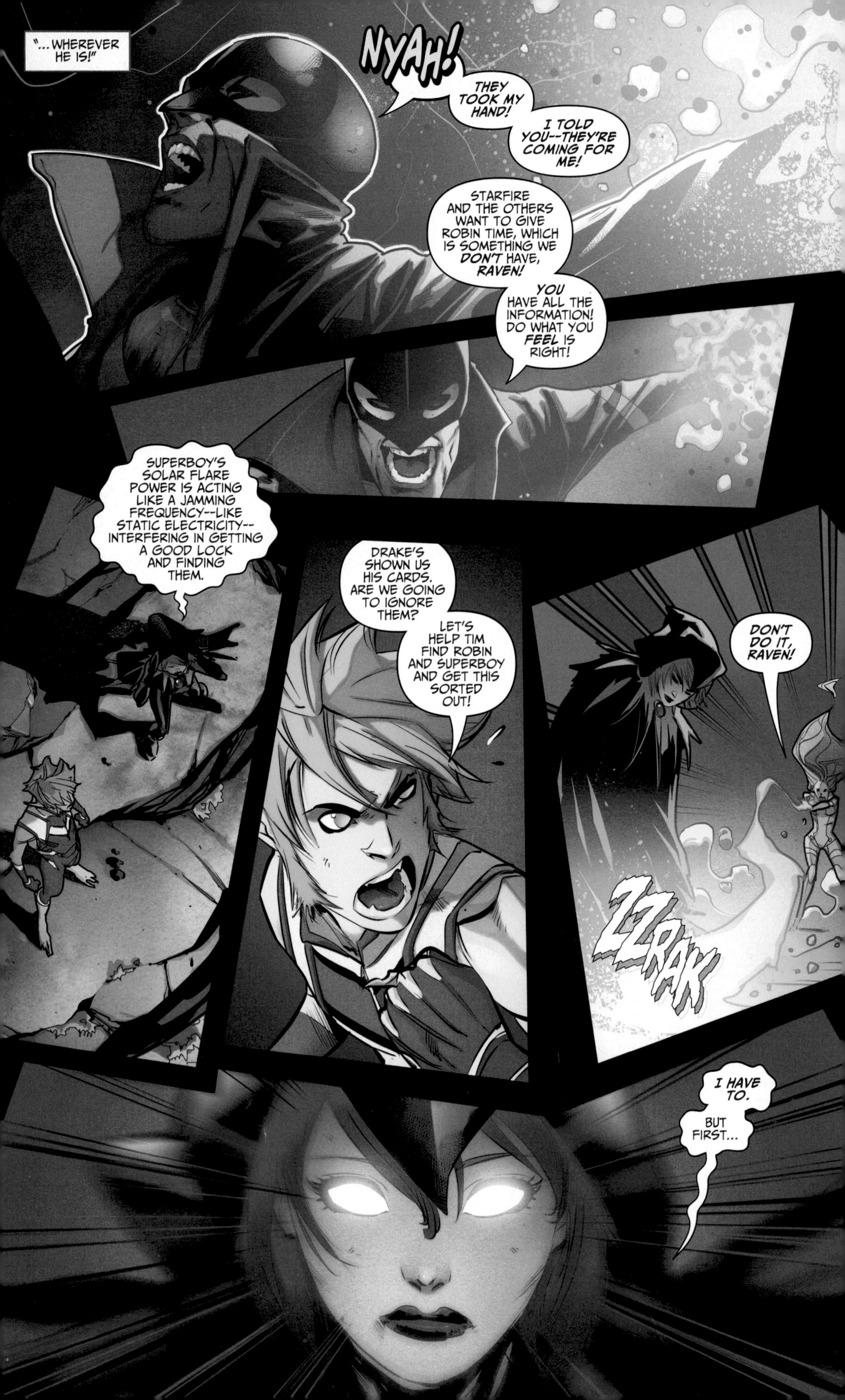
"...WHEREVER HE IS!"
NYAH!
THEY TOOK MY HAND!
I TOLD YOU--THEY'RE COMING FOR ME!
STARFIRE AND THE OTHERS WANT TO GIVE ROBIN TIME, WHICH IS SOMETHING WE DON'T HAVE, RAVEN!
YOU HAVE ALL THE INFORMATION! DO WHAT YOU FEEL IS RIGHT!
SUPERBOY'S SOLAR FLARE POWER IS ACTING LIKE A JAMMING FREQUENCY--LIKE STATIC ELECTRICITY--INTERFERING IN GETTING A GOOD LOCK AND FINDING THEM.
DRAKE'S SHOWN US HIS CARDS. ARE WE GOING TO IGNORE THEM?
LET'S HELP TIM FIND ROBIN AND SUPERBOY AND GET THIS SORTED OUT!
DON'T DO IT, RAVEN!
ZZRAK
I HAVE TO.
BUT FIRST...

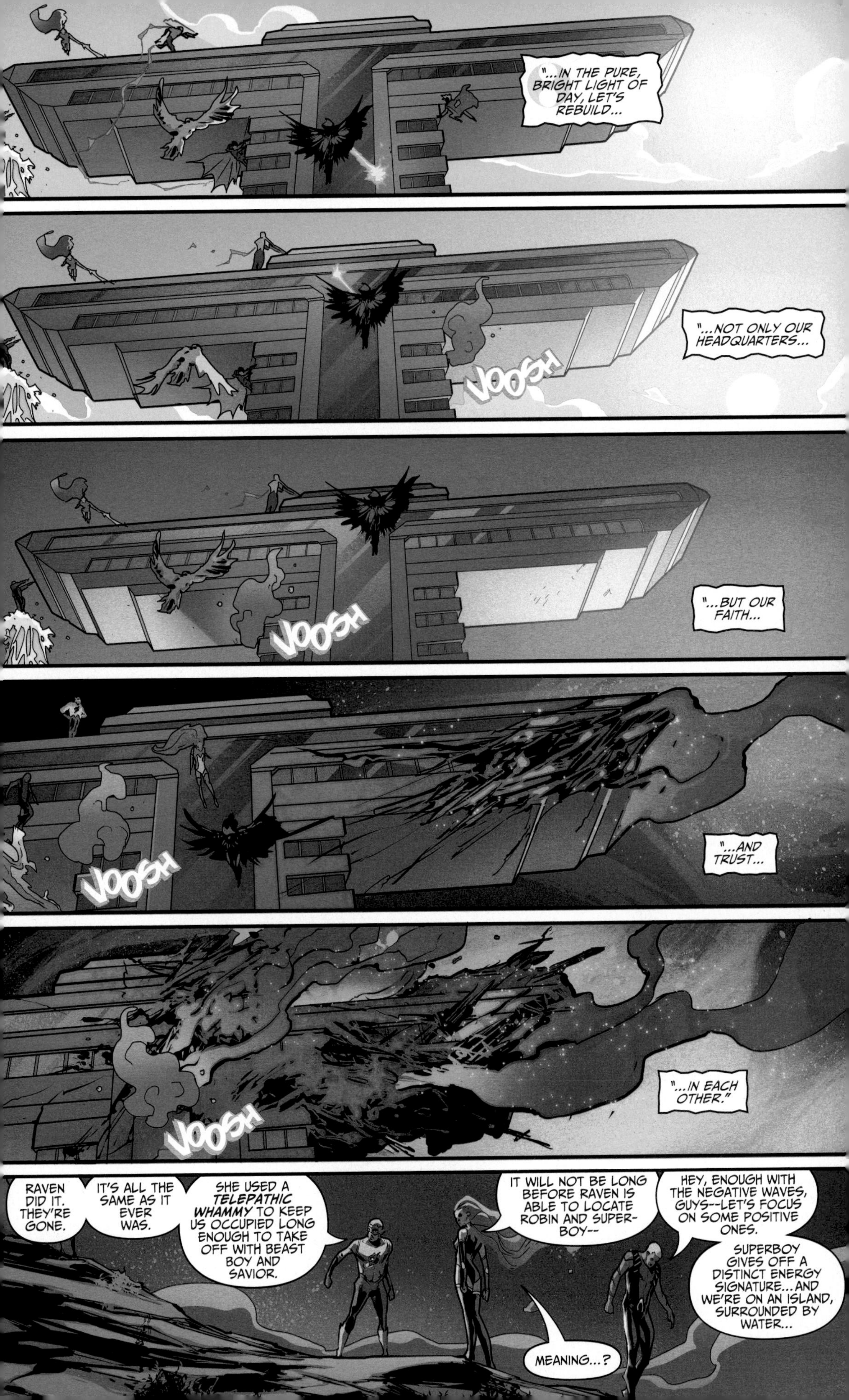
"...IN THE PURE, BRIGHT LIGHT OF DAY, LET'S REBUILD...
"...NOT ONLY OUR HEADQUARTERS...
VOOSH
"...BUT OUR FAITH...
VOOSH
"...AND TRUST...
VOOSH
"...IN EACH OTHER."
VOOSH
RAVEN DID IT. THEY'RE GONE.
IT'S ALL THE SAME AS IT EVER WAS.
SHE USED A ***TELEPATHIC WHAMMY*** TO KEEP US OCCUPIED LONG ENOUGH TO TAKE OFF WITH BEAST BOY AND SAVIOR.
IT WILL NOT BE LONG BEFORE RAVEN IS ABLE TO LOCATE ROBIN AND SUPER-BOY--
HEY, ENOUGH WITH THE NEGATIVE WAVES, GUYS--LET'S FOCUS ON SOME POSITIVE ONES.
SUPERBOY GIVES OFF A DISTINCT ENERGY SIGNATURE...AND WE'RE ON AN ISLAND, SURROUNDED BY WATER...
MEANING...?

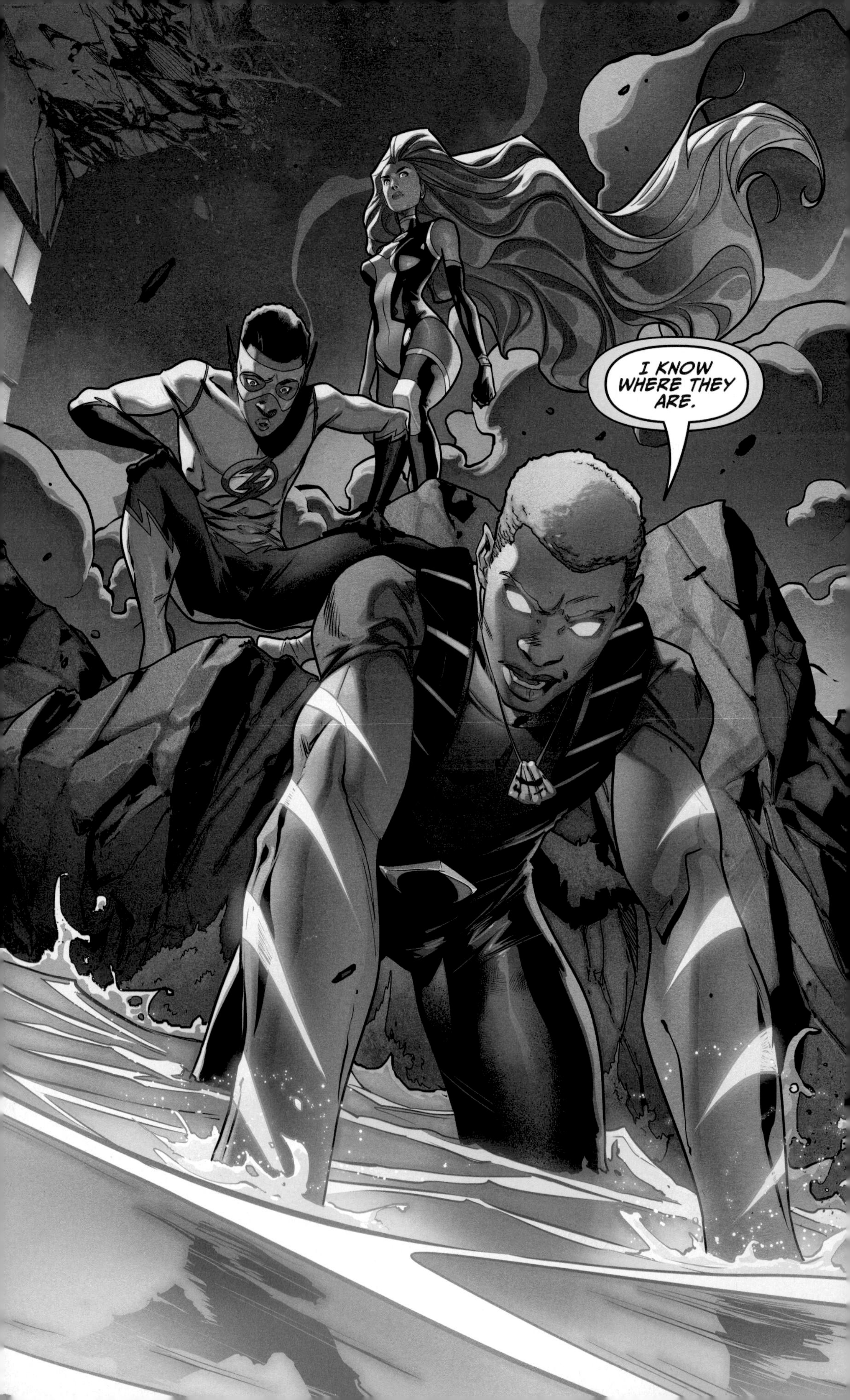
I KNOW WHERE THEY ARE.

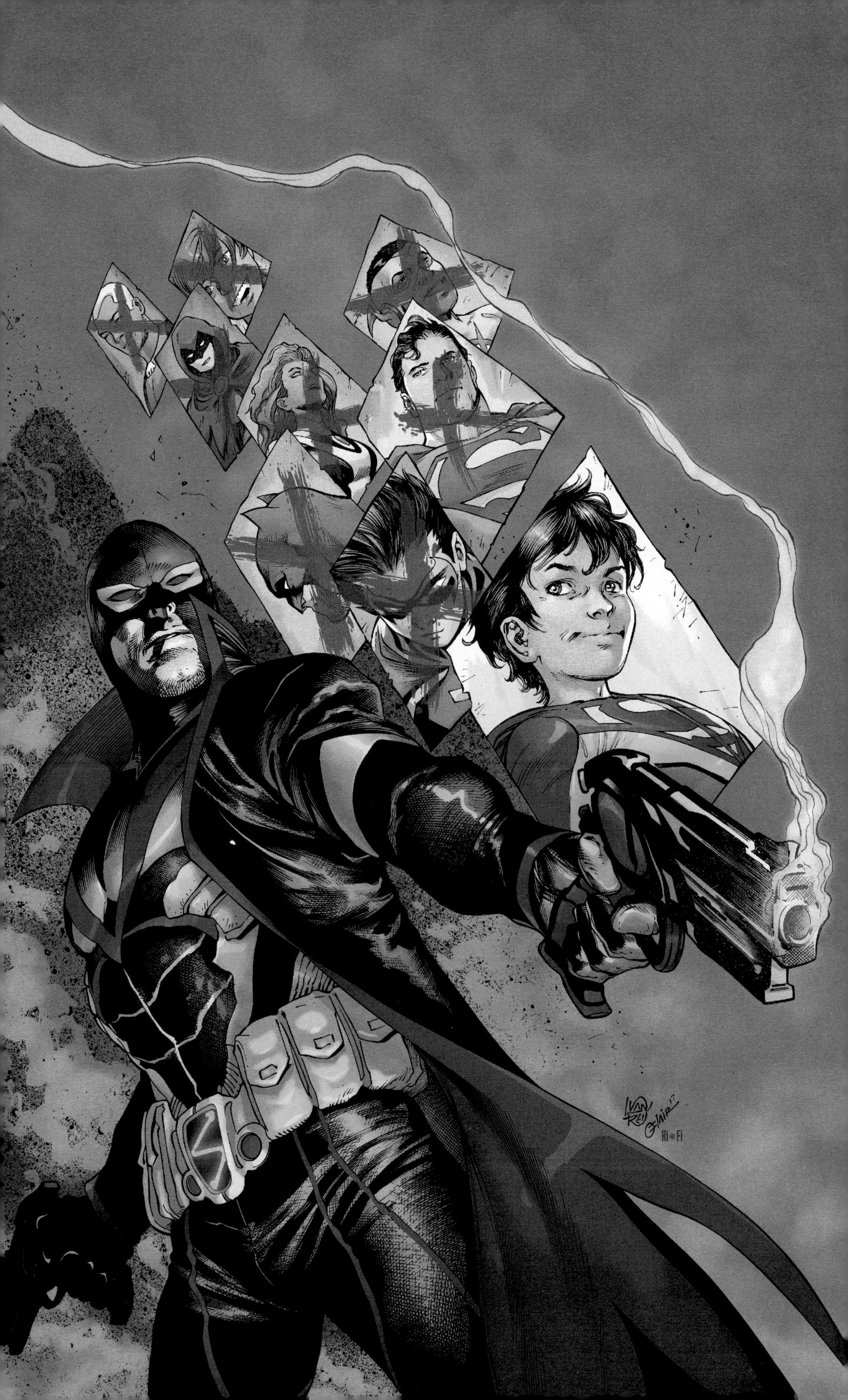

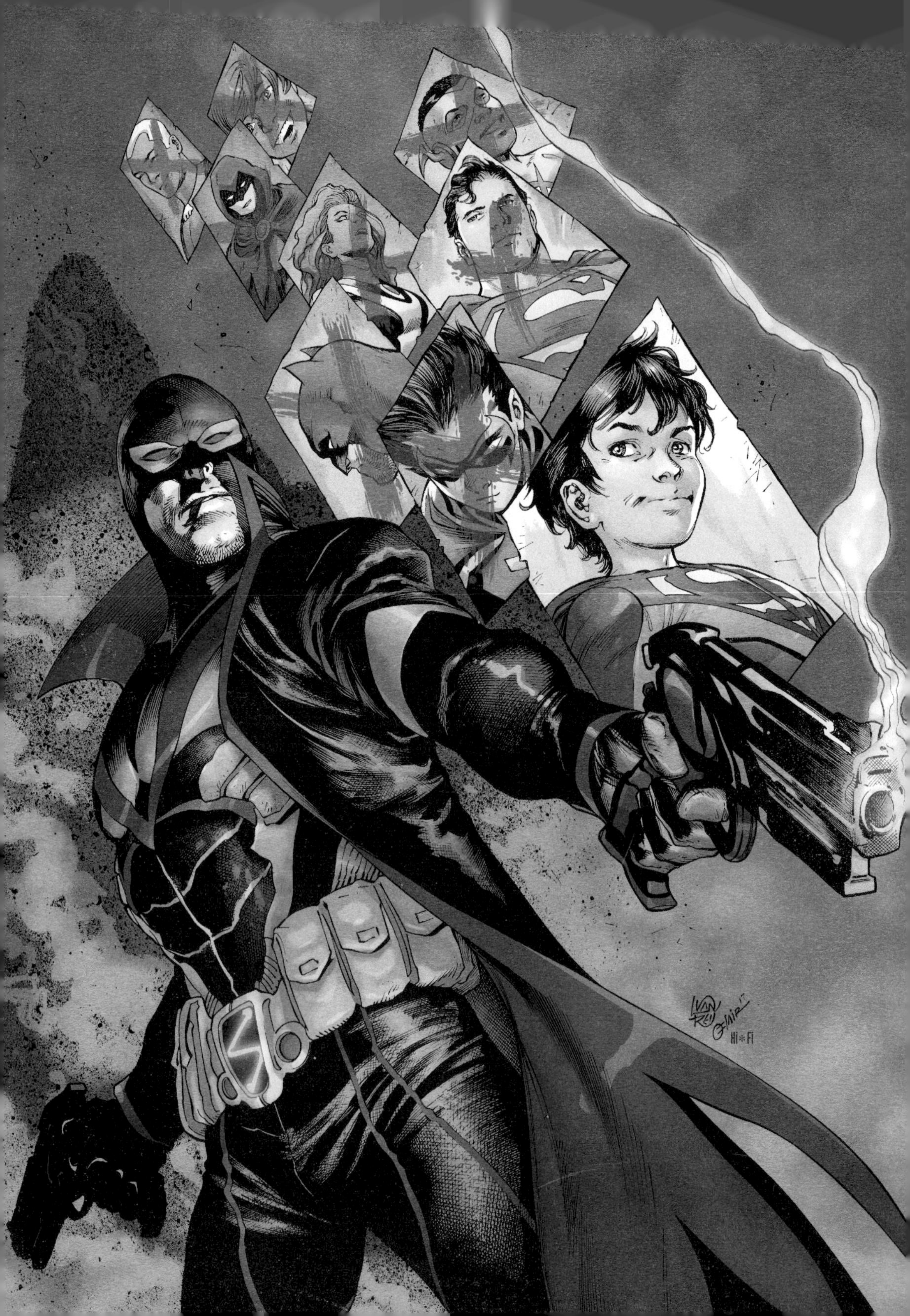

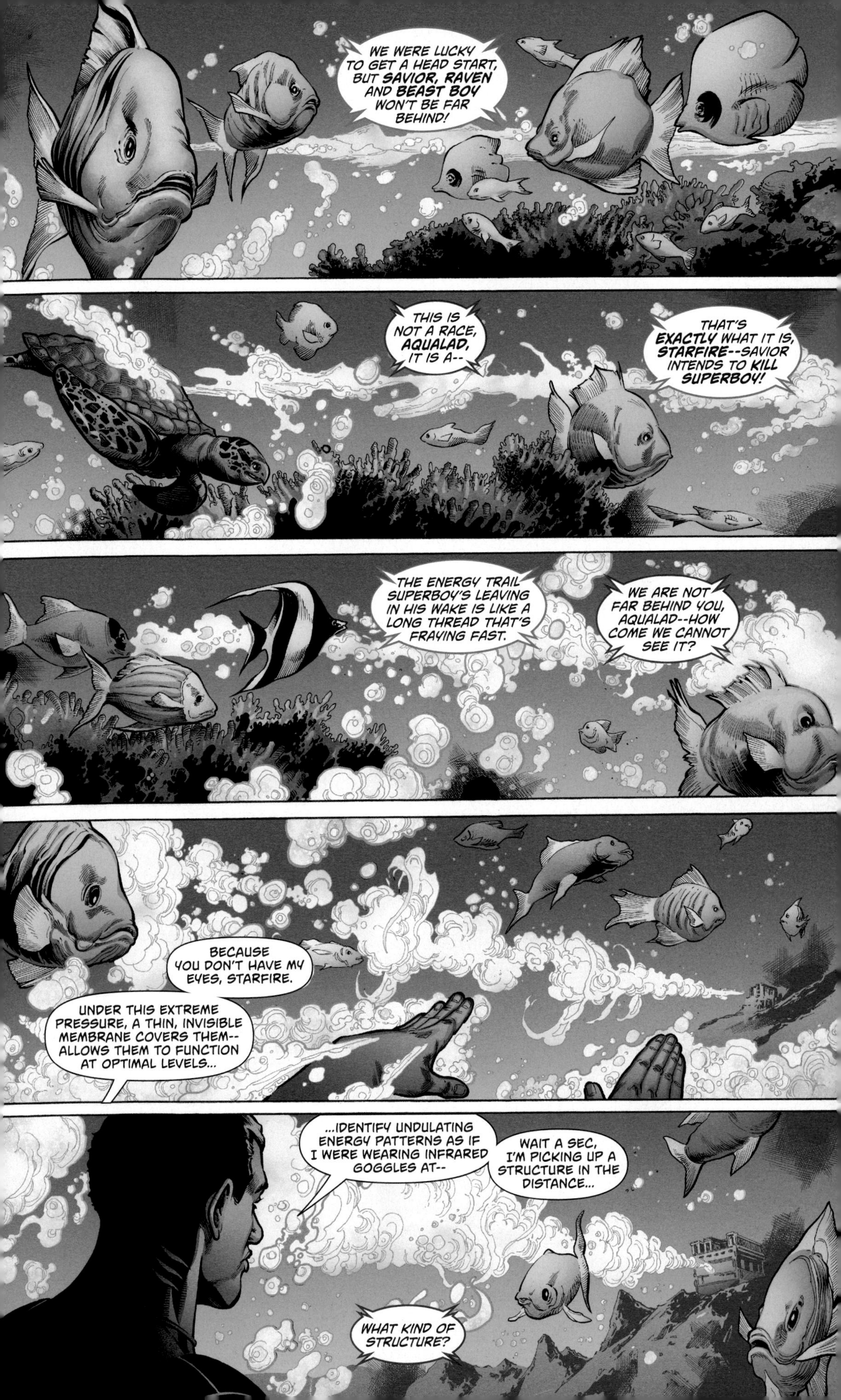

WE WERE LUCKY TO GET A HEAD START, BUT SAVIOR, RAVEN AND BEAST BOY WON'T BE FAR BEHIND!
THIS IS NOT A RACE, AQUALAD, IT IS A--
THAT'S EXACTLY WHAT IT IS, STARFIRE--SAVIOR INTENDS TO KILL SUPERBOY!
THE ENERGY TRAIL SUPERBOY'S LEAVING IN HIS WAKE IS LIKE A LONG THREAD THAT'S FRAYING FAST.
WE ARE NOT FAR BEHIND YOU, AQUALAD--HOW COME WE CANNOT SEE IT?
BECAUSE YOU DON'T HAVE MY EYES, STARFIRE.
UNDER THIS EXTREME PRESSURE, A THIN, INVISIBLE MEMBRANE COVERS THEM--ALLOWS THEM TO FUNCTION AT OPTIMAL LEVELS...
...IDENTIFY UNDULATING ENERGY PATTERNS AS IF I WERE WEARING INFRARED GOGGLES AT--
WAIT A SEC, I'M PICKING UP A STRUCTURE IN THE DISTANCE...
WHAT KIND OF STRUCTURE?

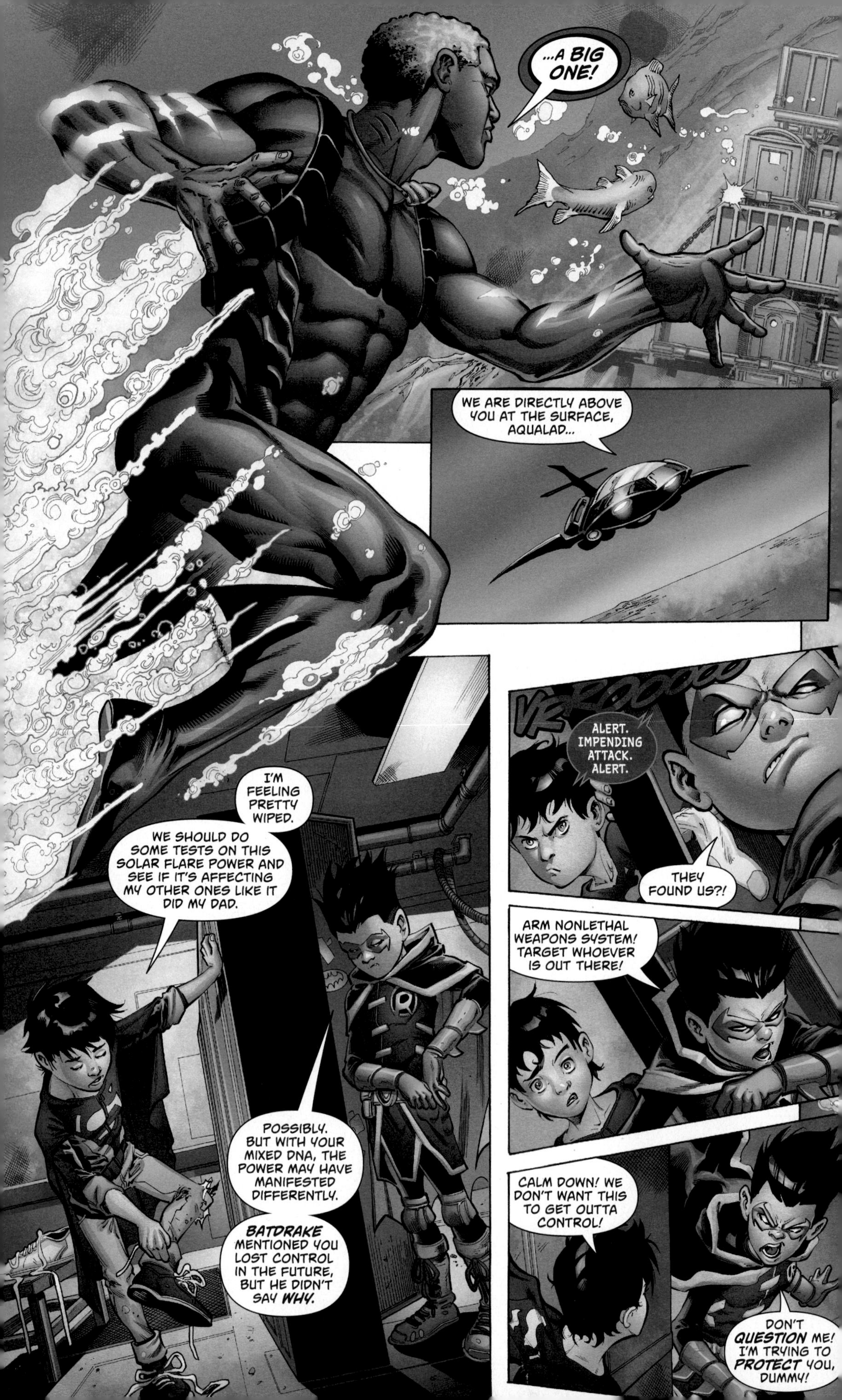

...A BIG ONE!
WE ARE DIRECTLY ABOVE YOU AT THE SURFACE, AQUALAD...
VRROOOOO
ALERT. IMPENDING ATTACK. ALERT.
THEY FOUND US?!
I'M FEELING PRETTY WIPED.
WE SHOULD DO SOME TESTS ON THIS SOLAR FLARE POWER AND SEE IF IT'S AFFECTING MY OTHER ONES LIKE IT DID MY DAD.
POSSIBLY. BUT WITH YOUR MIXED DNA, THE POWER MAY HAVE MANIFESTED DIFFERENTLY.
BATDRAKE MENTIONED YOU LOST CONTROL IN THE FUTURE, BUT HE DIDN'T SAY WHY.
ARM NONLETHAL WEAPONS SYSTEM! TARGET WHOEVER IS OUT THERE!
CALM DOWN! WE DON'T WANT THIS TO GET OUTTA CONTROL!
DON'T QUESTION ME! I'M TRYING TO PROTECT YOU, DUMMY!

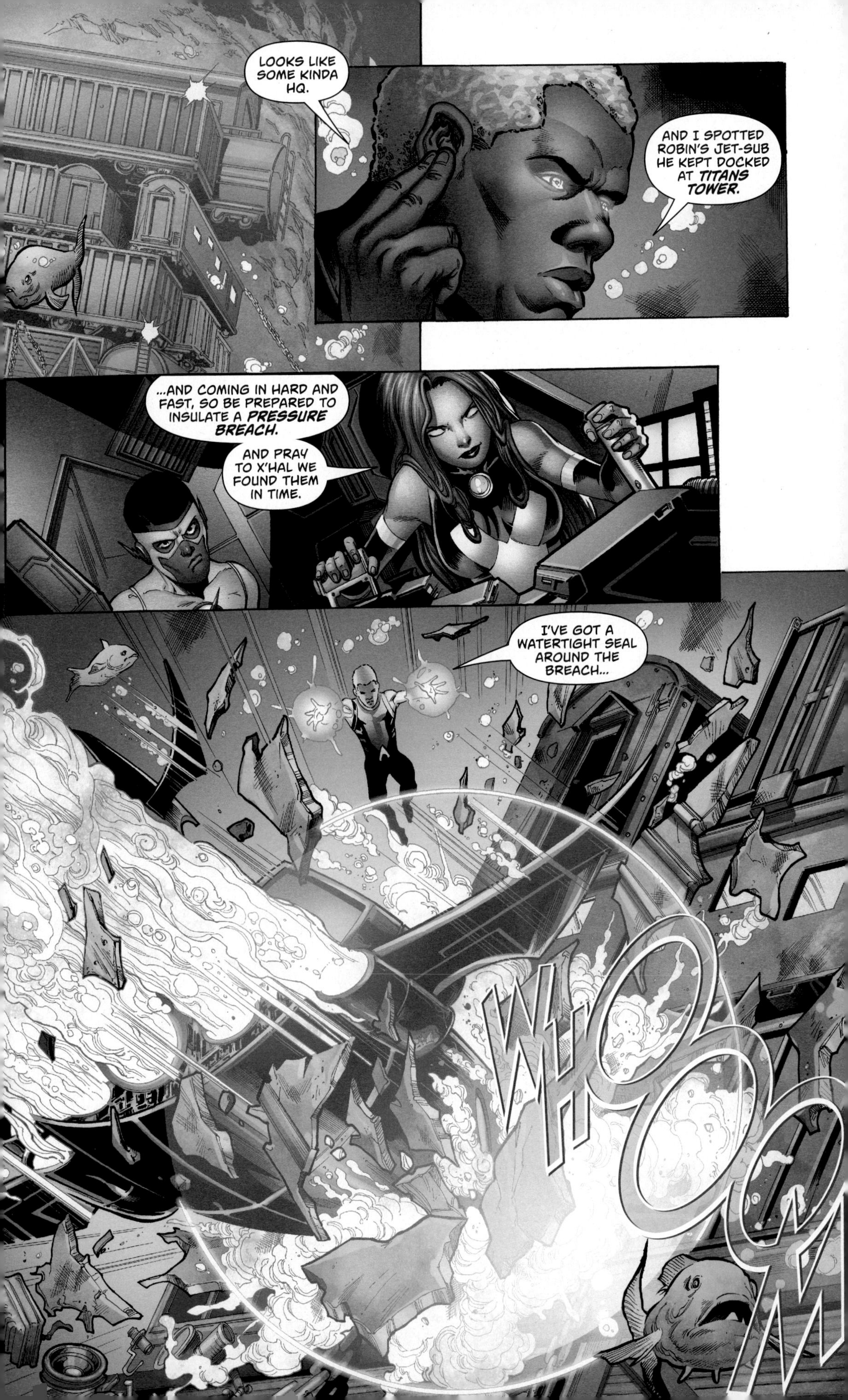
LOOKS LIKE SOME KINDA HQ.
AND I SPOTTED ROBIN'S JET-SUB HE KEPT DOCKED AT TITANS TOWER.
...AND COMING IN HARD AND FAST, SO BE PREPARED TO INSULATE A PRESSURE BREACH.
AND PRAY TO X'HAL WE FOUND THEM IN TIME.
I'VE GOT A WATERTIGHT SEAL AROUND THE BREACH...
WHOOOM

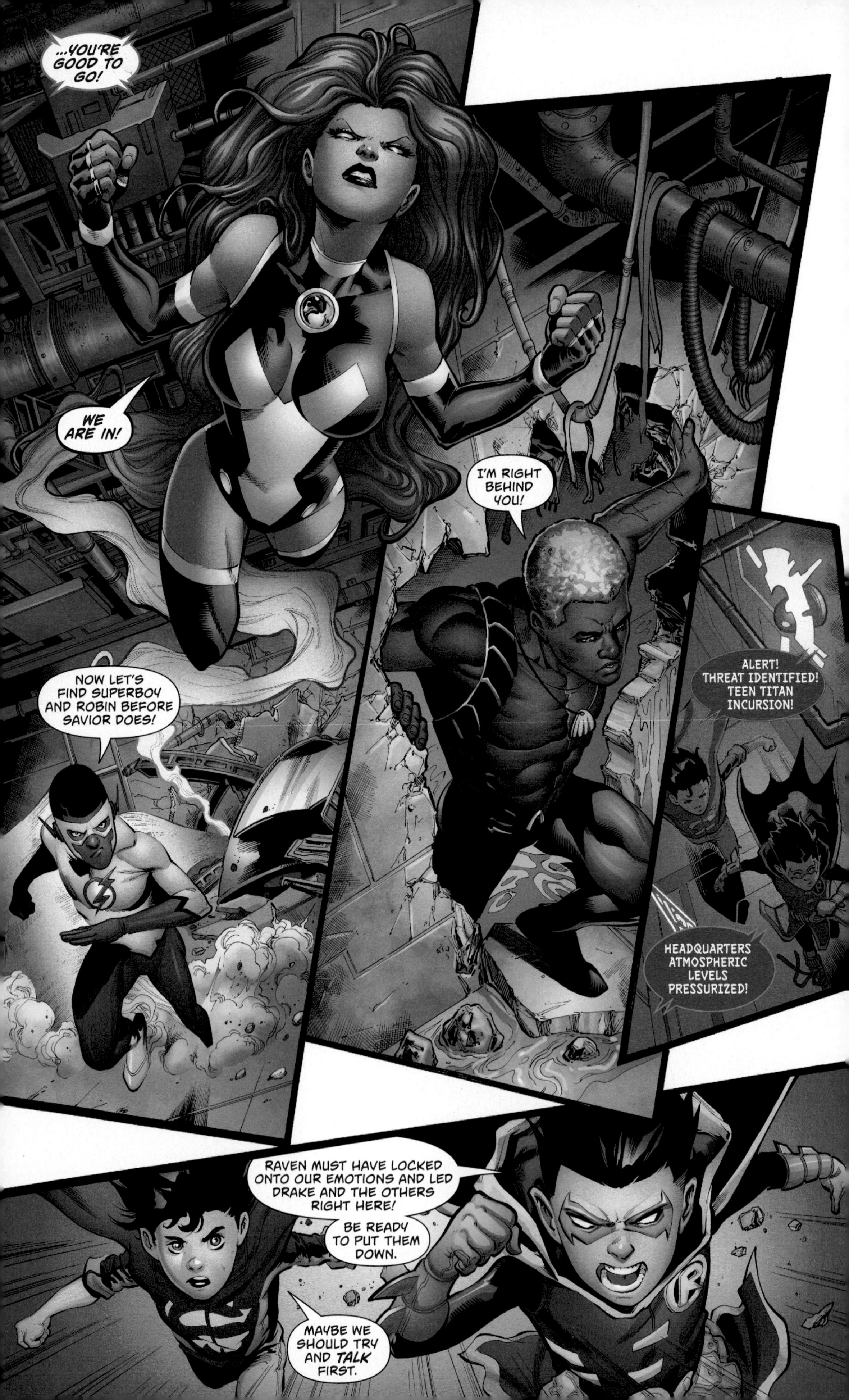
...YOU'RE GOOD TO GO!
WE ARE IN!
I'M RIGHT BEHIND YOU!
NOW LET'S FIND SUPERBOY AND ROBIN BEFORE SAVIOR DOES!
ALERT! THREAT IDENTIFIED! TEEN TITAN INCURSION!
HEADQUARTERS ATMOSPHERIC LEVELS PRESSURIZED!
RAVEN MUST HAVE LOCKED ONTO OUR EMOTIONS AND LED DRAKE AND THE OTHERS RIGHT HERE!
BE READY TO PUT THEM DOWN.
MAYBE WE SHOULD TRY AND TALK FIRST.

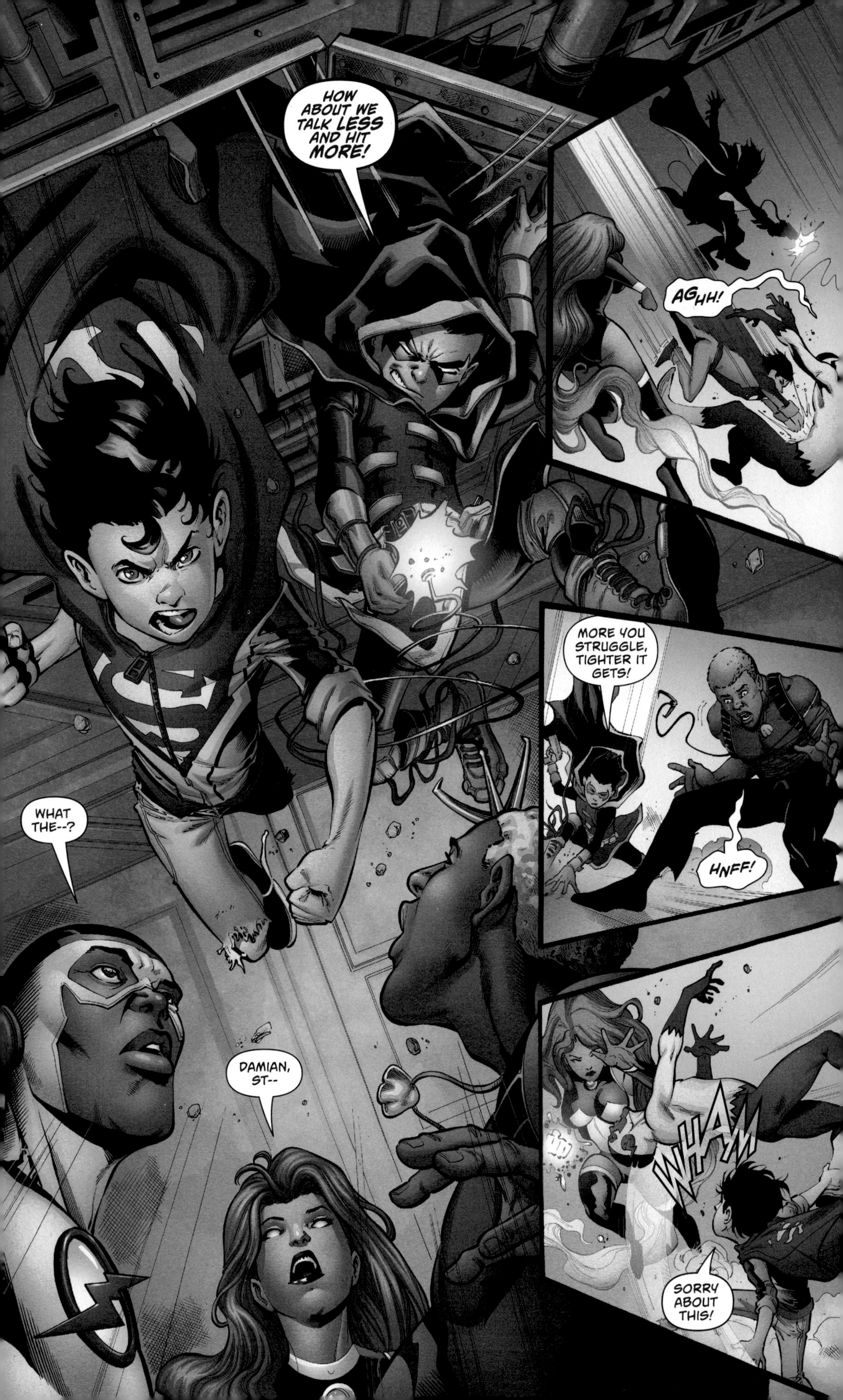
HOW ABOUT WE TALK LESS AND HIT MORE!
AGHH!
MORE YOU STRUGGLE, TIGHTER IT GETS!
HNFF!
WHAT THE--?
DAMIAN, ST--
WHAM
SORRY ABOUT THIS!

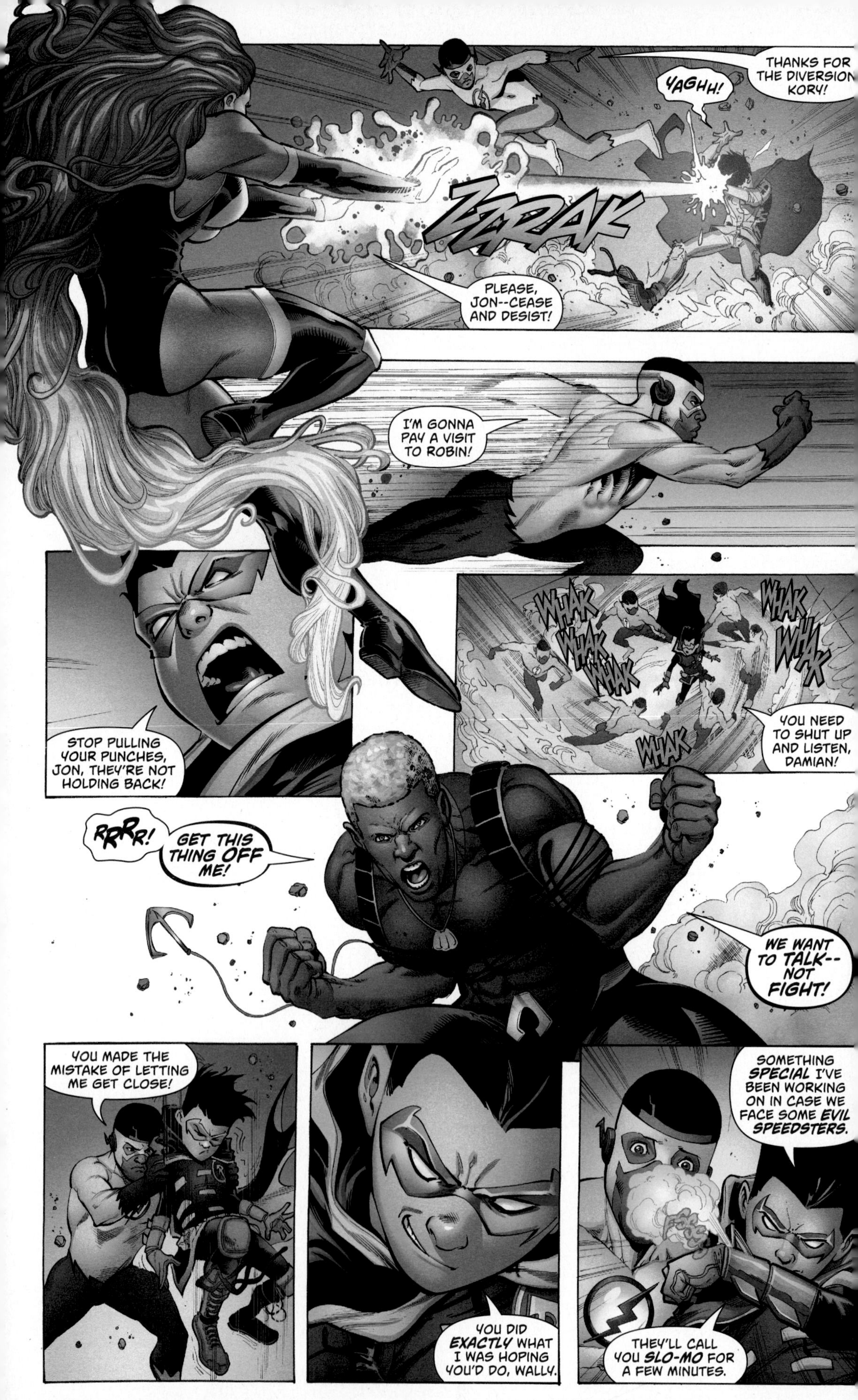

YAGHH!
THANKS FOR THE DIVERSION KORY!
ZZRAK
PLEASE, JON--CEASE AND DESIST!
I'M GONNA PAY A VISIT TO ROBIN!
STOP PULLING YOUR PUNCHES, JON, THEY'RE NOT HOLDING BACK!
WHAK WHAK WHAK
WHAK WHAK
WHAK
YOU NEED TO SHUT UP AND LISTEN, DAMIAN!
RRRR!
GET THIS THING OFF ME!
WE WANT TO TALK--NOT FIGHT!
YOU MADE THE MISTAKE OF LETTING ME GET CLOSE!
YOU DID EXACTLY WHAT I WAS HOPING YOU'D DO, WALLY.
SOMETHING SPECIAL I'VE BEEN WORKING ON IN CASE WE FACE SOME EVIL SPEEDSTERS.
THEY'LL CALL YOU SLO-MO FOR A FEW MINUTES.

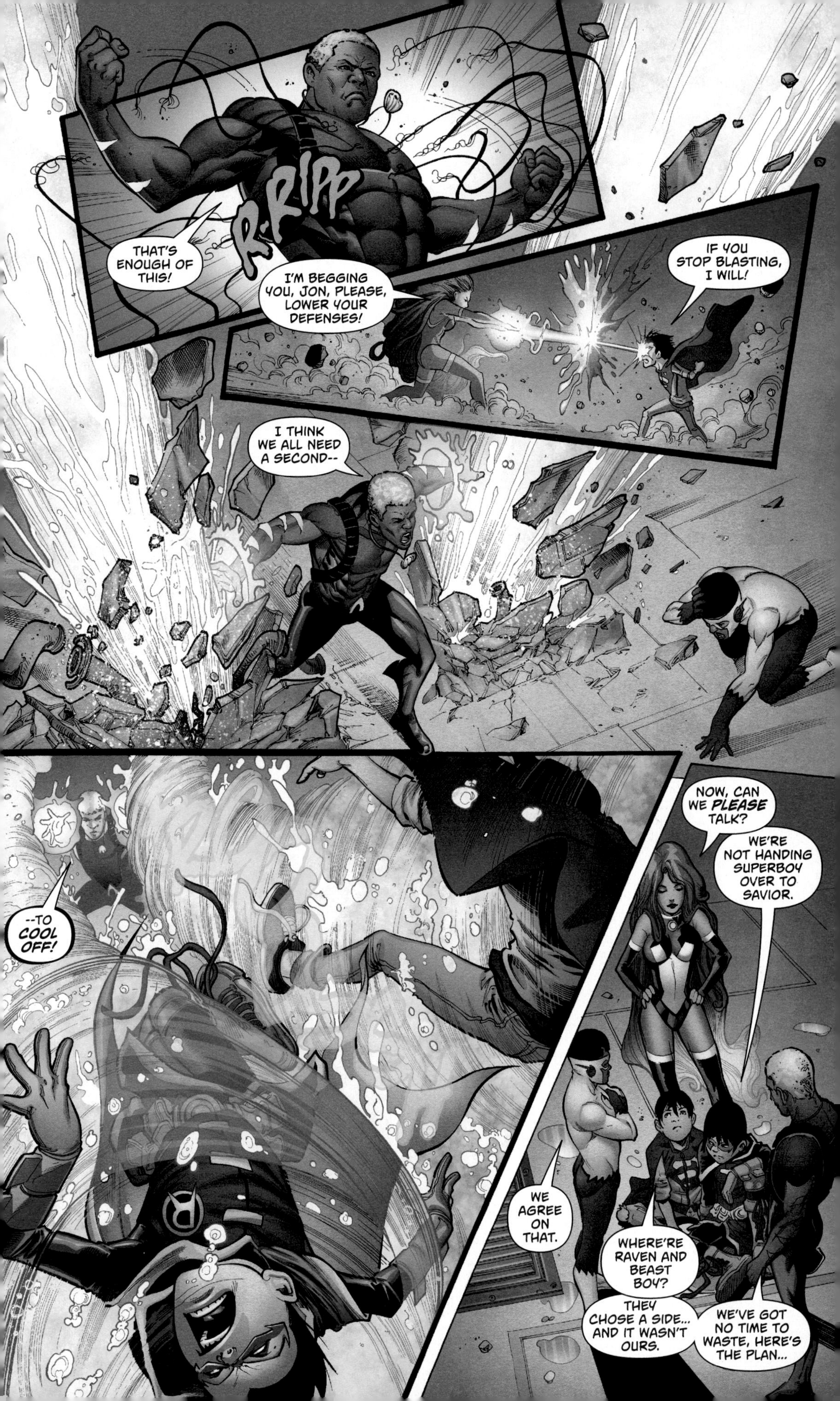
R-RIPP
THAT'S ENOUGH OF THIS!
I'M BEGGING YOU, JON, PLEASE, LOWER YOUR DEFENSES!
IF YOU STOP BLASTING, I WILL!
I THINK WE ALL NEED A SECOND--
--TO COOL OFF!
NOW, CAN WE PLEASE TALK?
WE'RE NOT HANDING SUPERBOY OVER TO SAVIOR.
WE AGREE ON THAT.
WHERE'RE RAVEN AND BEAST BOY?
THEY CHOSE A SIDE... AND IT WASN'T OURS.
WE'VE GOT NO TIME TO WASTE, HERE'S THE PLAN...

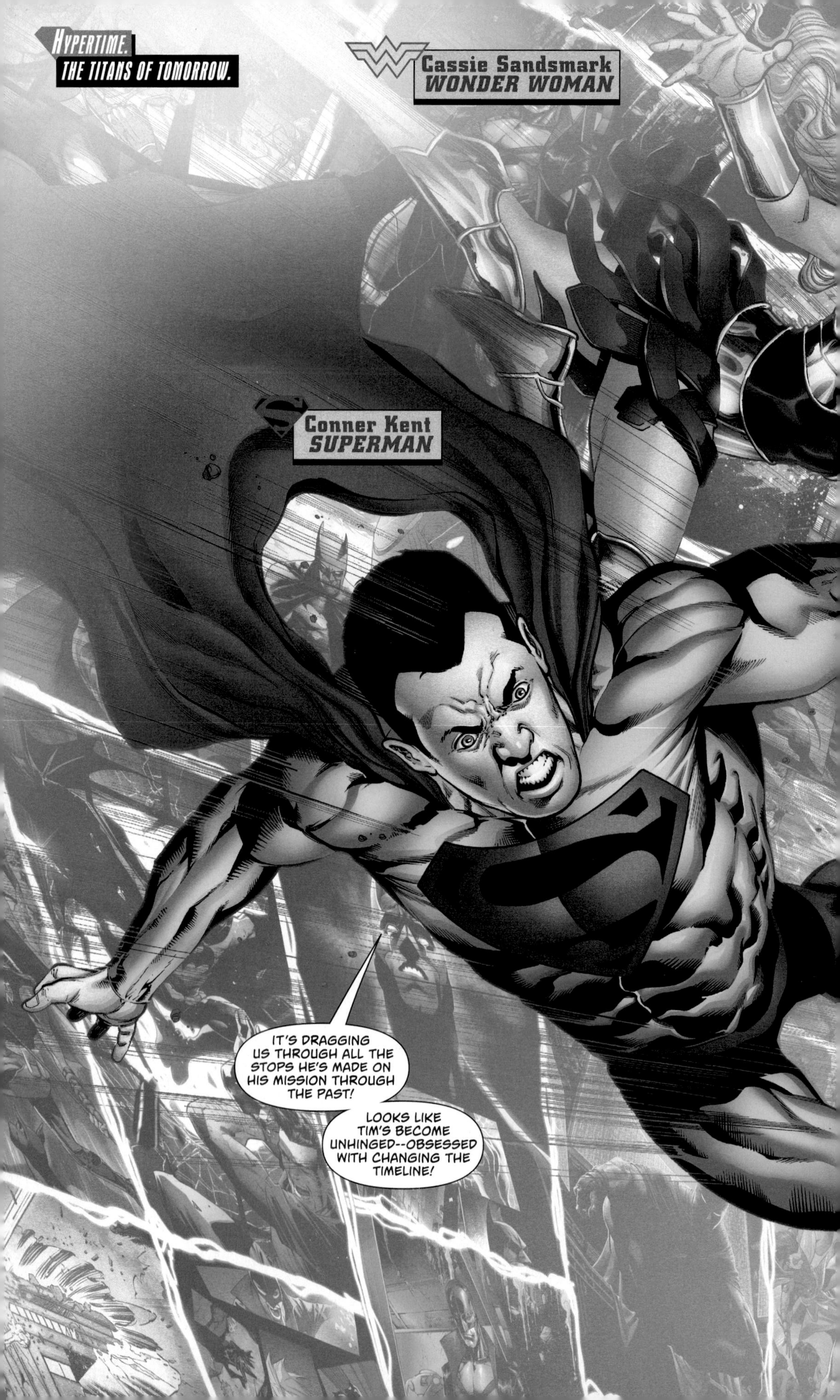
HYPERTIME.
THE TITANS OF TOMORROW.
Cassie Sandsmark WONDER WOMAN
Conner Kent SUPERMAN
IT'S DRAGGING US THROUGH ALL THE STOPS HE'S MADE ON HIS MISSION THROUGH THE PAST!
LOOKS LIKE TIM'S BECOME UNHINGED--OBSESSED WITH CHANGING THE TIMELINE!

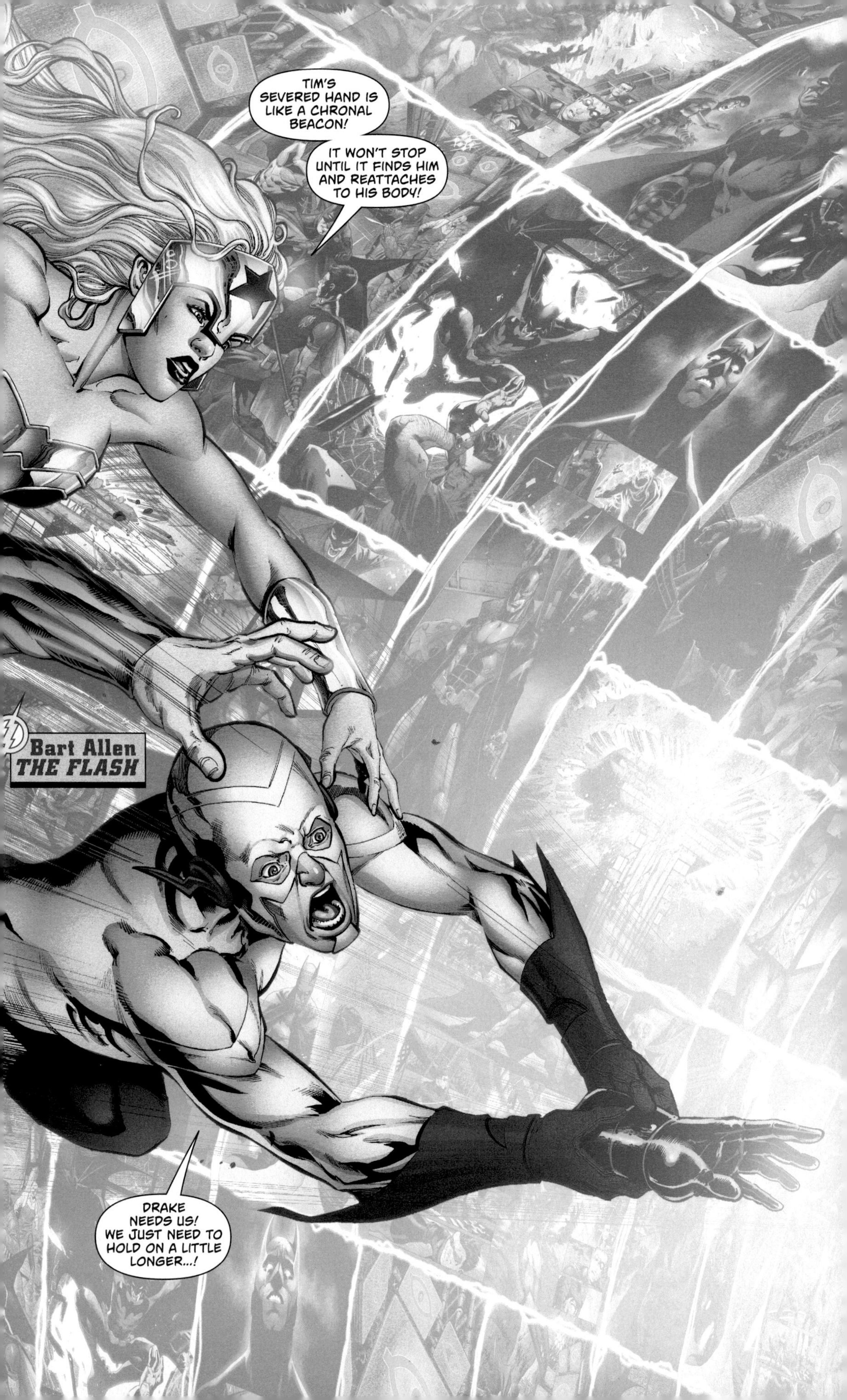
TIM'S SEVERED HAND IS LIKE A CHRONAL BEACON!
IT WON'T STOP UNTIL IT FINDS HIM AND REATTACHES TO HIS BODY!
Bart Allen THE FLASH
DRAKE NEEDS US! WE JUST NEED TO HOLD ON A LITTLE LONGER...!

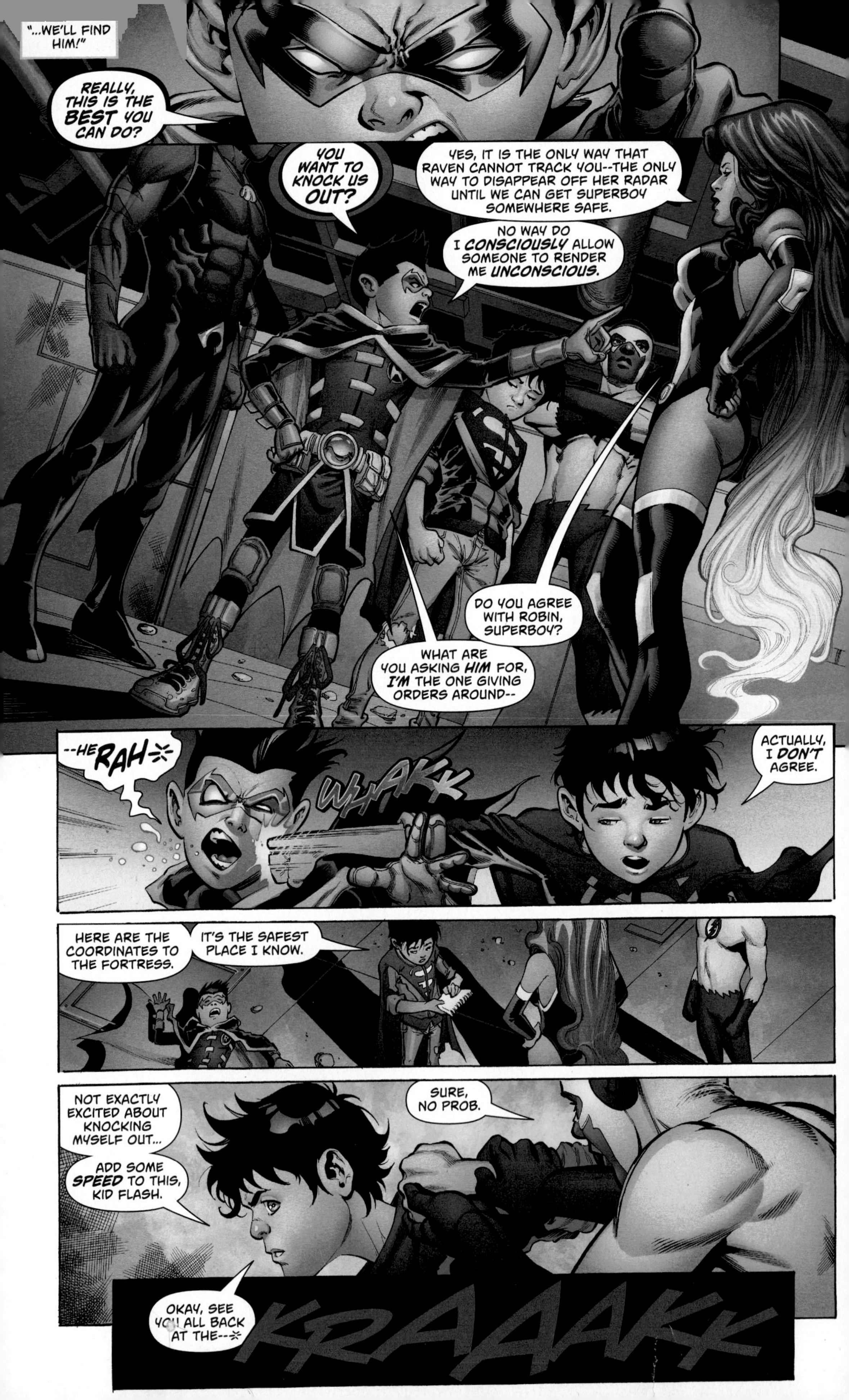
"...WE'LL FIND HIM!"
REALLY, THIS IS THE BEST YOU CAN DO?
YOU WANT TO KNOCK US OUT?
YES, IT IS THE ONLY WAY THAT RAVEN CANNOT TRACK YOU--THE ONLY WAY TO DISAPPEAR OFF HER RADAR UNTIL WE CAN GET SUPERBOY SOMEWHERE SAFE.
NO WAY DO I CONSCIOUSLY ALLOW SOMEONE TO RENDER ME UNCONSCIOUS.
DO YOU AGREE WITH ROBIN, SUPERBOY?
WHAT ARE YOU ASKING HIM FOR, I'M THE ONE GIVING ORDERS AROUND--
--HERAH
WHAKK
ACTUALLY, I DON'T AGREE.
HERE ARE THE COORDINATES TO THE FORTRESS.
IT'S THE SAFEST PLACE I KNOW.
NOT EXACTLY EXCITED ABOUT KNOCKING MYSELF OUT...
ADD SOME SPEED TO THIS, KID FLASH.
SURE, NO PROB.
OKAY, SEE YOU ALL BACK AT THE--
KRAAAKK

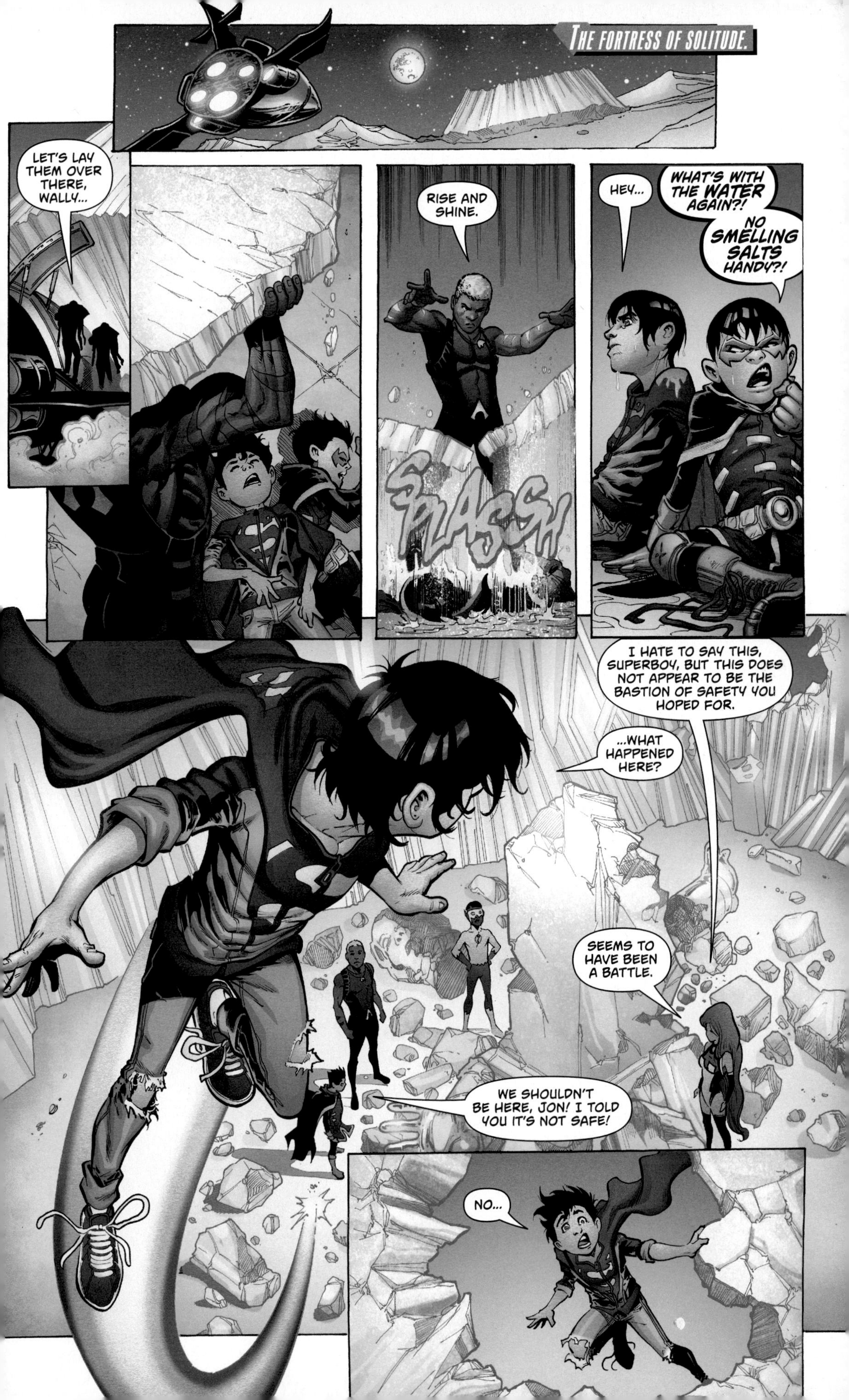
THE FORTRESS OF SOLITUDE.
LET'S LAY THEM OVER THERE, WALLY...
RISE AND SHINE.
SPLASH
HEY...
WHAT'S WITH THE WATER AGAIN?!
NO SMELLING SALTS HANDY?!
I HATE TO SAY THIS, SUPERBOY, BUT THIS DOES NOT APPEAR TO BE THE BASTION OF SAFETY YOU HOPED FOR.
...WHAT HAPPENED HERE?
SEEMS TO HAVE BEEN A BATTLE.
WE SHOULDN'T BE HERE, JON! I TOLD YOU IT'S NOT SAFE!
NO...

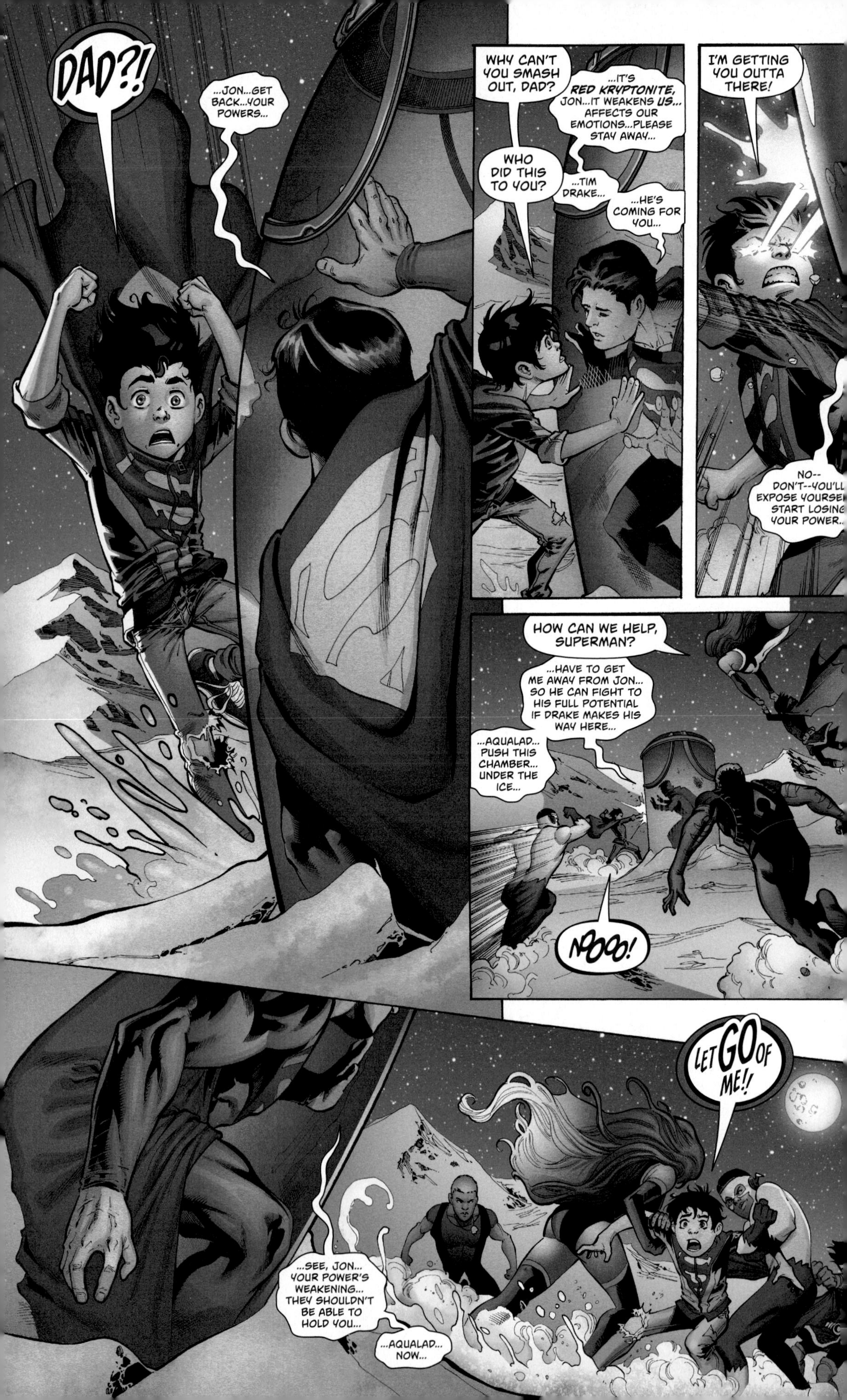
DAD?!
...JON...GET BACK...YOUR POWERS...
WHY CAN'T YOU SMASH OUT, DAD?
...IT'S RED KRYPTONITE, JON...IT WEAKENS US... AFFECTS OUR EMOTIONS...PLEASE STAY AWAY...
WHO DID THIS TO YOU?
...TIM DRAKE...
...HE'S COMING FOR YOU...
I'M GETTING YOU OUTTA THERE!
NO-- DON'T--YOU'LL EXPOSE YOURSE START LOSING YOUR POWER..
HOW CAN WE HELP, SUPERMAN?
...HAVE TO GET ME AWAY FROM JON... SO HE CAN FIGHT TO HIS FULL POTENTIAL IF DRAKE MAKES HIS WAY HERE...
...AQUALAD... PUSH THIS CHAMBER... UNDER THE ICE...
NOOOO!
LET GO OF ME!!
...SEE, JON... YOUR POWER'S WEAKENING... THEY SHOULDN'T BE ABLE TO HOLD YOU...
...AQUALAD... NOW...

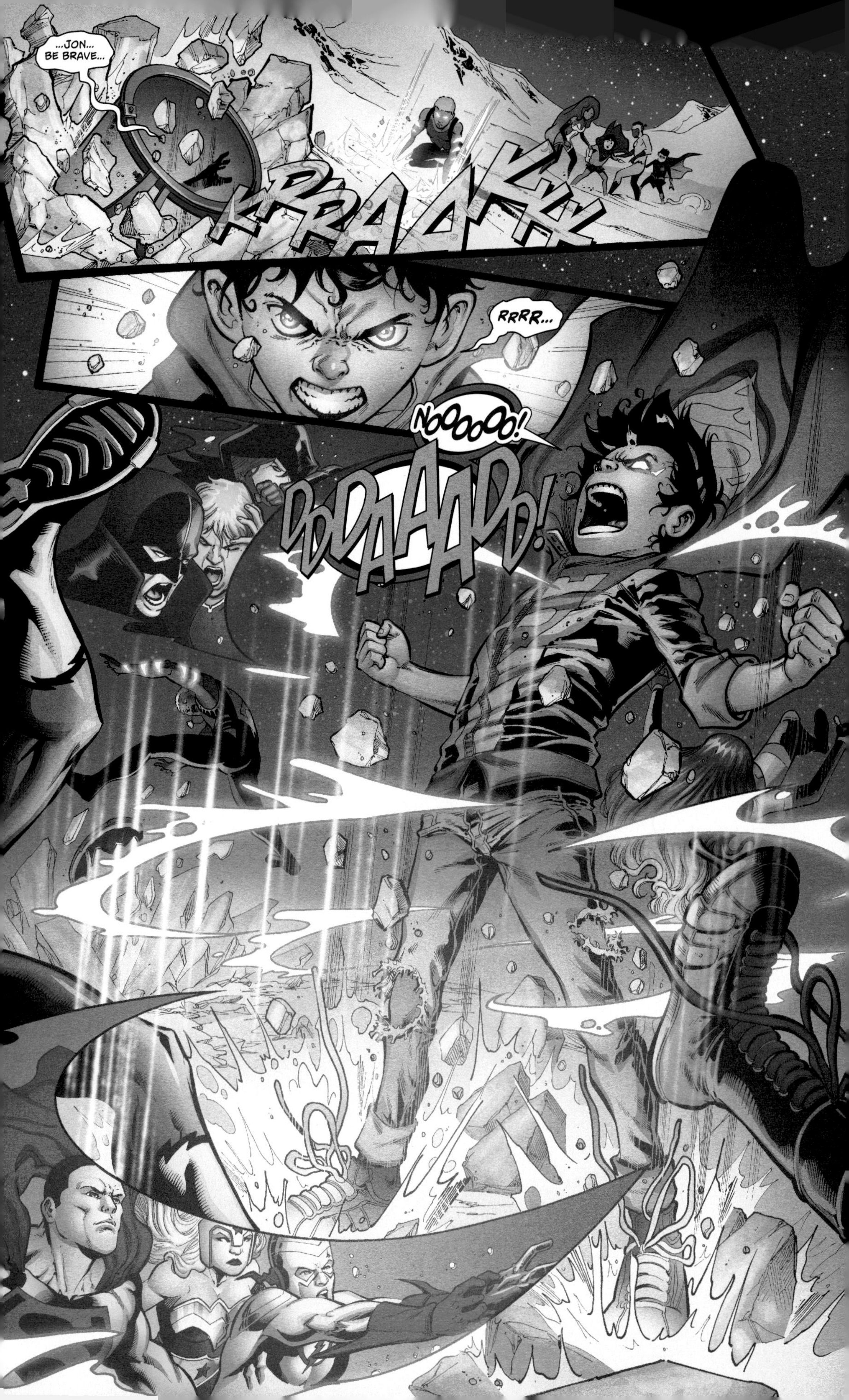
...JON... BE BRAVE...
KRRAKKK
RRRR...
NOOOOOO!
DOOAAADD!

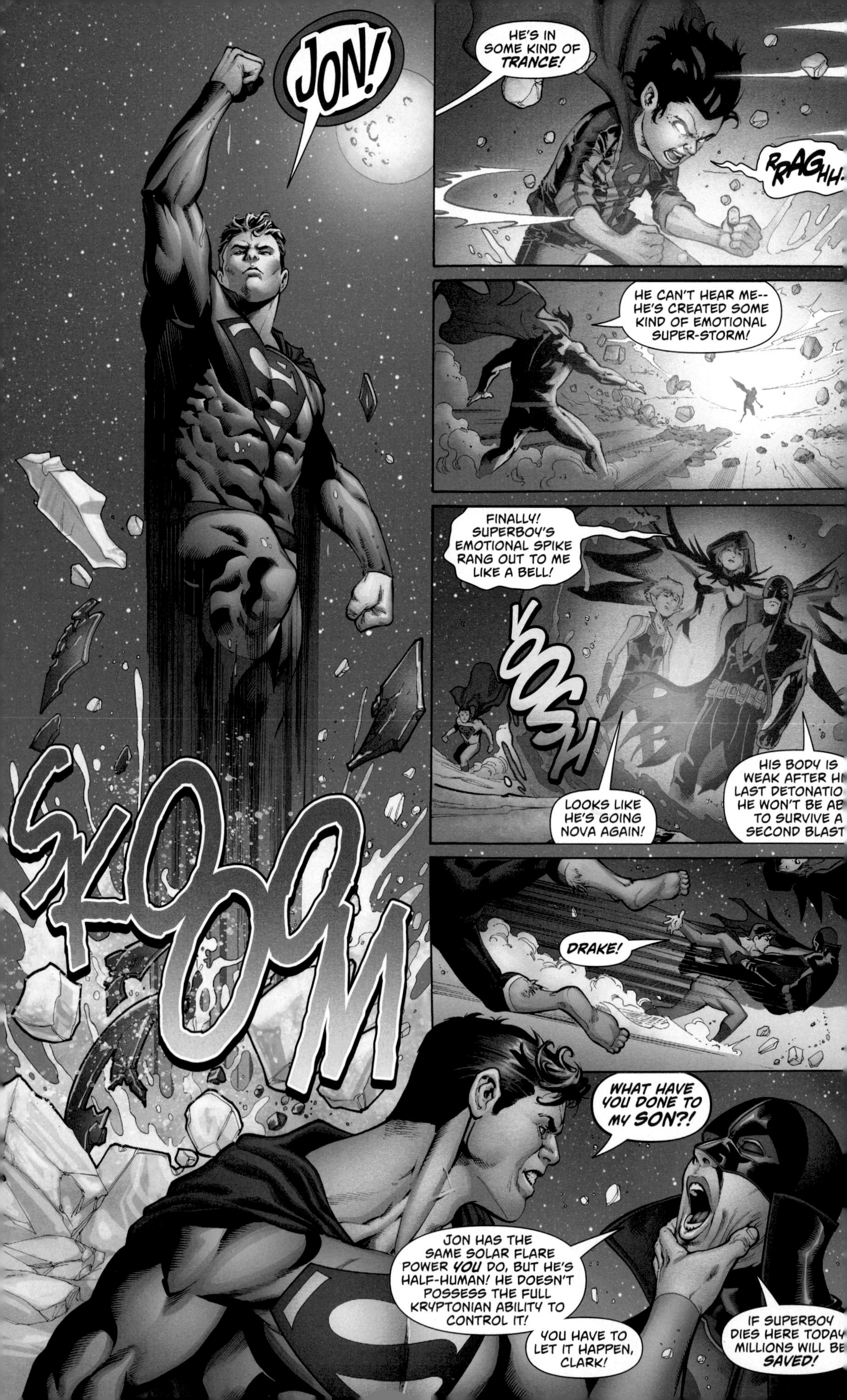
JON!
HE'S IN SOME KIND OF TRANCE!
RRAGHH
HE CAN'T HEAR ME-- HE'S CREATED SOME KIND OF EMOTIONAL SUPER-STORM!
FINALLY! SUPERBOY'S EMOTIONAL SPIKE RANG OUT TO ME LIKE A BELL!
VOOSH
LOOKS LIKE HE'S GOING NOVA AGAIN!
HIS BODY IS WEAK AFTER HI LAST DETONATIO HE WON'T BE AB TO SURVIVE A SECOND BLAST
SKOOM
DRAKE!
WHAT HAVE YOU DONE TO MY SON?!
JON HAS THE SAME SOLAR FLARE POWER YOU DO, BUT HE'S HALF-HUMAN! HE DOESN'T POSSESS THE FULL KRYPTONIAN ABILITY TO CONTROL IT!
YOU HAVE TO LET IT HAPPEN, CLARK!
IF SUPERBOY DIES HERE TODAY MILLIONS WILL BE SAVED!

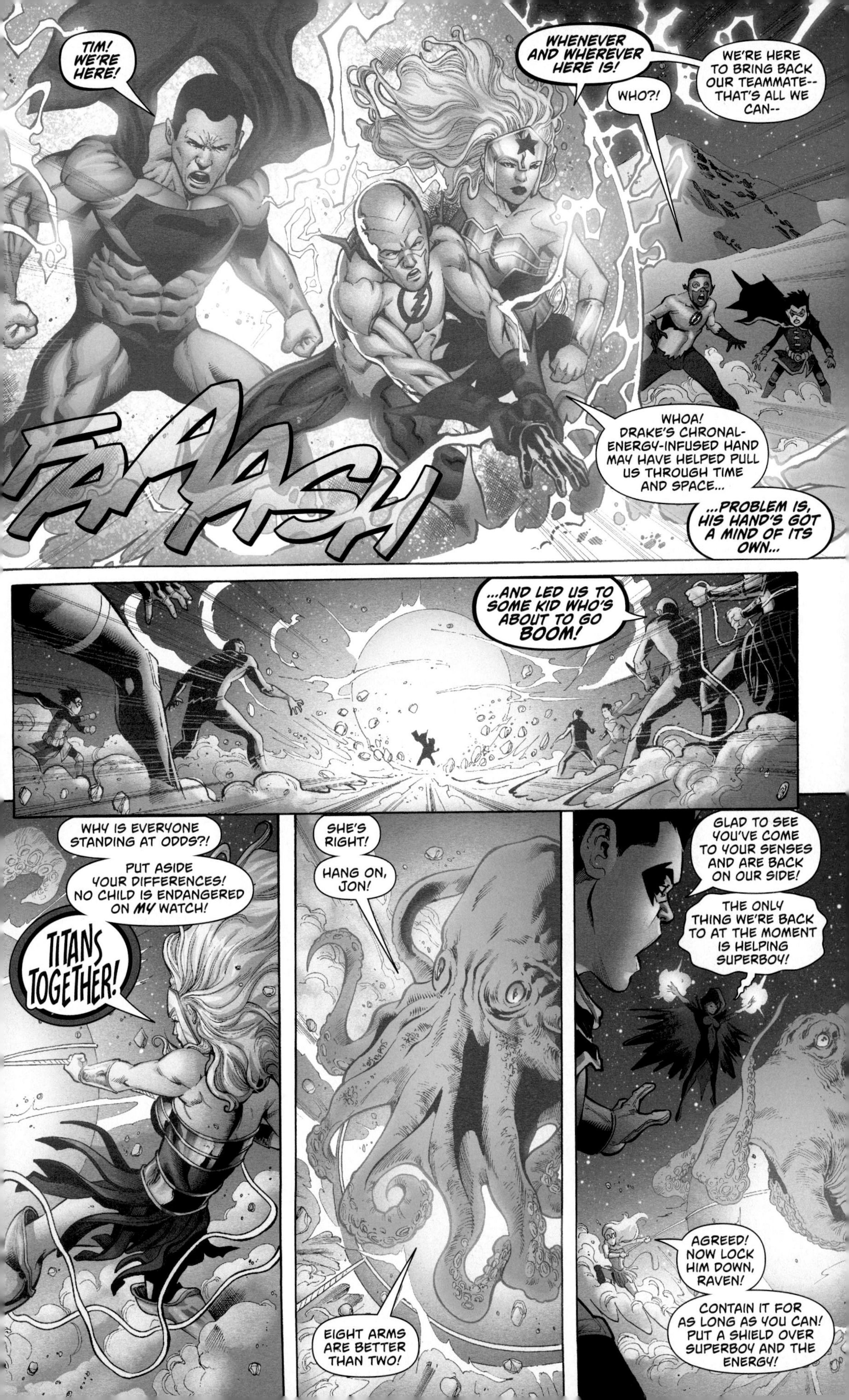
TIM! WE'RE HERE!
WHENEVER AND WHEREVER HERE IS!
WHO?!
WE'RE HERE TO BRING BACK OUR TEAMMATE-- THAT'S ALL WE CAN--
FAAASH
WHOA! DRAKE'S CHRONAL-ENERGY-INFUSED HAND MAY HAVE HELPED PULL US THROUGH TIME AND SPACE...
...PROBLEM IS, HIS HAND'S GOT A MIND OF ITS OWN...
...AND LED US TO SOME KID WHO'S ABOUT TO GO BOOM!
WHY IS EVERYONE STANDING AT ODDS?!
PUT ASIDE YOUR DIFFERENCES! NO CHILD IS ENDANGERED ON MY WATCH!
TITANS TOGETHER!
SHE'S RIGHT!
HANG ON, JON!
EIGHT ARMS ARE BETTER THAN TWO!
GLAD TO SEE YOU'VE COME TO YOUR SENSES AND ARE BACK ON OUR SIDE!
THE ONLY THING WE'RE BACK TO AT THE MOMENT IS HELPING SUPERBOY!
AGREED! NOW LOCK HIM DOWN, RAVEN!
CONTAIN IT FOR AS LONG AS YOU CAN! PUT A SHIELD OVER SUPERBOY AND THE ENERGY!

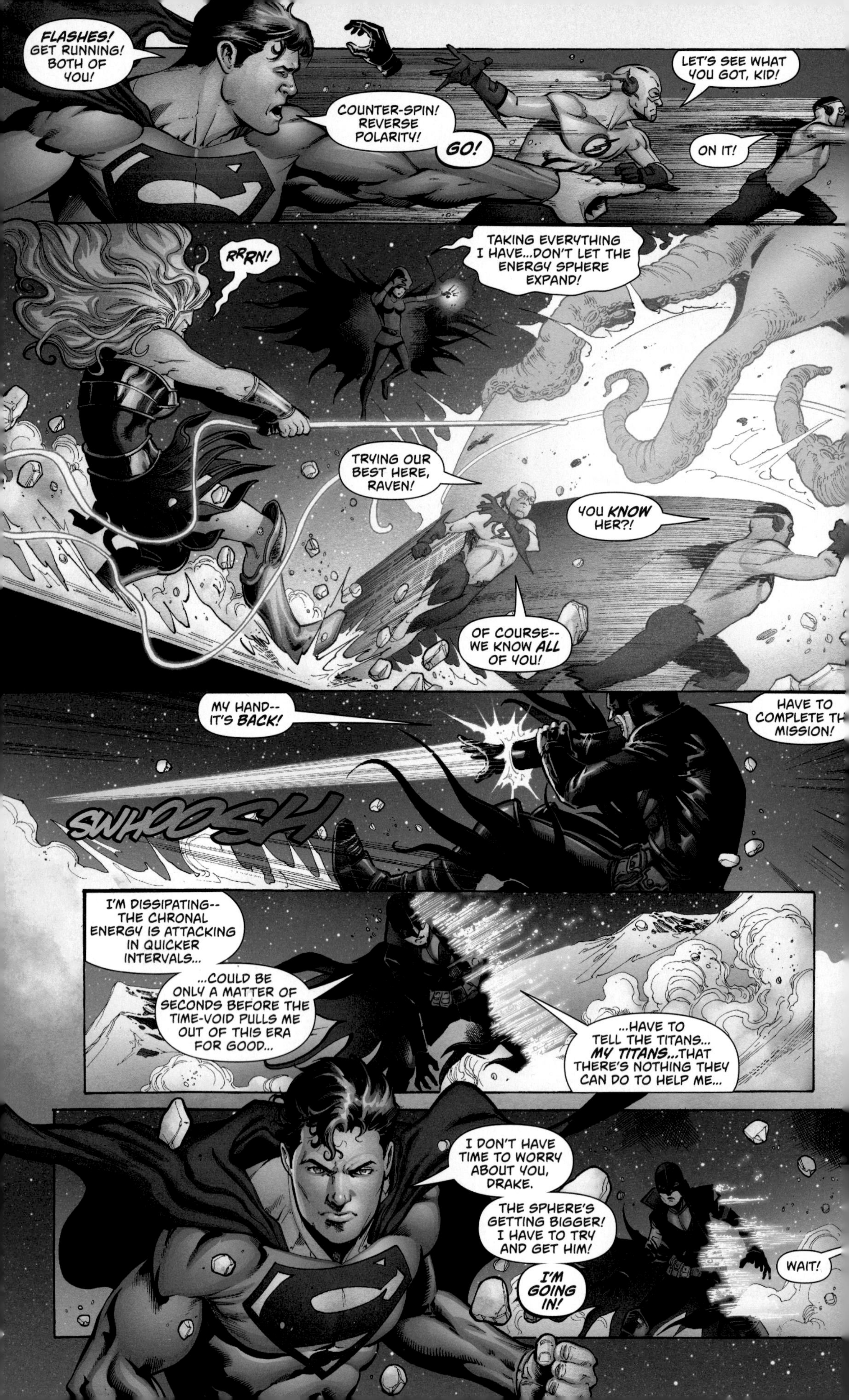
FLASHES! GET RUNNING! BOTH OF YOU!
COUNTER-SPIN! REVERSE POLARITY!
GO!
LET'S SEE WHAT YOU GOT, KID!
ON IT!
RRRN!
TAKING EVERYTHING I HAVE...DON'T LET THE ENERGY SPHERE EXPAND!
TRYING OUR BEST HERE, RAVEN!
YOU KNOW HER?!
OF COURSE-- WE KNOW ALL OF YOU!
MY HAND-- IT'S BACK!
HAVE TO COMPLETE TH MISSION!
SWHOOSH
I'M DISSIPATING-- THE CHRONAL ENERGY IS ATTACKING IN QUICKER INTERVALS...
...COULD BE ONLY A MATTER OF SECONDS BEFORE THE TIME-VOID PULLS ME OUT OF THIS ERA FOR GOOD...
...HAVE TO TELL THE TITANS... MY TITANS...THAT THERE'S NOTHING THEY CAN DO TO HELP ME...
I DON'T HAVE TIME TO WORRY ABOUT YOU, DRAKE.
THE SPHERE'S GETTING BIGGER! I HAVE TO TRY AND GET HIM!
I'M GOING IN!
WAIT!

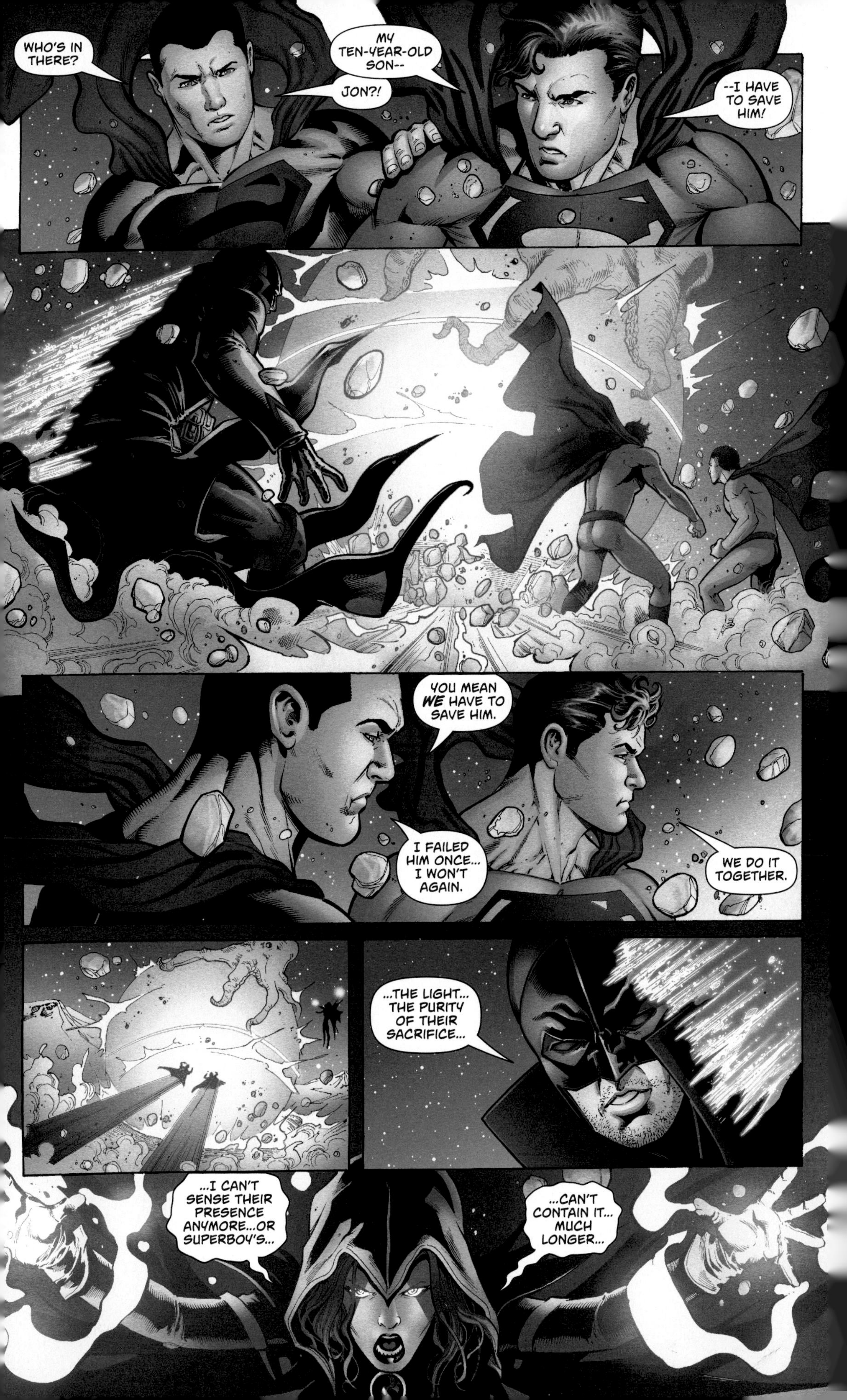
WHO'S IN THERE?
MY TEN-YEAR-OLD SON--
JON?!
--I HAVE TO SAVE HIM!
YOU MEAN *WE* HAVE TO SAVE HIM.
I FAILED HIM ONCE... I WON'T AGAIN.
WE DO IT TOGETHER.
...THE LIGHT... THE PURITY OF THEIR SACRIFICE...
...I CAN'T SENSE THEIR PRESENCE ANYMORE...OR SUPERBOY'S...
...CAN'T CONTAIN IT... MUCH LONGER...

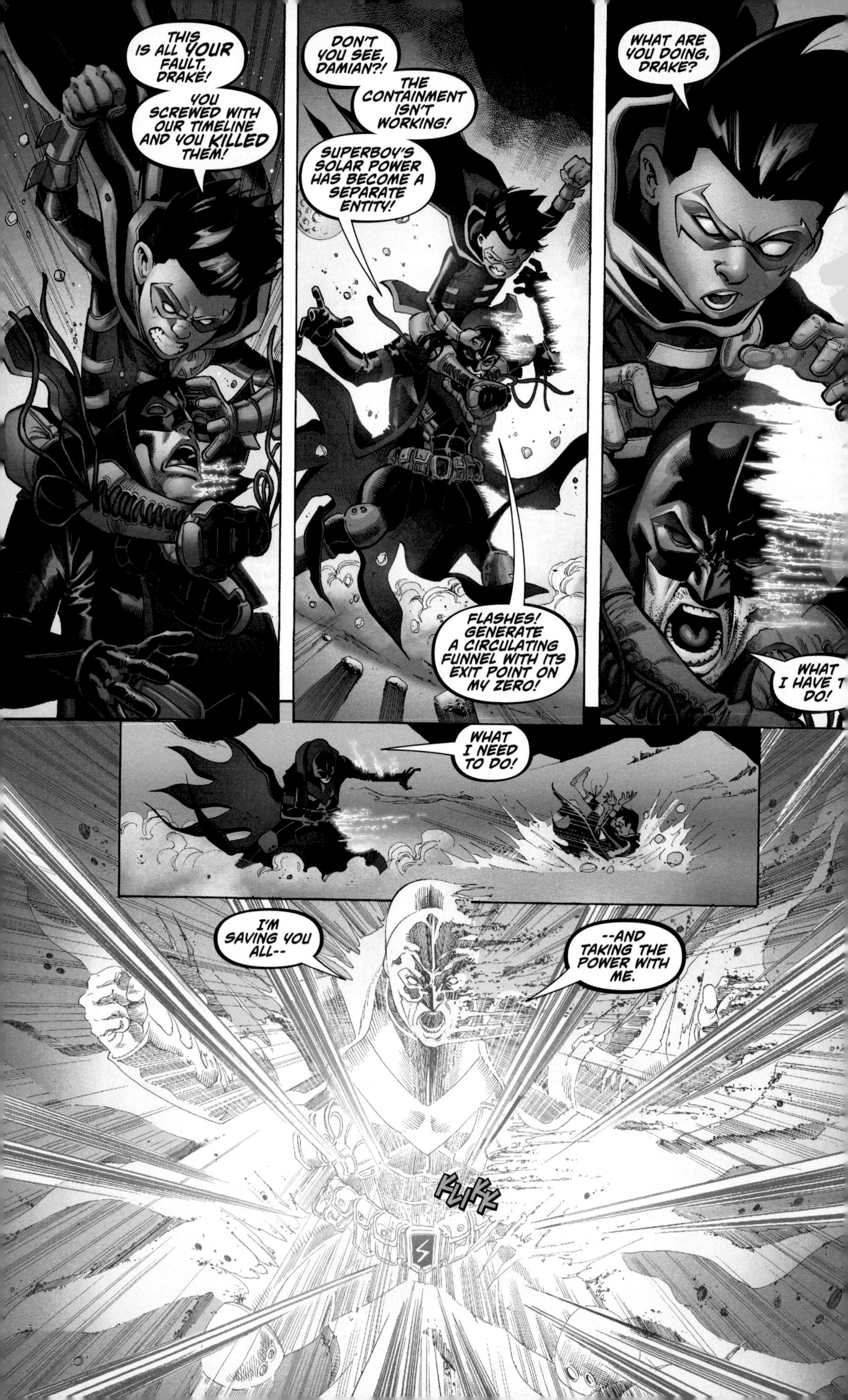
THIS IS ALL YOUR FAULT, DRAKE!
YOU SCREWED WITH OUR TIMELINE AND YOU KILLED THEM!
DON'T YOU SEE, DAMIAN?!
THE CONTAINMENT ISN'T WORKING!
SUPERBOY'S SOLAR POWER HAS BECOME A SEPARATE ENTITY!
FLASHES! GENERATE A CIRCULATING FUNNEL WITH ITS EXIT POINT ON MY ZERO!
WHAT ARE YOU DOING, DRAKE?
WHAT I HAVE T DO!
WHAT I NEED TO DO!
I'M SAVING YOU ALL--
--AND TAKING THE POWER WITH ME.
KLIKK

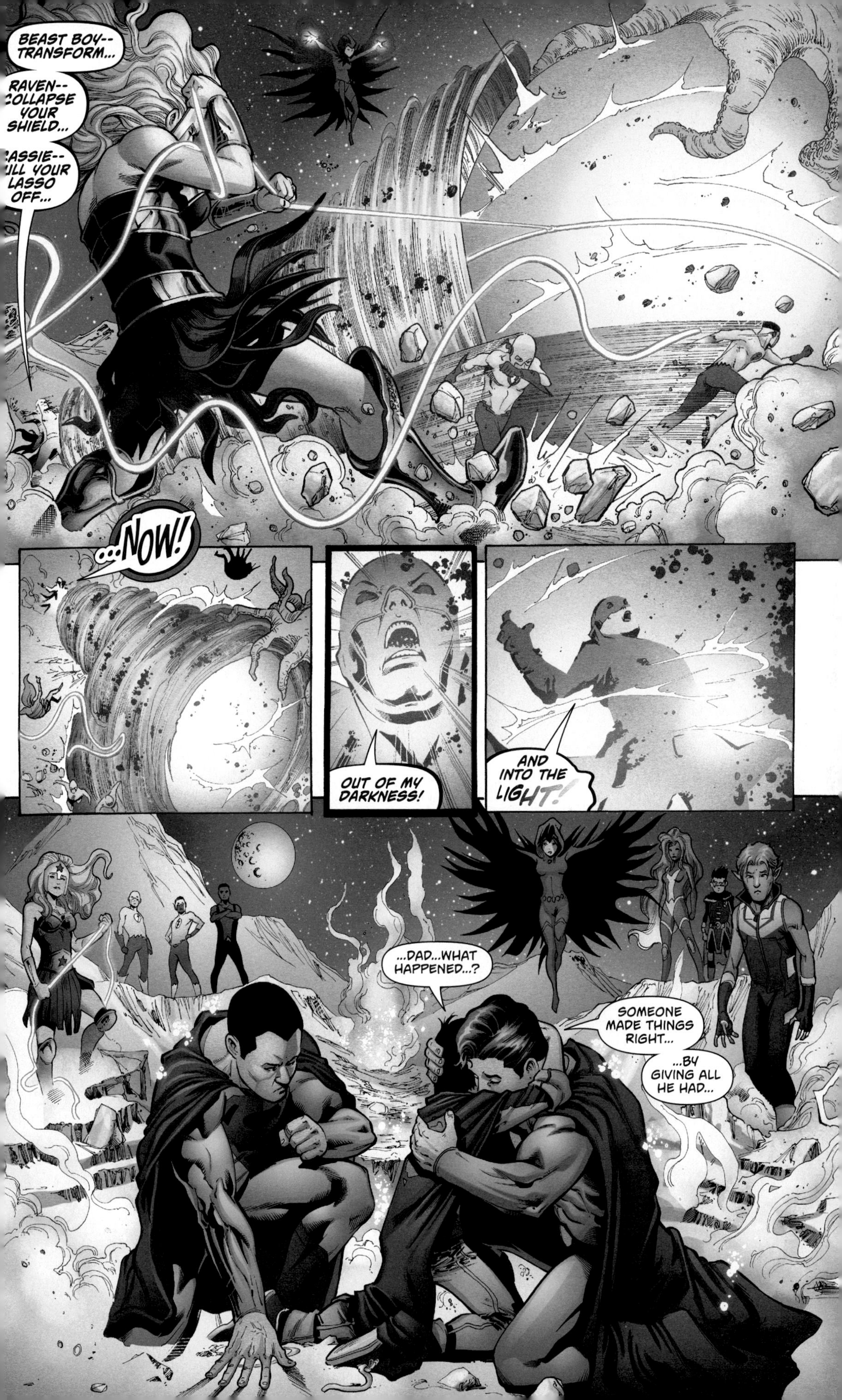
BEAST BOY-- TRANSFORM...
RAVEN-- COLLAPSE YOUR SHIELD...
CASSIE-- PULL YOUR LASSO OFF...
...NOW!
OUT OF MY DARKNESS!
AND INTO THE LIGHT!
...DAD...WHAT HAPPENED...?
SOMEONE MADE THINGS RIGHT...
...BY GIVING ALL HE HAD...

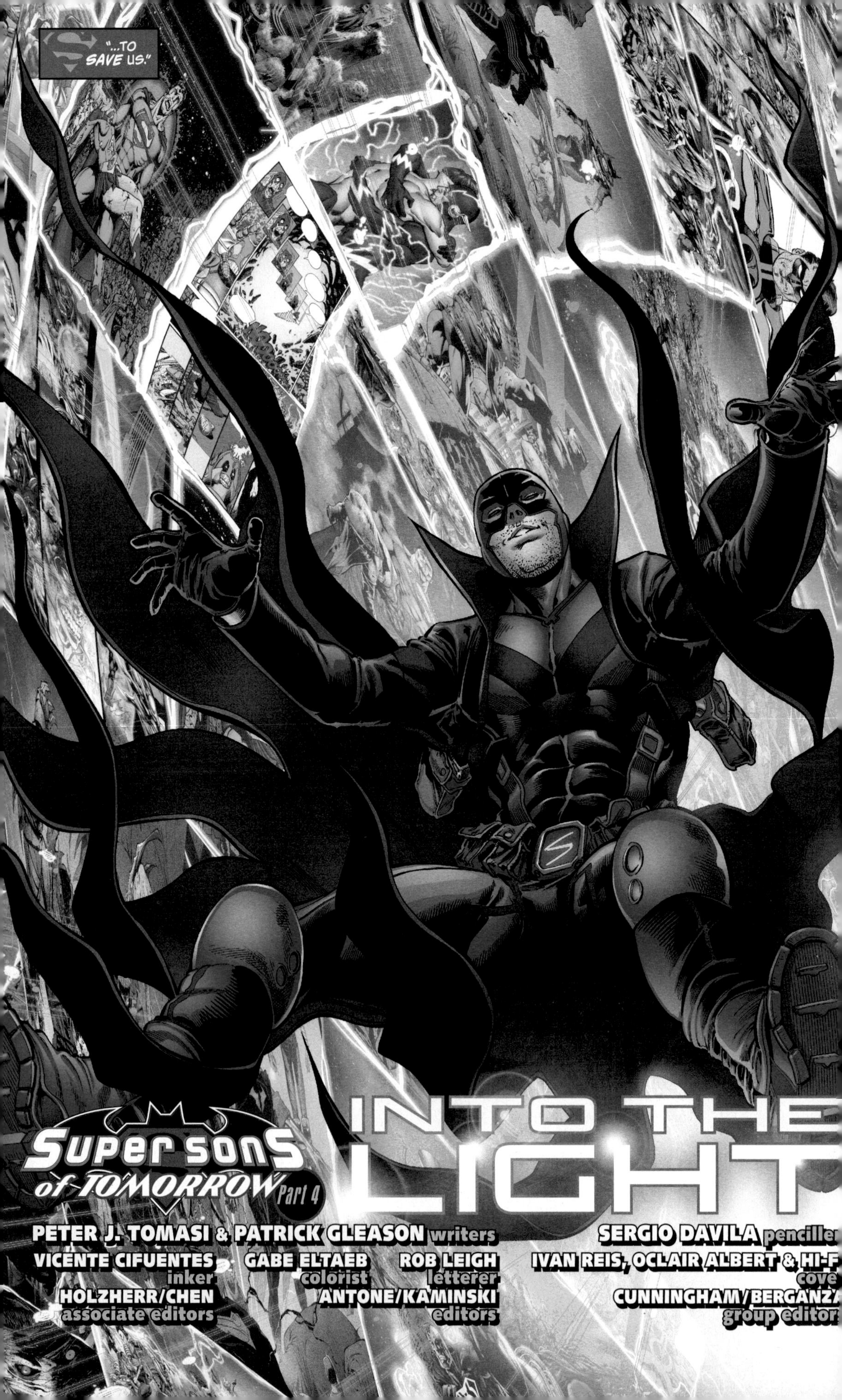
"...TO SAVE US."
Super Sons of TOMORROW Part 4
INTO THE LIGHT
PETER J. TOMASI & PATRICK GLEASON writers
SERGIO DAVILA penciller
VICENTE CIFUENTES inker
GABE ELTAEB colorist
ROB LEIGH letterer
IVAN REIS, OCLAIR ALBERT & HI-FI cover
HOLZHERR/CHEN associate editors
ANTONE/KAMINSKI editors
CUNNINGHAM/BERGANZA group editor

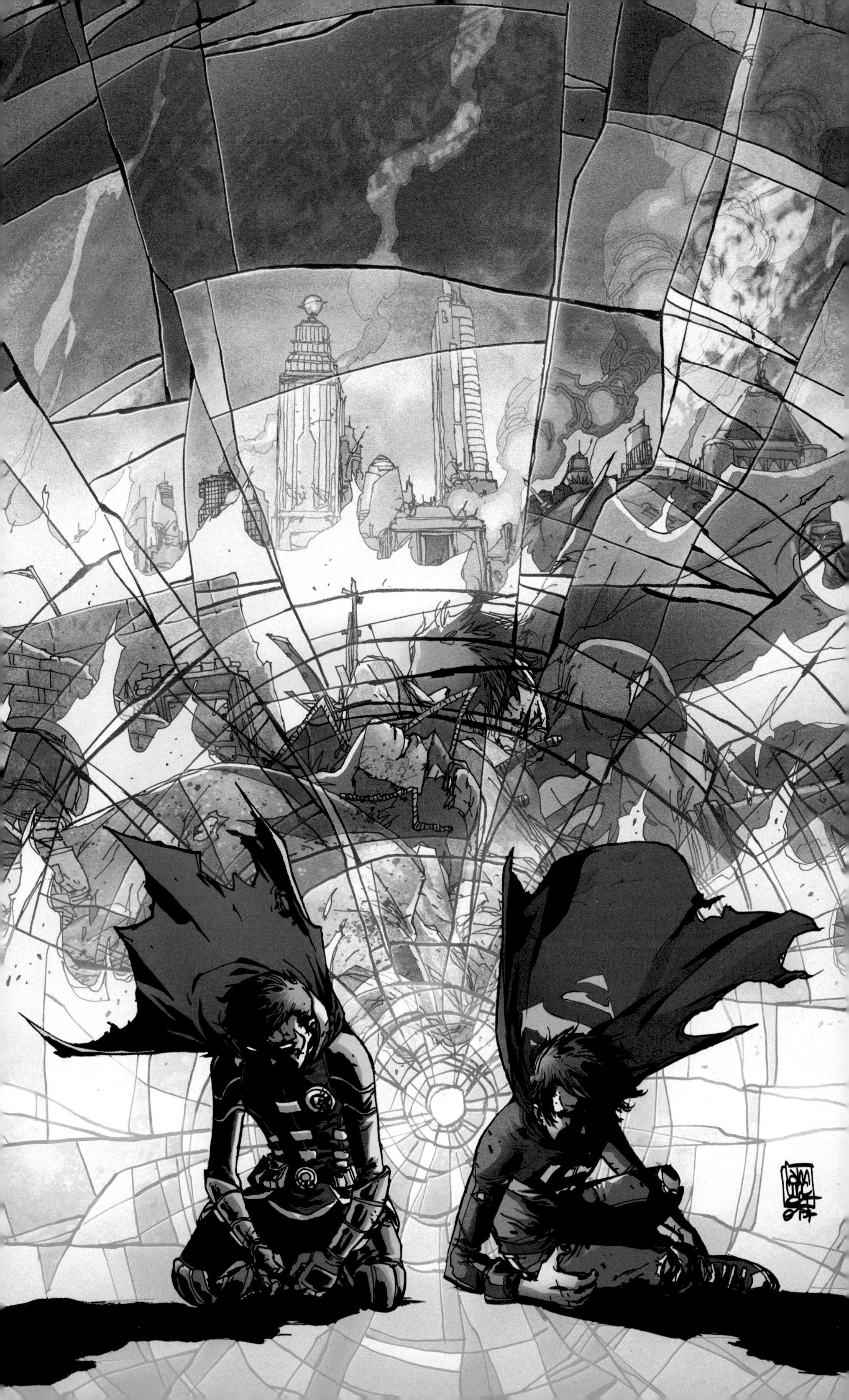

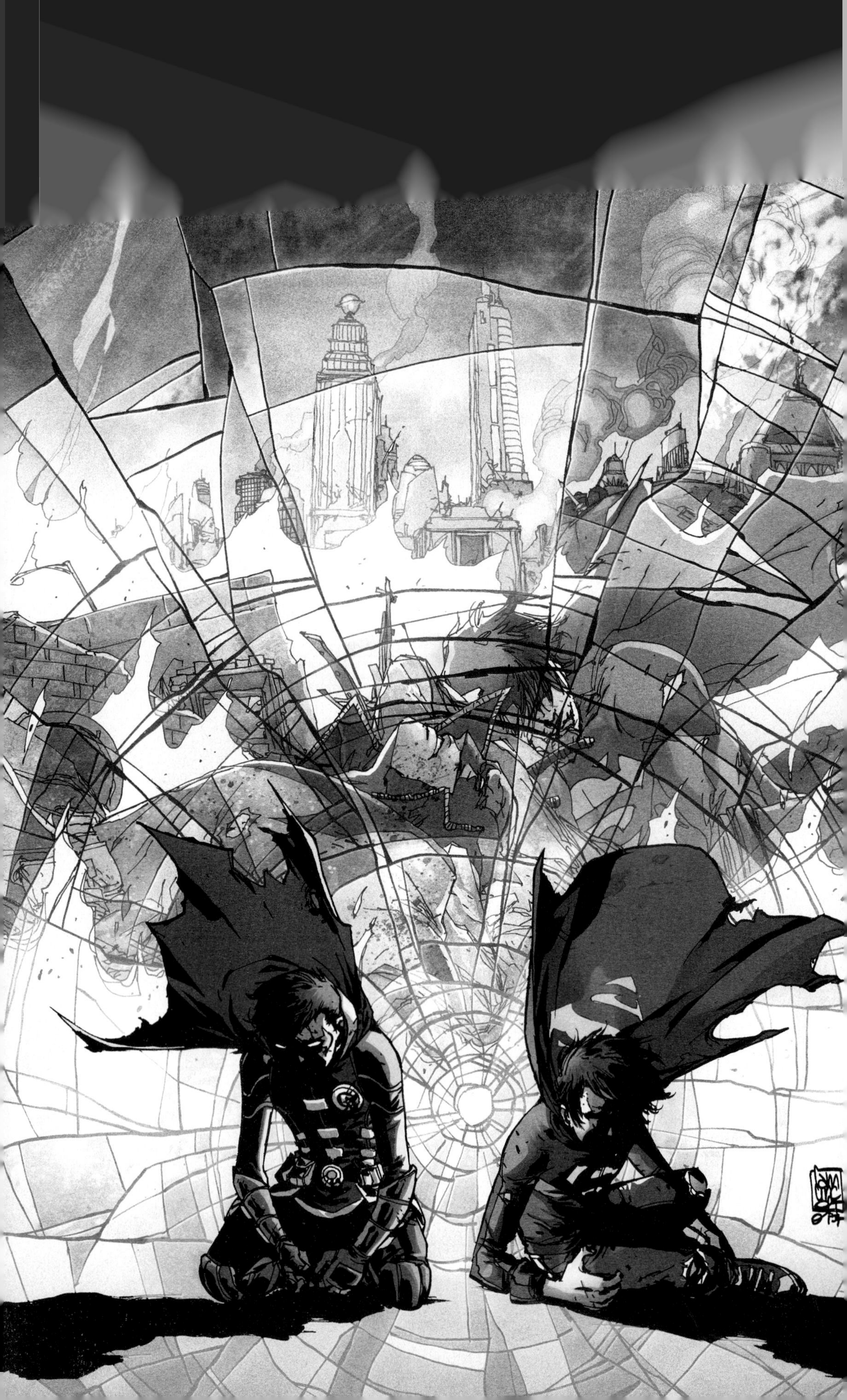

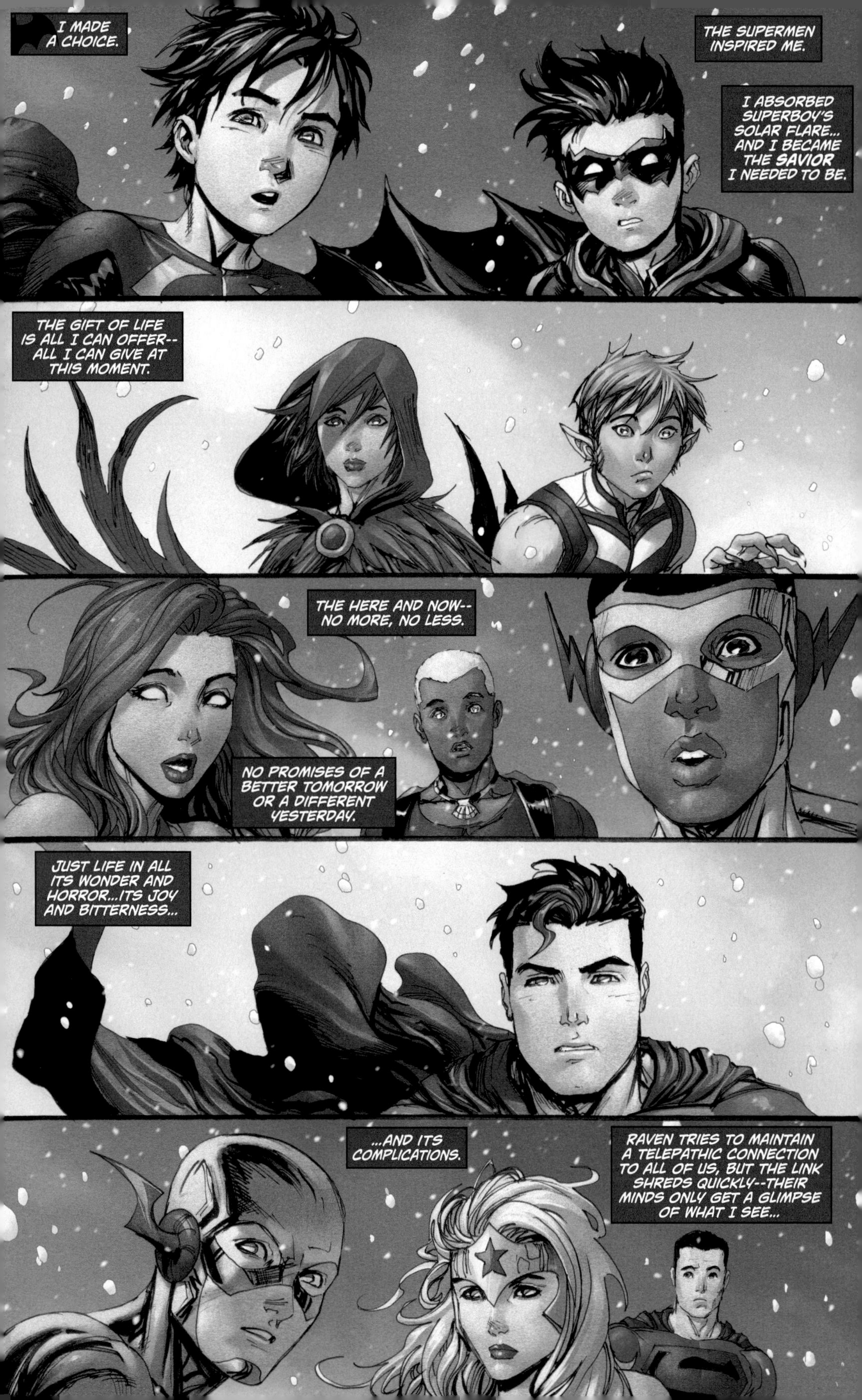

I MADE A CHOICE.
THE SUPERMEN INSPIRED ME.
I ABSORBED SUPERBOY'S SOLAR FLARE... AND I BECAME THE SAVIOR I NEEDED TO BE.
THE GIFT OF LIFE IS ALL I CAN OFFER-- ALL I CAN GIVE AT THIS MOMENT.
THE HERE AND NOW-- NO MORE, NO LESS.
NO PROMISES OF A BETTER TOMORROW OR A DIFFERENT YESTERDAY.
JUST LIFE IN ALL ITS WONDER AND HORROR...ITS JOY AND BITTERNESS...
...AND ITS COMPLICATIONS.
RAVEN TRIES TO MAINTAIN A TELEPATHIC CONNECTION TO ALL OF US, BUT THE LINK SHREDS QUICKLY--THEIR MINDS ONLY GET A GLIMPSE OF WHAT I SEE...

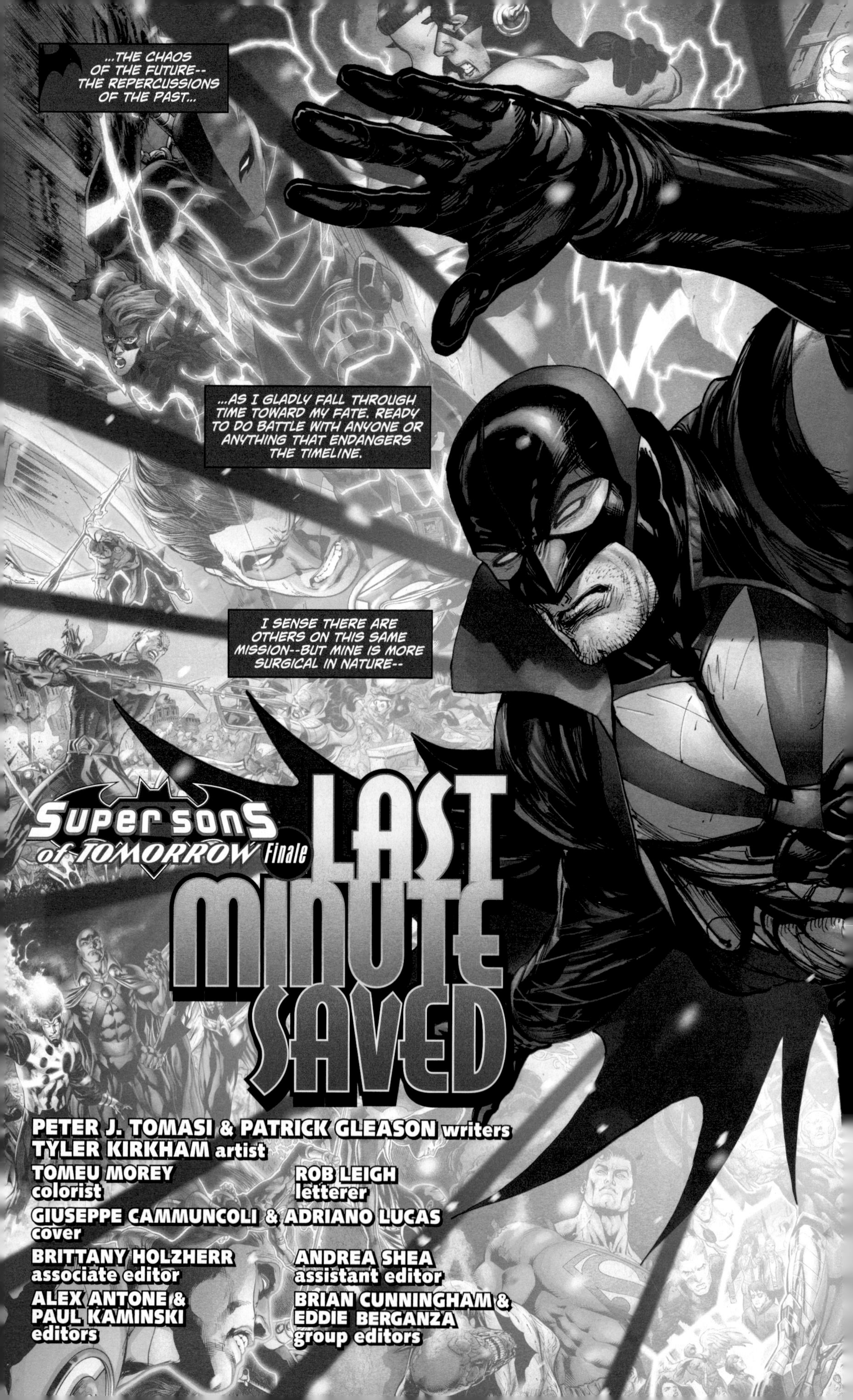
...THE CHAOS OF THE FUTURE-- THE REPERCUSSIONS OF THE PAST...
...AS I GLADLY FALL THROUGH TIME TOWARD MY FATE. READY TO DO BATTLE WITH ANYONE OR ANYTHING THAT ENDANGERS THE TIMELINE.
I SENSE THERE ARE OTHERS ON THIS SAME MISSION--BUT MINE IS MORE SURGICAL IN NATURE--
SUPER SONS of TOMORROW Finale
LAST MINUTE SAVED
PETER J. TOMASI & PATRICK GLEASON writers
TYLER KIRKHAM artist
TOMEU MOREY colorist
ROB LEIGH letterer
GIUSEPPE CAMMUNCOLI & ADRIANO LUCAS cover
BRITTANY HOLZHERR associate editor
ANDREA SHEA assistant editor
ALEX ANTONE & PAUL KAMINSKI editors
BRIAN CUNNINGHAM & EDDIE BERGANZA group editors

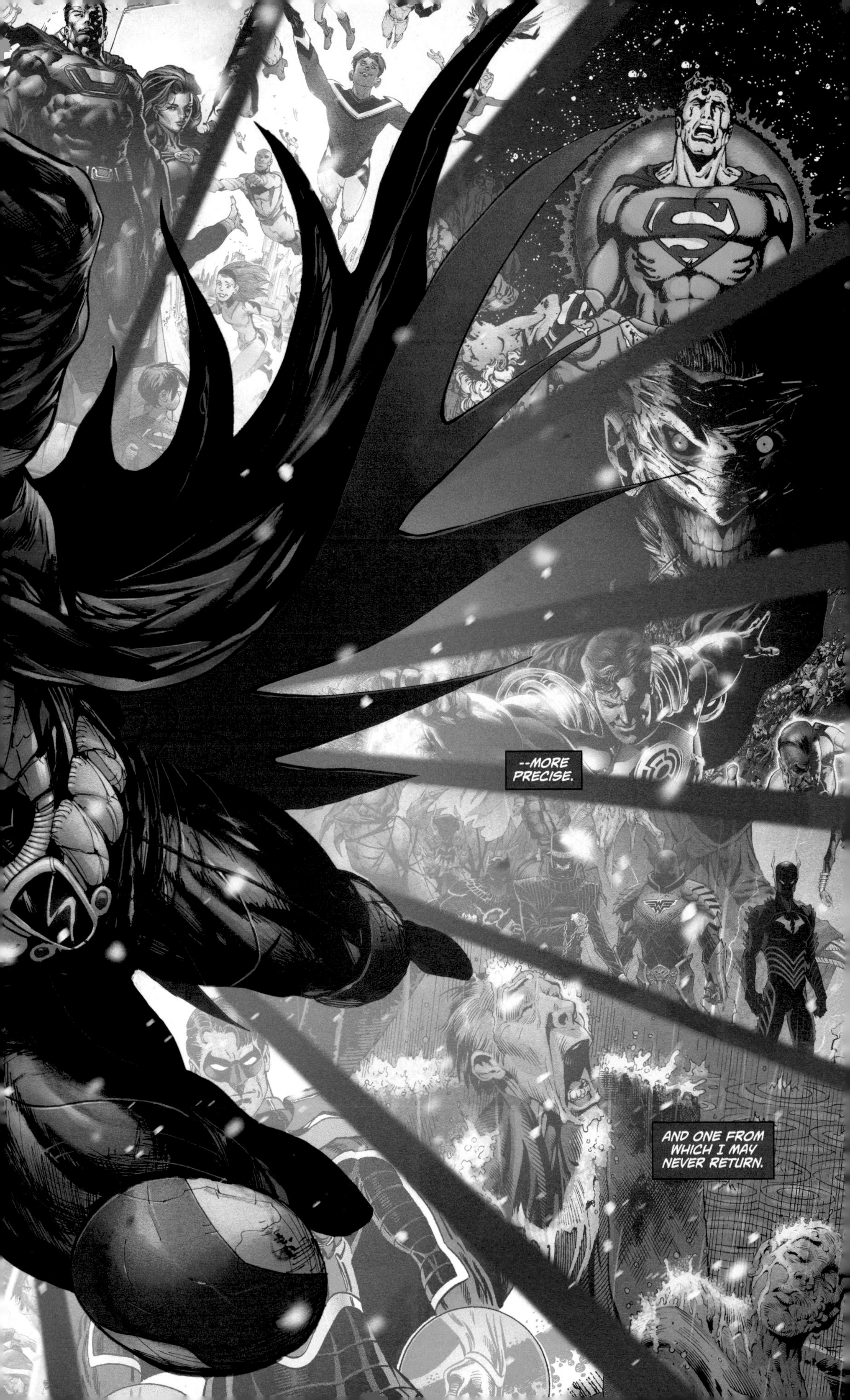
--MORE PRECISE.
AND ONE FROM WHICH I MAY NEVER RETURN.

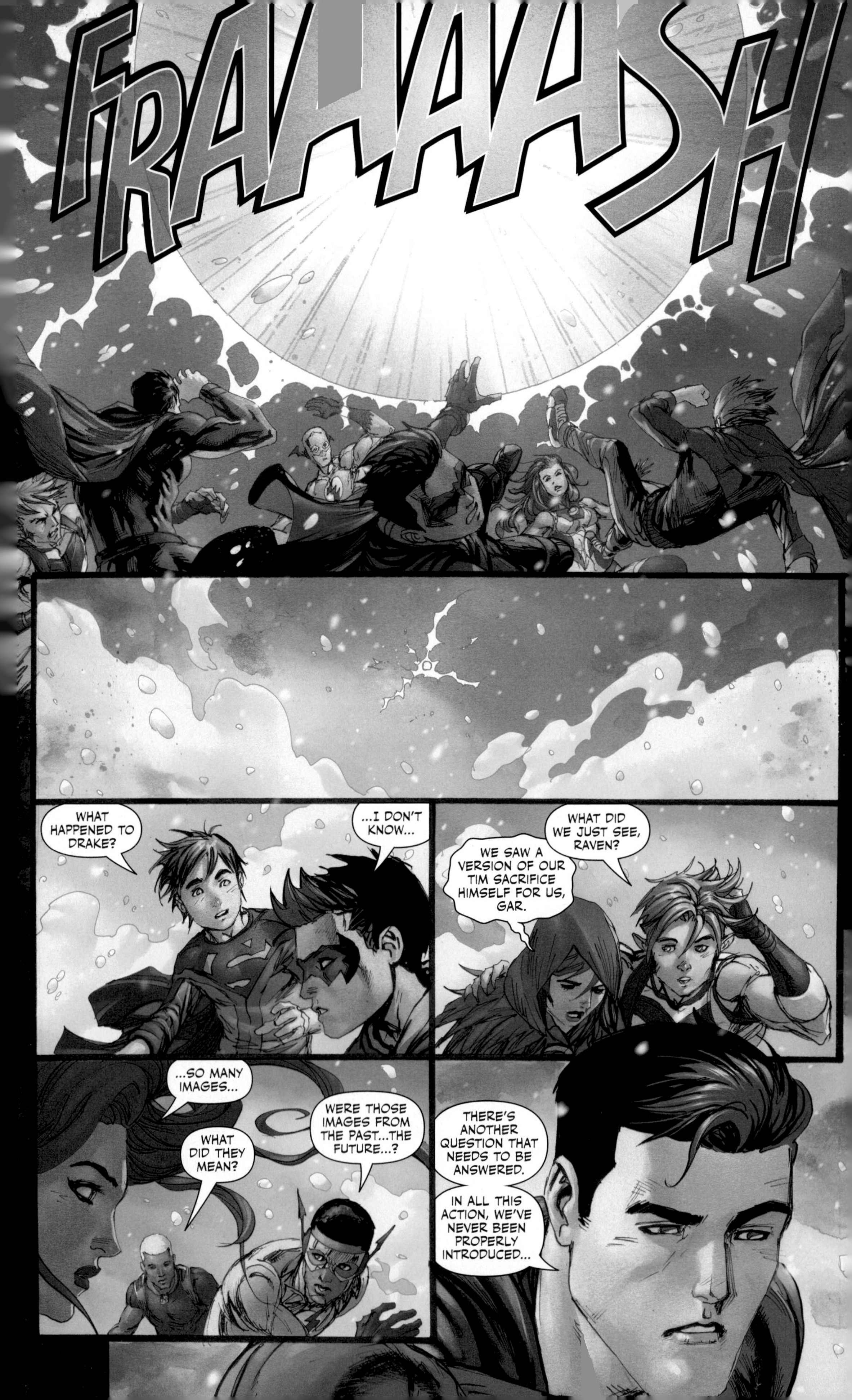
FRAAAASH
WHAT HAPPENED TO DRAKE?
...I DON'T KNOW...
WHAT DID WE JUST SEE, RAVEN?
WE SAW A VERSION OF OUR TIM SACRIFICE HIMSELF FOR US, GAR.
...SO MANY IMAGES...
WHAT DID THEY MEAN?
WERE THOSE IMAGES FROM THE PAST...THE FUTURE...?
THERE'S ANOTHER QUESTION THAT NEEDS TO BE ANSWERED.
IN ALL THIS ACTION, WE'VE NEVER BEEN PROPERLY INTRODUCED...

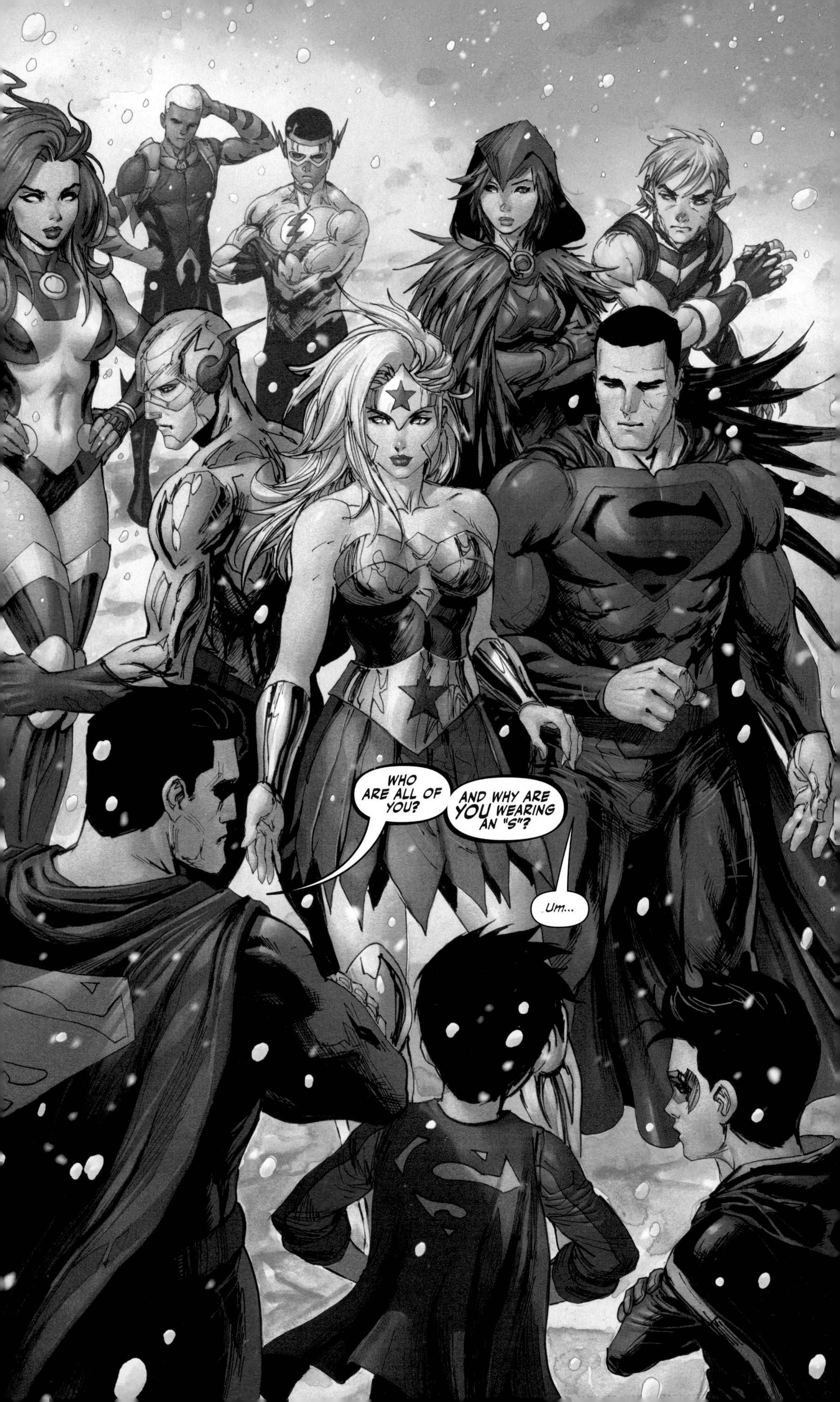
WHO ARE ALL OF YOU?
AND WHY ARE YOU WEARING AN "S"?
Um...

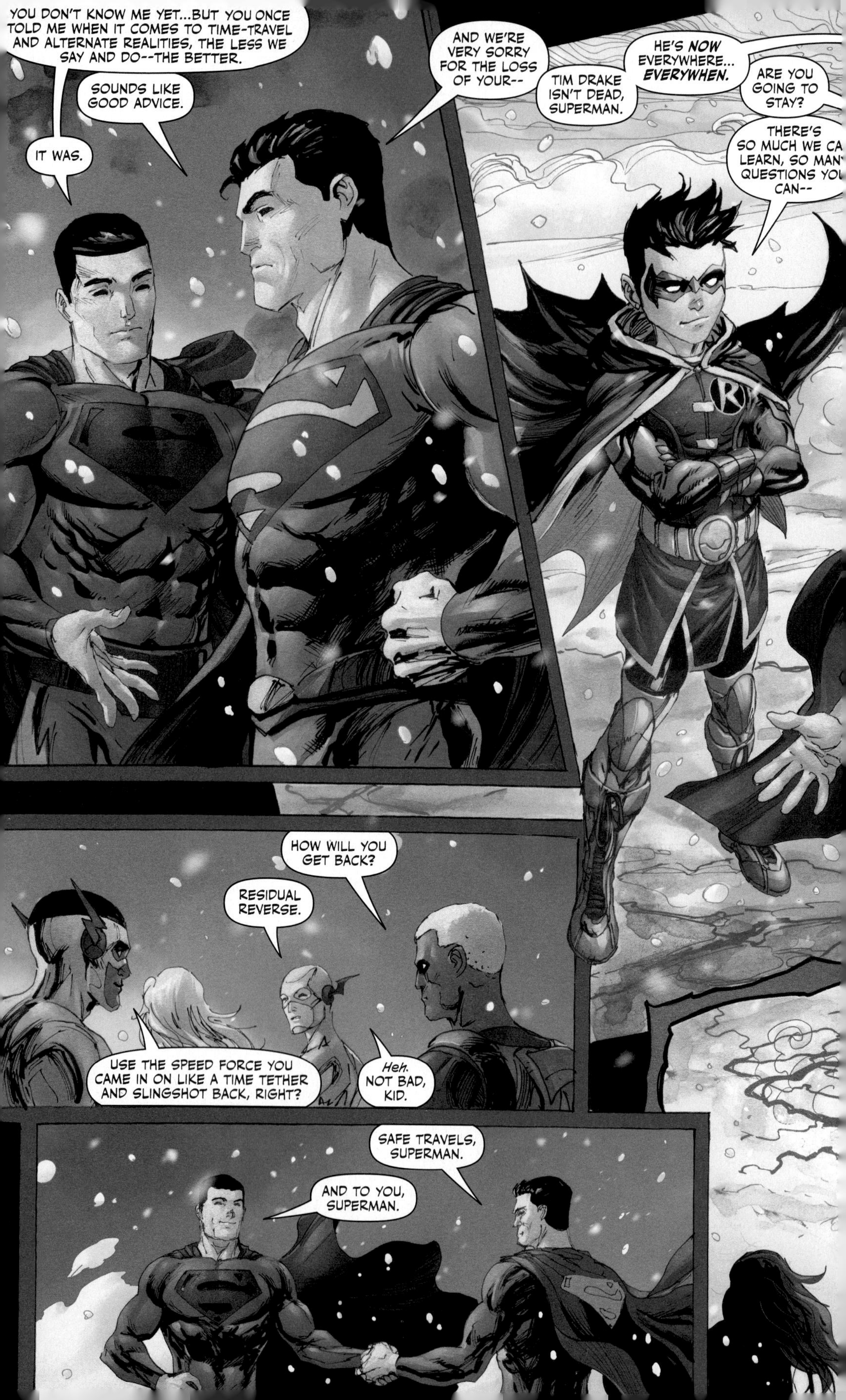
YOU DON'T KNOW ME YET...BUT YOU ONCE TOLD ME WHEN IT COMES TO TIME-TRAVEL AND ALTERNATE REALITIES, THE LESS WE SAY AND DO--THE BETTER.
SOUNDS LIKE GOOD ADVICE.
IT WAS.
AND WE'RE VERY SORRY FOR THE LOSS OF YOUR--
TIM DRAKE ISN'T DEAD, SUPERMAN.
HE'S NOW EVERYWHERE... EVERYWHEN.
ARE YOU GOING TO STAY?
THERE'S SO MUCH WE CA LEARN, SO MAN QUESTIONS YOU CAN--
HOW WILL YOU GET BACK?
RESIDUAL REVERSE.
USE THE SPEED FORCE YOU CAME IN ON LIKE A TIME TETHER AND SLINGSHOT BACK, RIGHT?
Heh. NOT BAD, KID.
SAFE TRAVELS, SUPERMAN.
AND TO YOU, SUPERMAN.

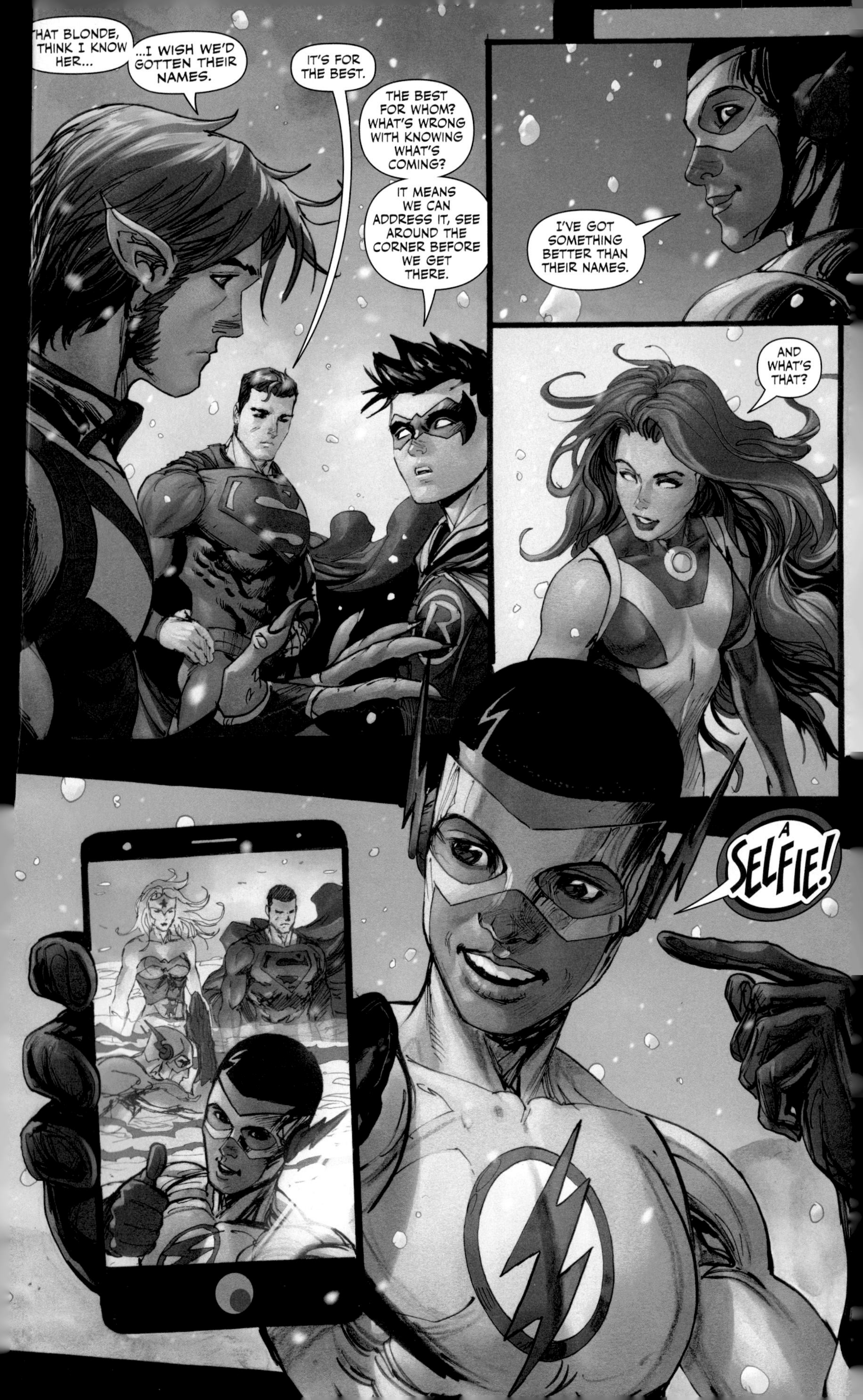
THAT BLONDE, THINK I KNOW HER...
...I WISH WE'D GOTTEN THEIR NAMES.
IT'S FOR THE BEST.
THE BEST FOR WHOM? WHAT'S WRONG WITH KNOWING WHAT'S COMING?
IT MEANS WE CAN ADDRESS IT, SEE AROUND THE CORNER BEFORE WE GET THERE.
I'VE GOT SOMETHING BETTER THAN THEIR NAMES.
AND WHAT'S THAT?
A SELFIE!

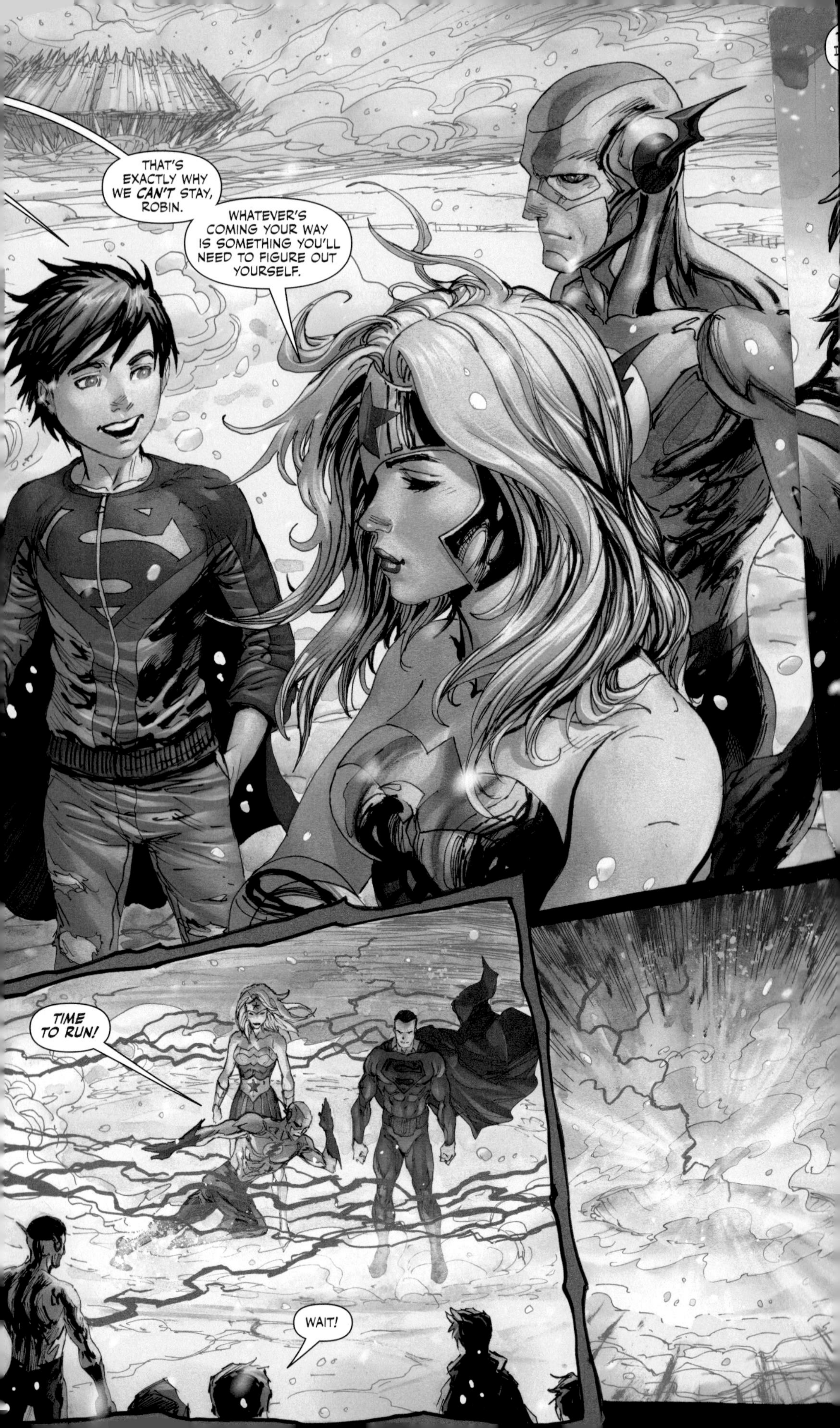
THAT'S EXACTLY WHY WE *CAN'T* STAY, ROBIN.
WHATEVER'S COMING YOUR WAY IS SOMETHING YOU'LL NEED TO FIGURE OUT YOURSELF.
TIME TO RUN!
WAIT!

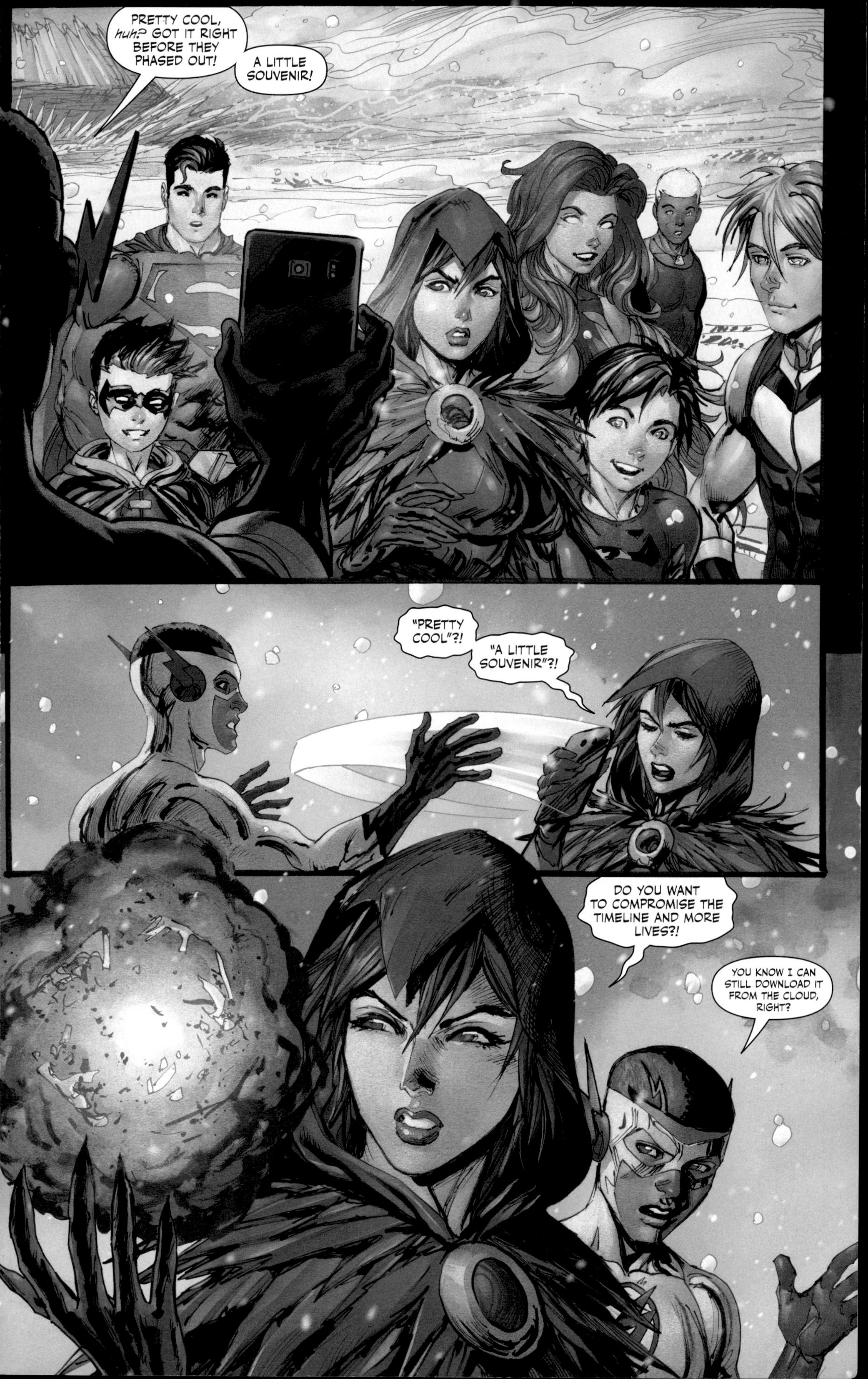
PRETTY COOL, *huh?* GOT IT RIGHT BEFORE THEY PHASED OUT!
A LITTLE SOUVENIR!
"PRETTY COOL"?!
"A LITTLE SOUVENIR"?!
DO YOU WANT TO COMPROMISE THE TIMELINE AND MORE LIVES?!
YOU KNOW I CAN STILL DOWNLOAD IT FROM THE CLOUD, RIGHT?

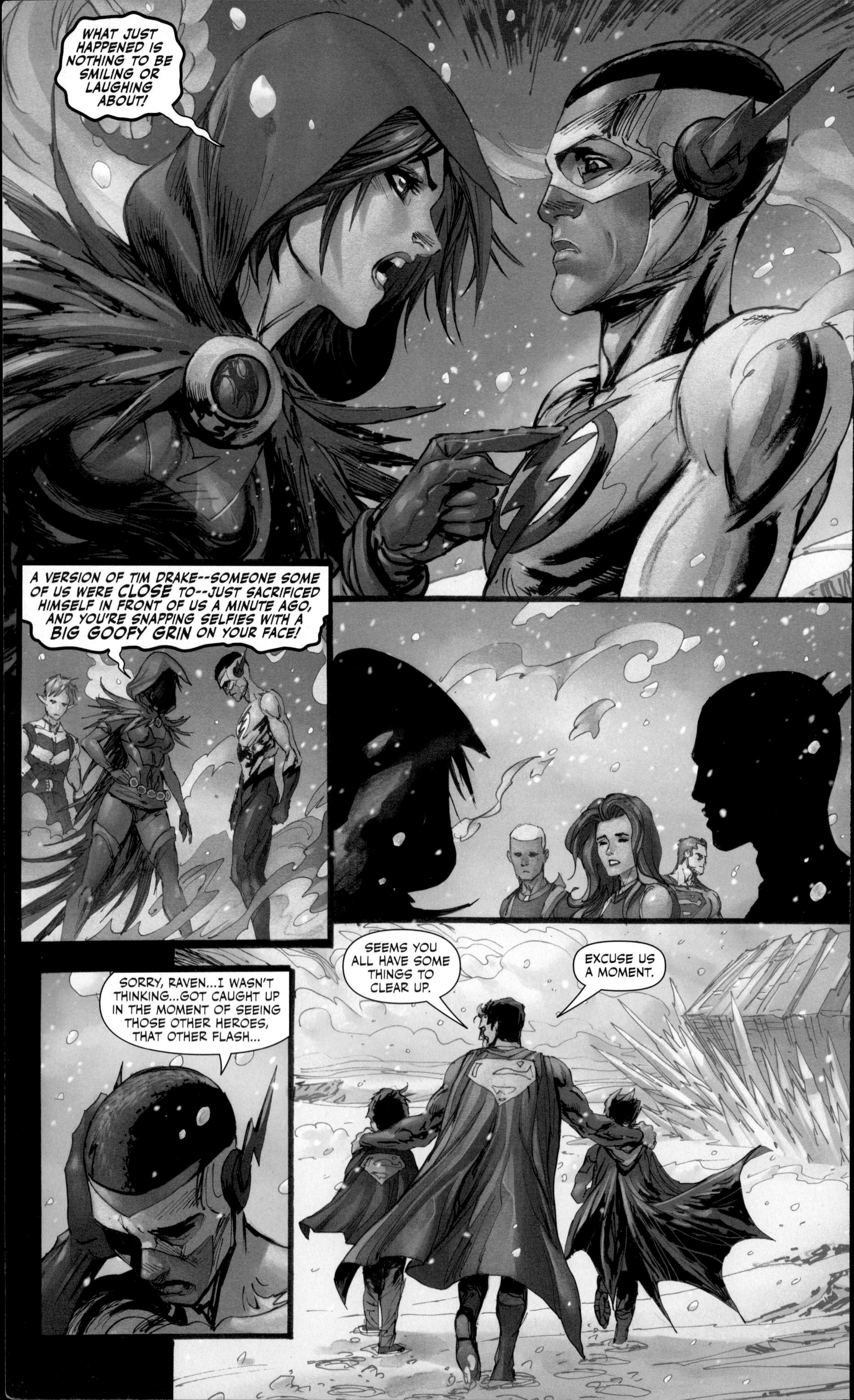
WHAT JUST HAPPENED IS NOTHING TO BE SMILING OR LAUGHING ABOUT!
A VERSION OF TIM DRAKE--SOMEONE SOME OF US WERE CLOSE TO--JUST SACRIFICED HIMSELF IN FRONT OF US A MINUTE AGO, AND YOU'RE SNAPPING SELFIES WITH A BIG GOOFY GRIN ON YOUR FACE!
SORRY, RAVEN...I WASN'T THINKING...GOT CAUGHT UP IN THE MOMENT OF SEEING THOSE OTHER HEROES, THAT OTHER FLASH...
SEEMS YOU ALL HAVE SOME THINGS TO CLEAR UP.
EXCUSE US A MOMENT.

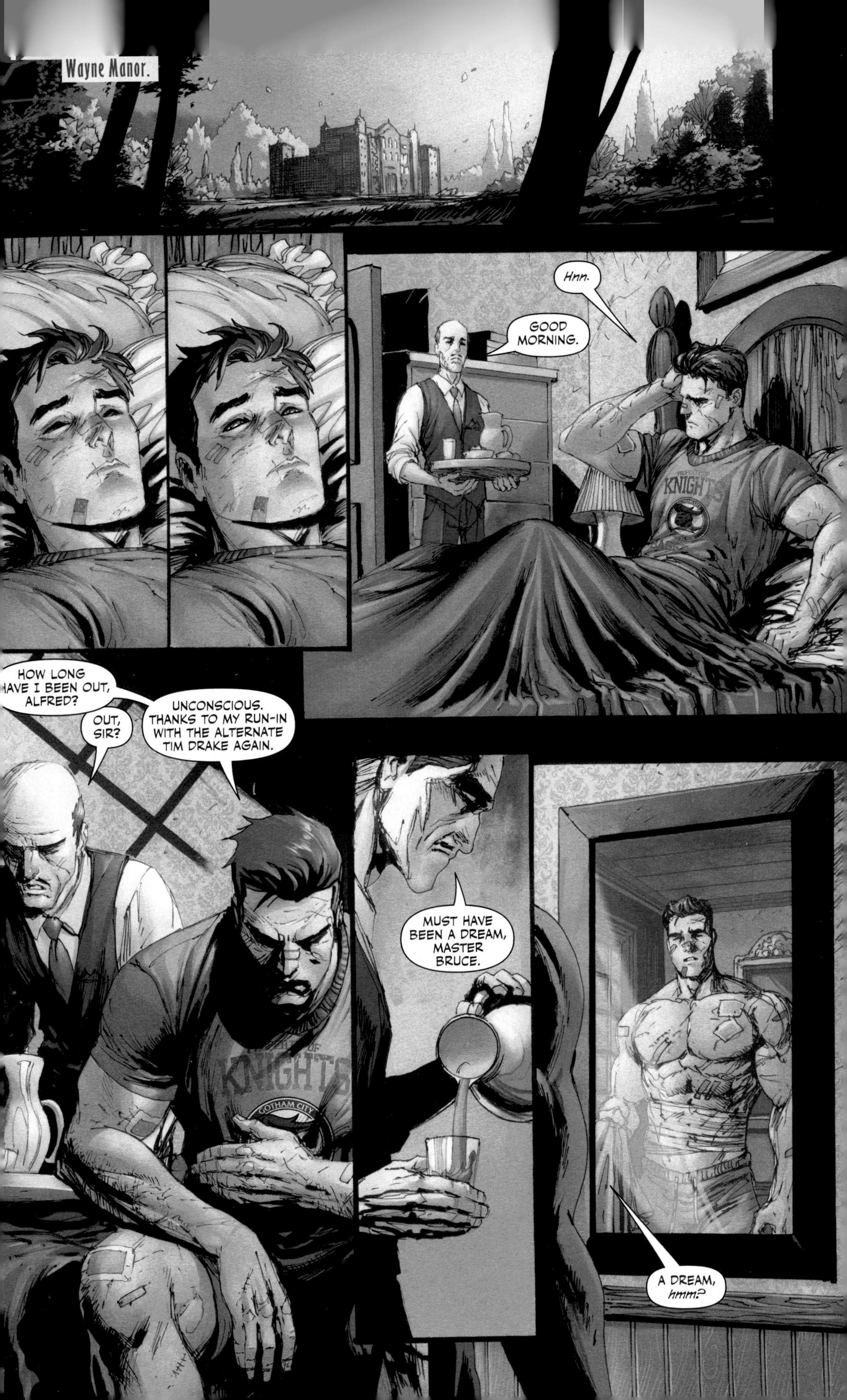

Wayne Manor.
GOOD MORNING.
Hnn.
HOW LONG HAVE I BEEN OUT, ALFRED?
OUT, SIR?
UNCONSCIOUS. THANKS TO MY RUN-IN WITH THE ALTERNATE TIM DRAKE AGAIN.
MUST HAVE BEEN A DREAM, MASTER BRUCE.
A DREAM, hmm?

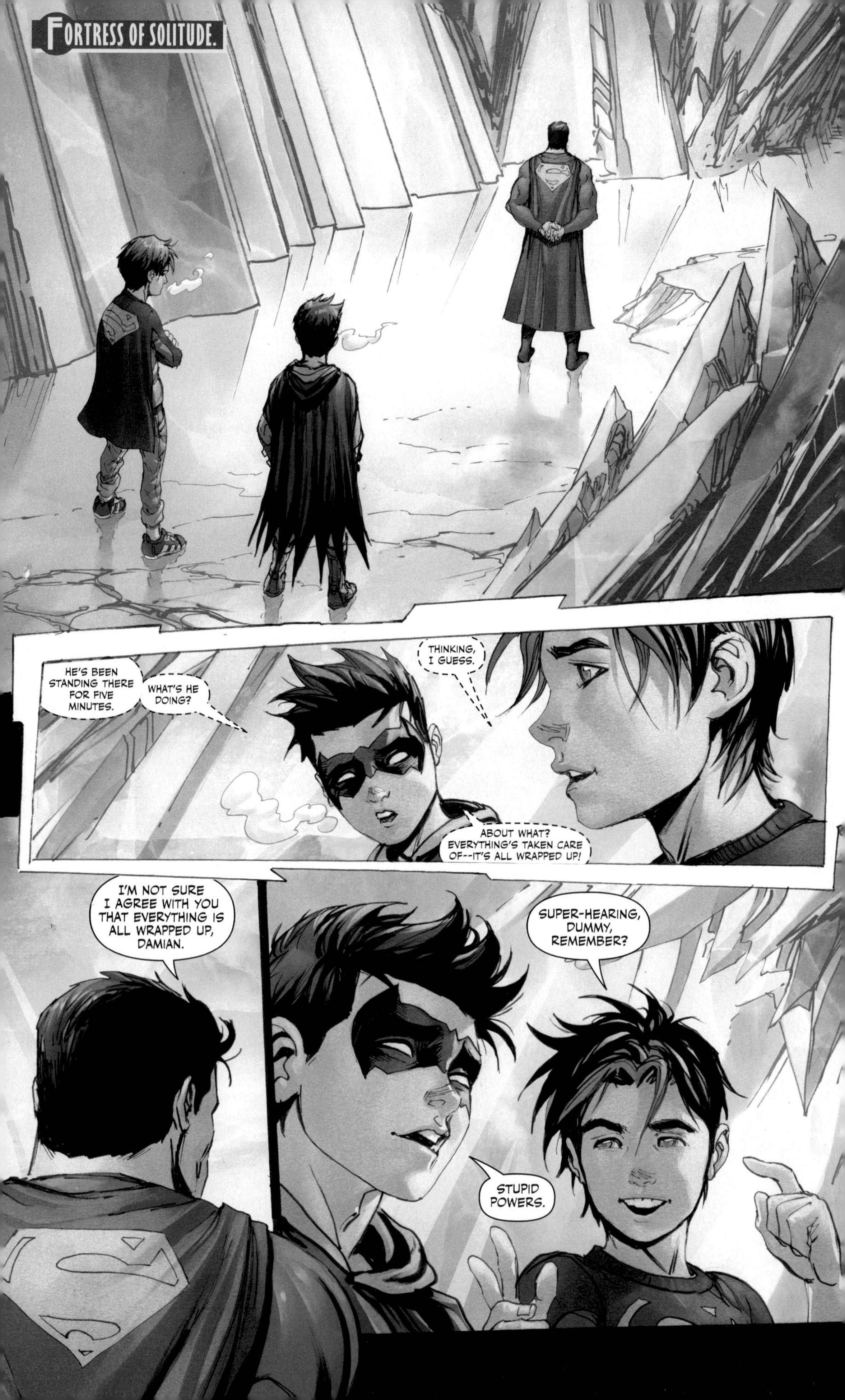
FORTRESS OF SOLITUDE.
HE'S BEEN STANDING THERE FOR FIVE MINUTES.
WHAT'S HE DOING?
THINKING, I GUESS.
ABOUT WHAT? EVERYTHING'S TAKEN CARE OF--IT'S ALL WRAPPED UP!
I'M NOT SURE I AGREE WITH YOU THAT EVERYTHING IS ALL WRAPPED UP, DAMIAN.
SUPER-HEARING, DUMMY, REMEMBER?
STUPID POWERS.

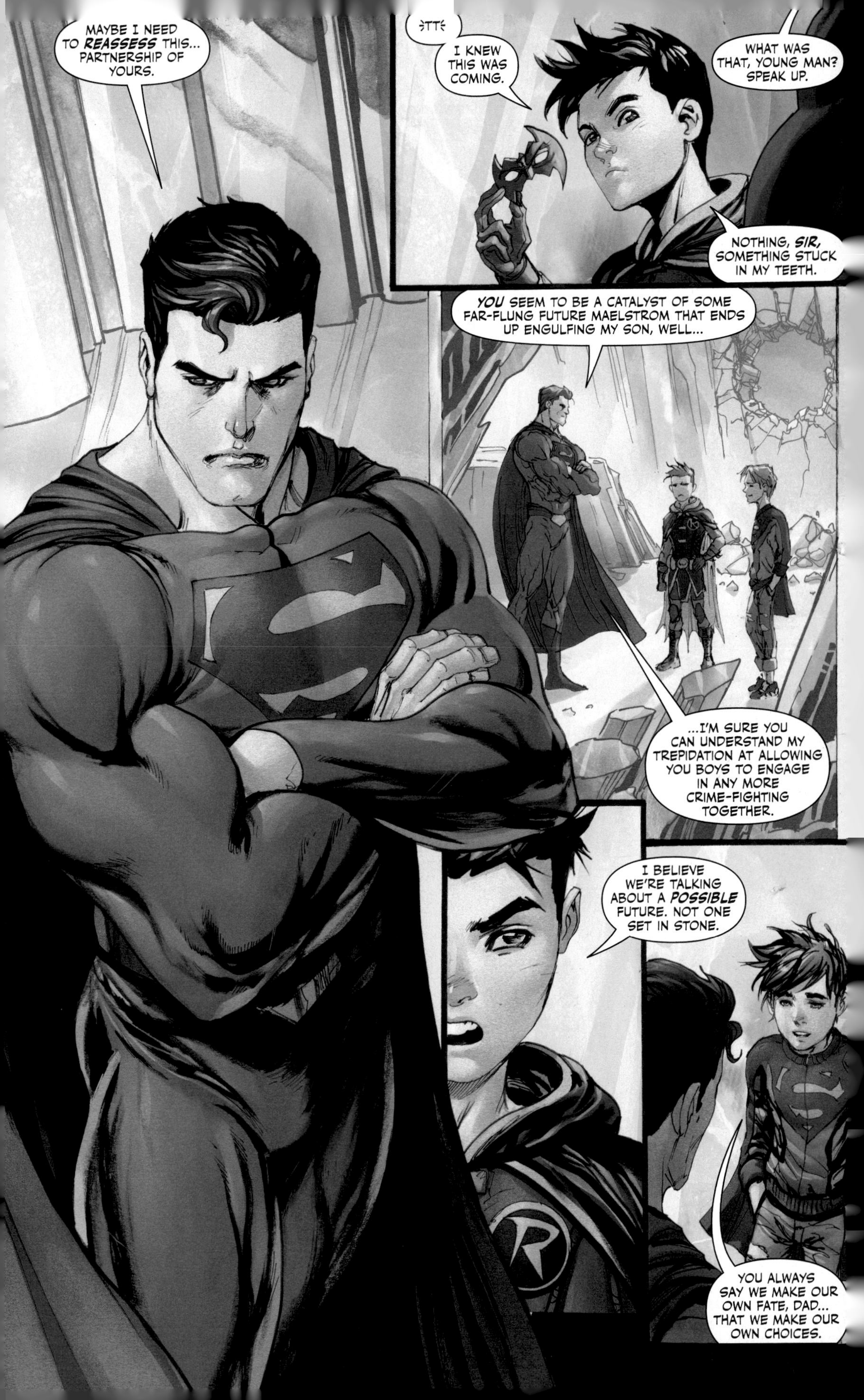
MAYBE I NEED TO *REASSESS* THIS... PARTNERSHIP OF YOURS.
TT
I KNEW THIS WAS COMING.
WHAT WAS THAT, YOUNG MAN? SPEAK UP.
NOTHING, *SIR,* SOMETHING STUCK IN MY TEETH.
YOU SEEM TO BE A CATALYST OF SOME FAR-FLUNG FUTURE MAELSTROM THAT ENDS UP ENGULFING MY SON, WELL...
...I'M SURE YOU CAN UNDERSTAND MY TREPIDATION AT ALLOWING YOU BOYS TO ENGAGE IN ANY MORE CRIME-FIGHTING TOGETHER.
I BELIEVE WE'RE TALKING ABOUT A *POSSIBLE* FUTURE. NOT ONE SET IN STONE.
YOU ALWAYS SAY WE MAKE OUR OWN FATE, DAD... THAT WE MAKE OUR OWN CHOICES.

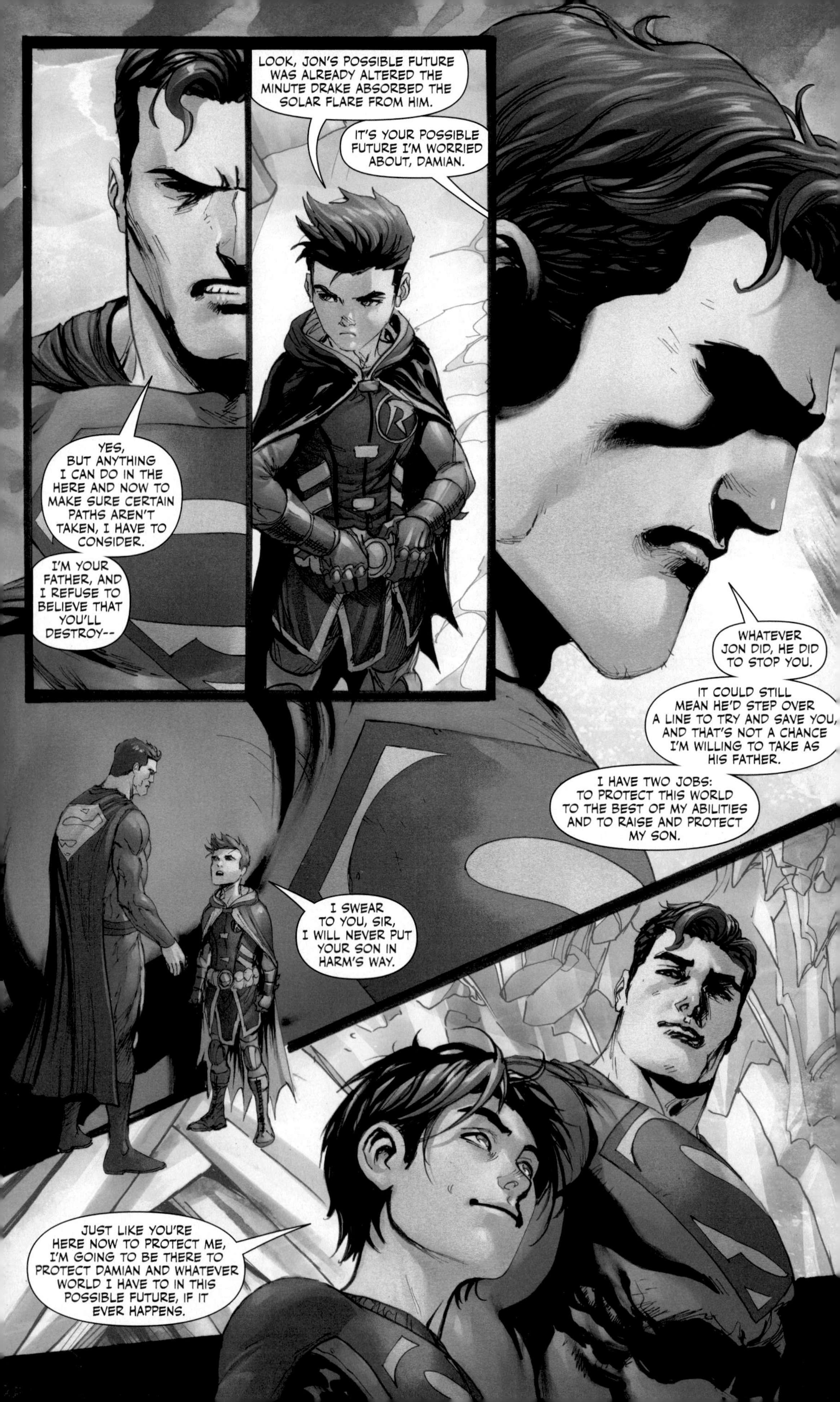
LOOK, JON'S POSSIBLE FUTURE WAS ALREADY ALTERED THE MINUTE DRAKE ABSORBED THE SOLAR FLARE FROM HIM.
IT'S YOUR POSSIBLE FUTURE I'M WORRIED ABOUT, DAMIAN.
YES, BUT ANYTHING I CAN DO IN THE HERE AND NOW TO MAKE SURE CERTAIN PATHS AREN'T TAKEN, I HAVE TO CONSIDER.
I'M YOUR FATHER, AND I REFUSE TO BELIEVE THAT YOU'LL DESTROY--
WHATEVER JON DID, HE DID TO STOP YOU.
IT COULD STILL MEAN HE'D STEP OVER A LINE TO TRY AND SAVE YOU, AND THAT'S NOT A CHANCE I'M WILLING TO TAKE AS HIS FATHER.
I HAVE TWO JOBS: TO PROTECT THIS WORLD TO THE BEST OF MY ABILITIES AND TO RAISE AND PROTECT MY SON.
I SWEAR TO YOU, SIR, I WILL NEVER PUT YOUR SON IN HARM'S WAY.
JUST LIKE YOU'RE HERE NOW TO PROTECT ME, I'M GOING TO BE THERE TO PROTECT DAMIAN AND WHATEVER WORLD I HAVE TO IN THIS POSSIBLE FUTURE, IF IT EVER HAPPENS.

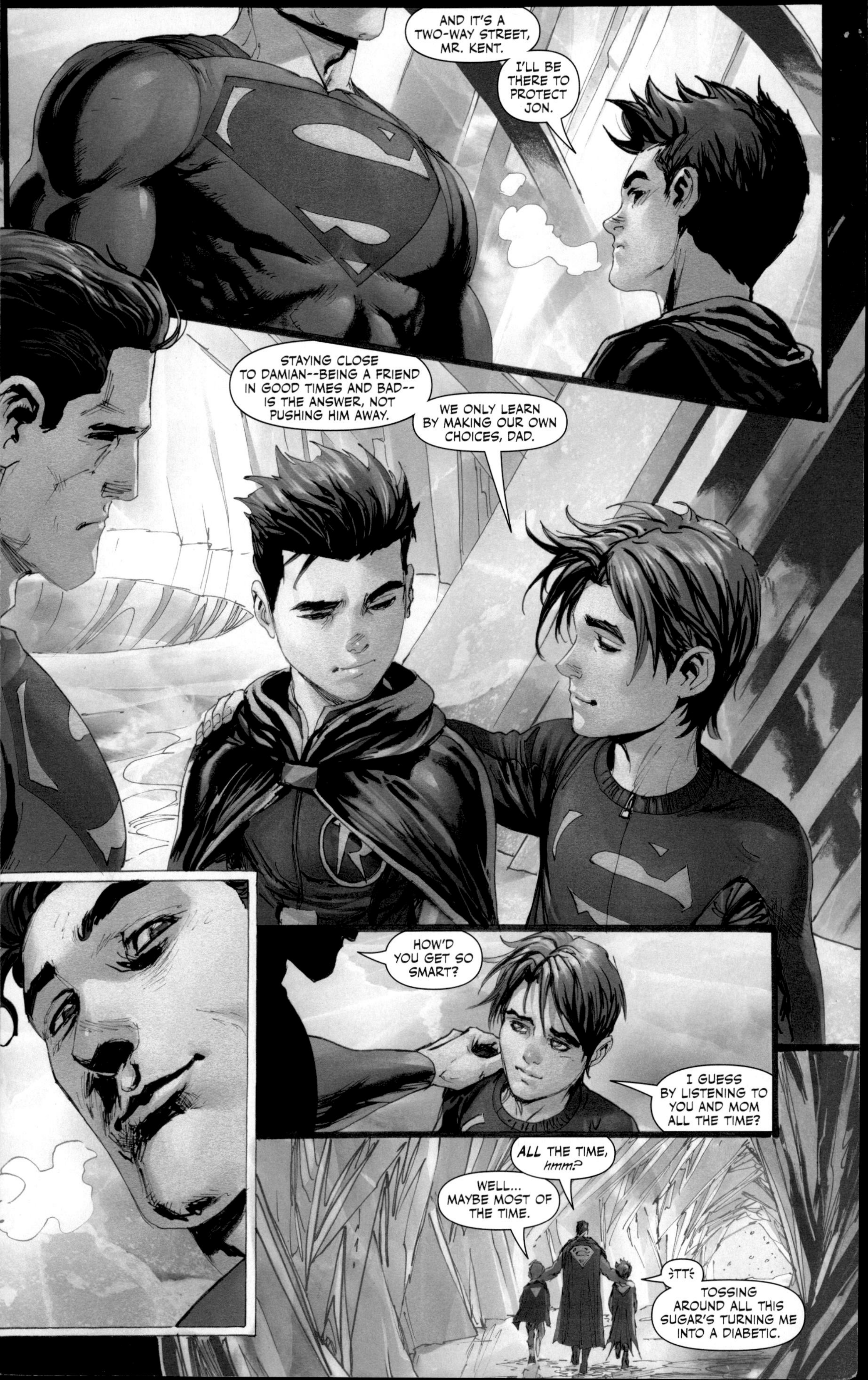
AND IT'S A TWO-WAY STREET, MR. KENT.
I'LL BE THERE TO PROTECT JON.
STAYING CLOSE TO DAMIAN--BEING A FRIEND IN GOOD TIMES AND BAD--IS THE ANSWER, NOT PUSHING HIM AWAY.
WE ONLY LEARN BY MAKING OUR OWN CHOICES, DAD.
HOW'D YOU GET SO SMART?
I GUESS BY LISTENING TO YOU AND MOM ALL THE TIME?
ALL THE TIME, hmm?
WELL... MAYBE MOST OF THE TIME.
-TT-
TOSSING AROUND ALL THIS SUGAR'S TURNING ME INTO A DIABETIC.

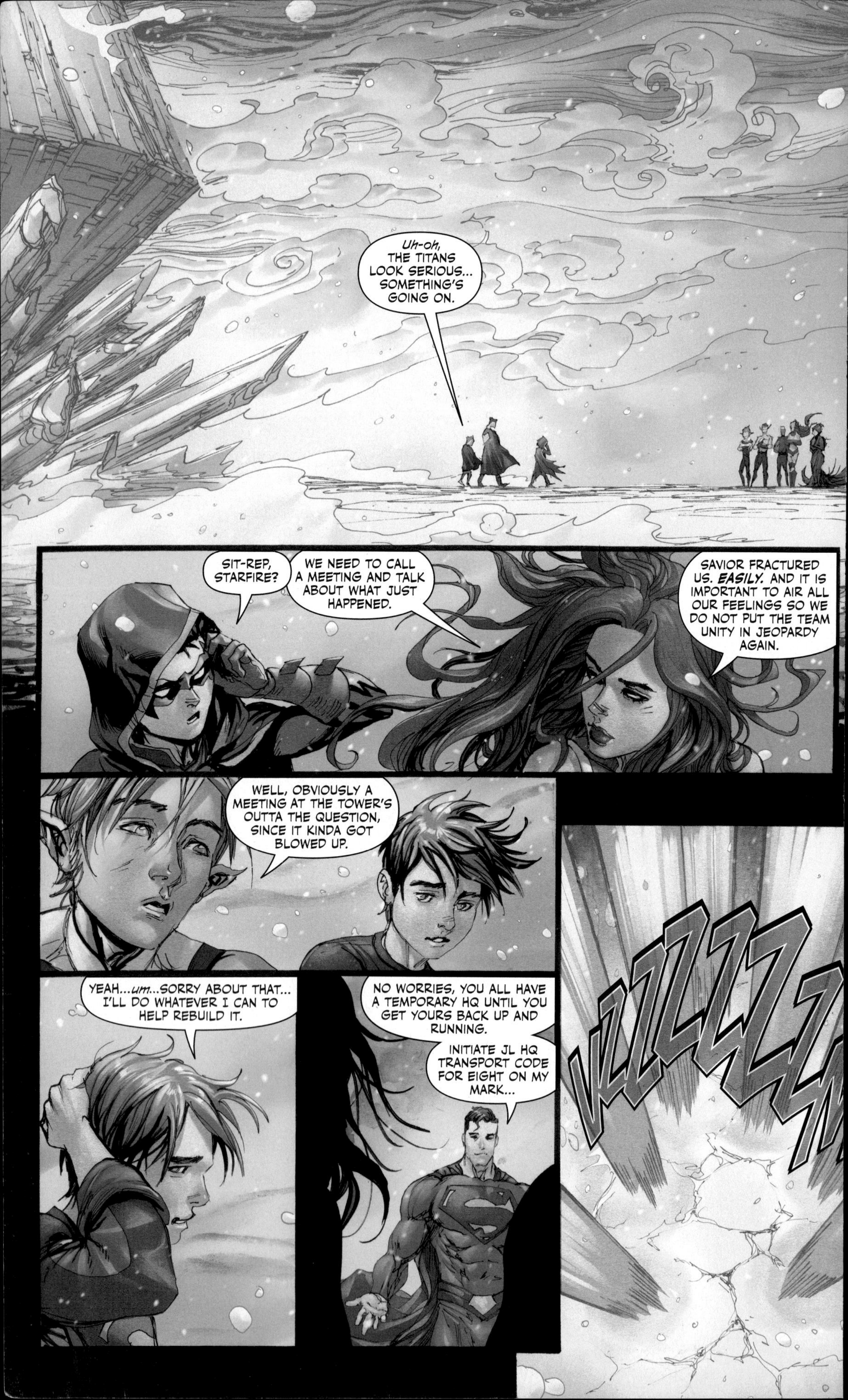
Uh-oh, THE TITANS LOOK SERIOUS... SOMETHING'S GOING ON.
SIT-REP, STARFIRE?
WE NEED TO CALL A MEETING AND TALK ABOUT WHAT JUST HAPPENED.
SAVIOR FRACTURED US. ***EASILY.*** AND IT IS IMPORTANT TO AIR ALL OUR FEELINGS SO WE DO NOT PUT THE TEAM UNITY IN JEOPARDY AGAIN.
WELL, OBVIOUSLY A MEETING AT THE TOWER'S OUTTA THE QUESTION, SINCE IT KINDA GOT BLOWED UP.
YEAH...*UM*...SORRY ABOUT THAT... I'LL DO WHATEVER I CAN TO HELP REBUILD IT.
NO WORRIES, YOU ALL HAVE A TEMPORARY HQ UNTIL YOU GET YOURS BACK UP AND RUNNING.
INITIATE JL HQ TRANSPORT CODE FOR EIGHT ON MY MARK...
VZZZZZM

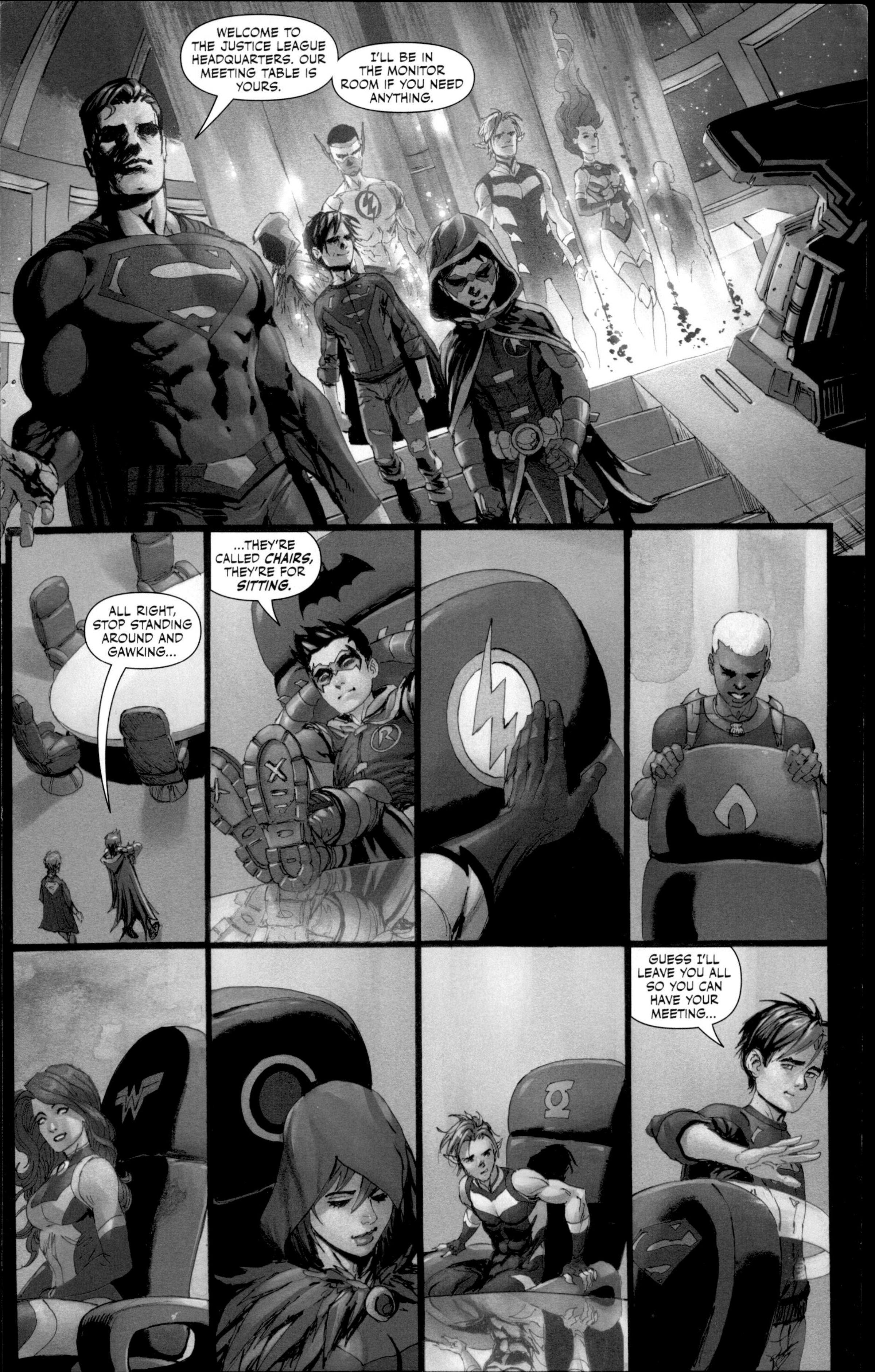
WELCOME TO THE JUSTICE LEAGUE HEADQUARTERS. OUR MEETING TABLE IS YOURS.
I'LL BE IN THE MONITOR ROOM IF YOU NEED ANYTHING.
ALL RIGHT, STOP STANDING AROUND AND GAWKING...
...THEY'RE CALLED CHAIRS, THEY'RE FOR SITTING.
GUESS I'LL LEAVE YOU ALL SO YOU CAN HAVE YOUR MEETING...

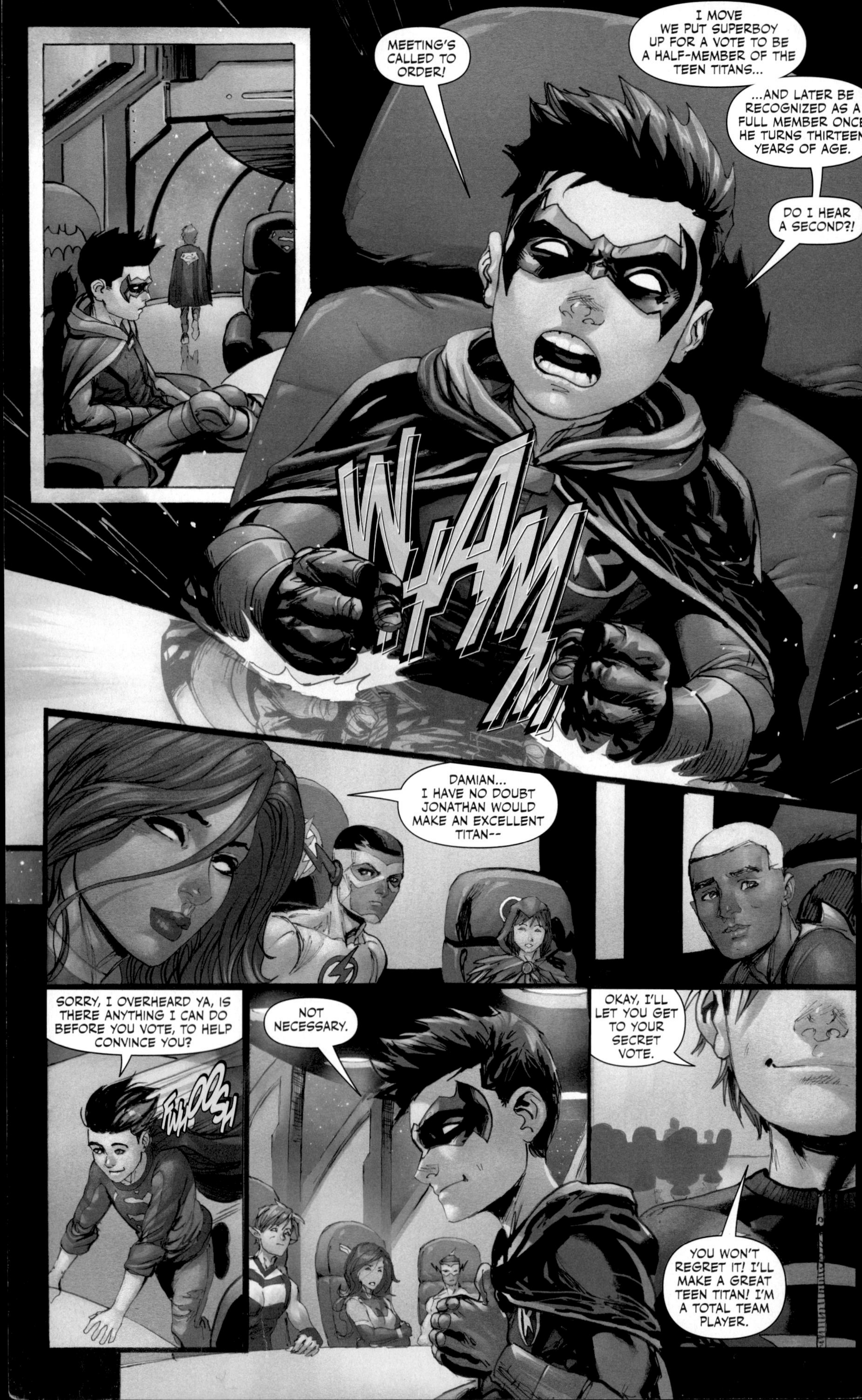
MEETING'S CALLED TO ORDER!
I MOVE WE PUT SUPERBOY UP FOR A VOTE TO BE A HALF-MEMBER OF THE TEEN TITANS...
...AND LATER BE RECOGNIZED AS A FULL MEMBER ONCE HE TURNS THIRTEEN YEARS OF AGE.
DO I HEAR A SECOND?!
WHAM
DAMIAN... I HAVE NO DOUBT JONATHAN WOULD MAKE AN EXCELLENT TITAN--
SORRY, I OVERHEARD YA, IS THERE ANYTHING I CAN DO BEFORE YOU VOTE, TO HELP CONVINCE YOU?
FWOOOSH
NOT NECESSARY.
OKAY, I'LL LET YOU GET TO YOUR SECRET VOTE.
YOU WON'T REGRET IT! I'LL MAKE A GREAT TEEN TITAN! I'M A TOTAL TEAM PLAYER.

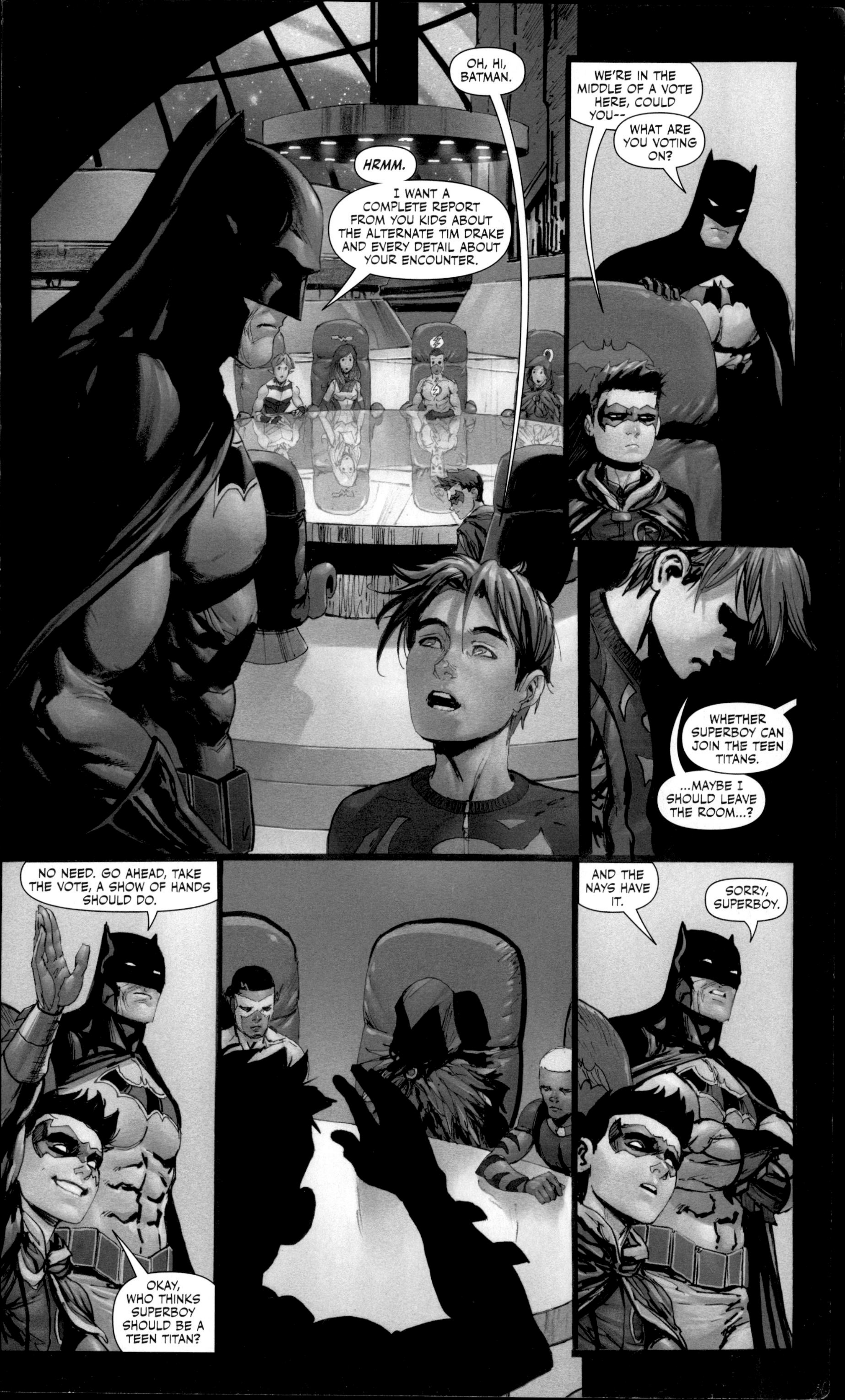
OH, HI, BATMAN.
HRMM.
I WANT A COMPLETE REPORT FROM YOU KIDS ABOUT THE ALTERNATE TIM DRAKE AND EVERY DETAIL ABOUT YOUR ENCOUNTER.
WE'RE IN THE MIDDLE OF A VOTE HERE, COULD YOU--
WHAT ARE YOU VOTING ON?
WHETHER SUPERBOY CAN JOIN THE TEEN TITANS.
...MAYBE I SHOULD LEAVE THE ROOM...?
NO NEED. GO AHEAD, TAKE THE VOTE, A SHOW OF HANDS SHOULD DO.
OKAY, WHO THINKS SUPERBOY SHOULD BE A TEEN TITAN?
AND THE NAYS HAVE IT.
SORRY, SUPERBOY.

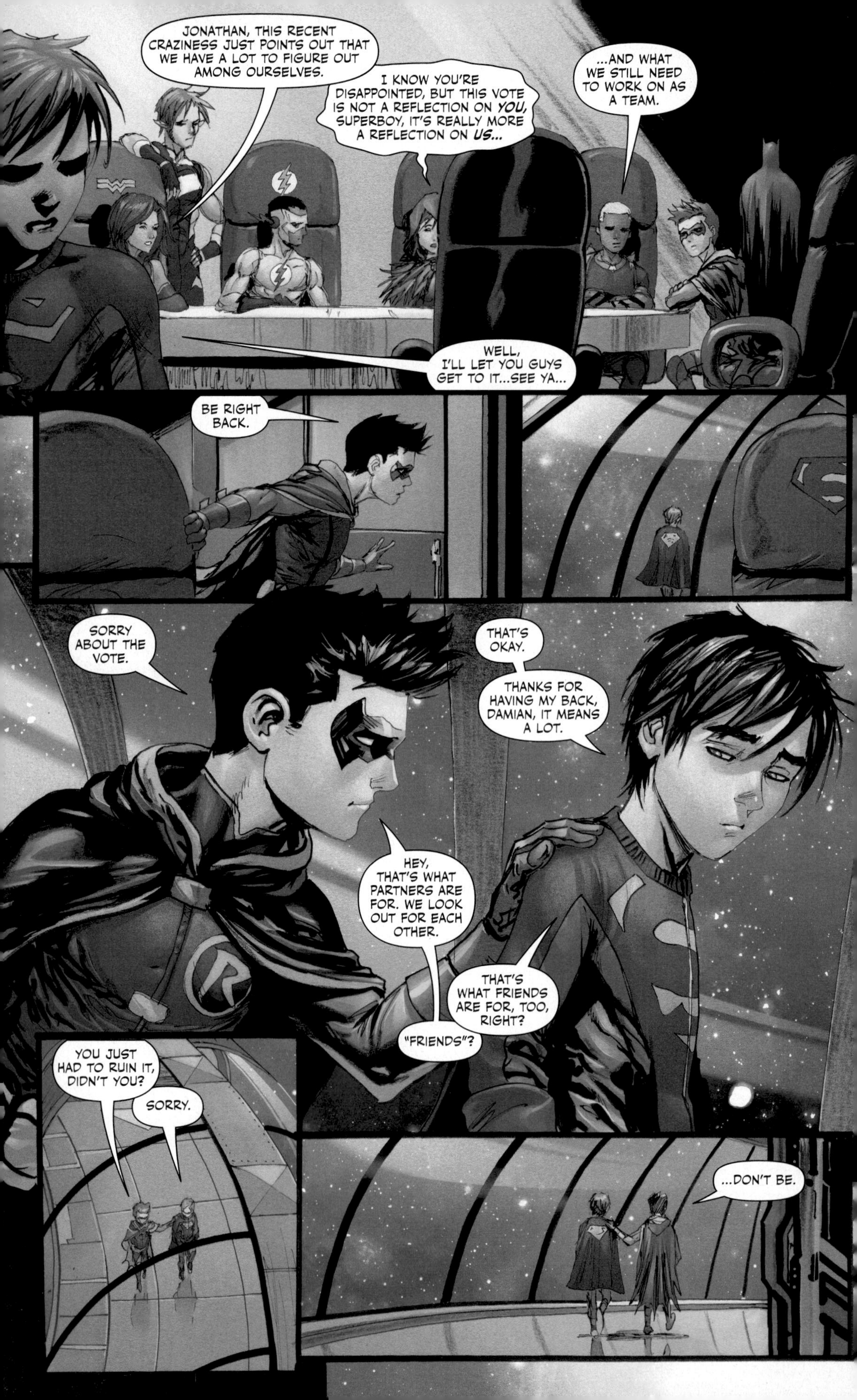
JONATHAN, THIS RECENT CRAZINESS JUST POINTS OUT THAT WE HAVE A LOT TO FIGURE OUT AMONG OURSELVES.
I KNOW YOU'RE DISAPPOINTED, BUT THIS VOTE IS NOT A REFLECTION ON *YOU*, SUPERBOY, IT'S REALLY MORE A REFLECTION ON *US*...
...AND WHAT WE STILL NEED TO WORK ON AS A TEAM.
WELL, I'LL LET YOU GUYS GET TO IT...SEE YA...
BE RIGHT BACK.
SORRY ABOUT THE VOTE.
THAT'S OKAY.
THANKS FOR HAVING MY BACK, DAMIAN, IT MEANS A LOT.
HEY, THAT'S WHAT PARTNERS ARE FOR. WE LOOK OUT FOR EACH OTHER.
THAT'S WHAT FRIENDS ARE FOR, TOO, RIGHT?
"FRIENDS"?
YOU JUST HAD TO RUIN IT, DIDN'T YOU?
SORRY.
...DON'T BE.

Super Sons of Tomorrow

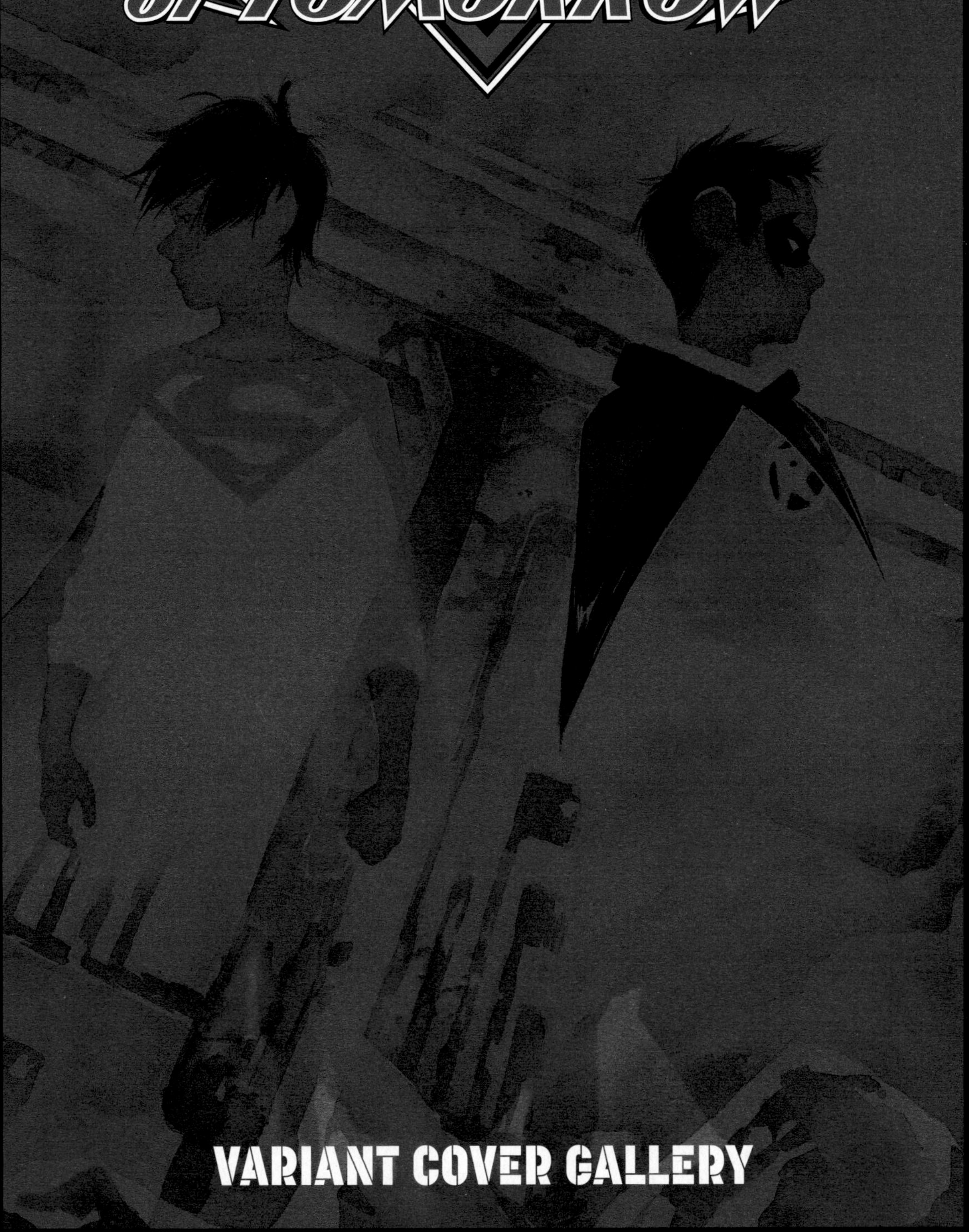

VARIANT COVER GALLERY

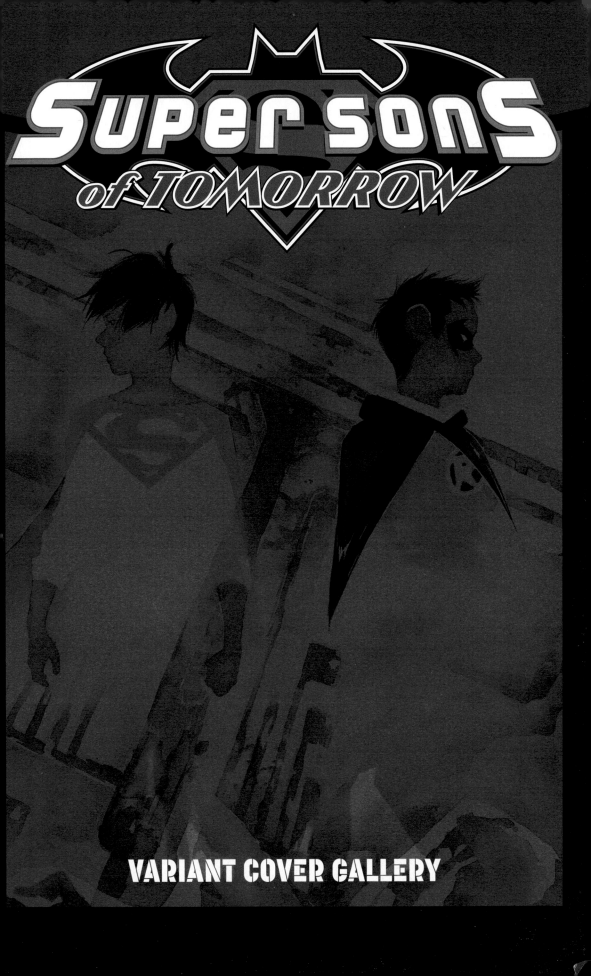

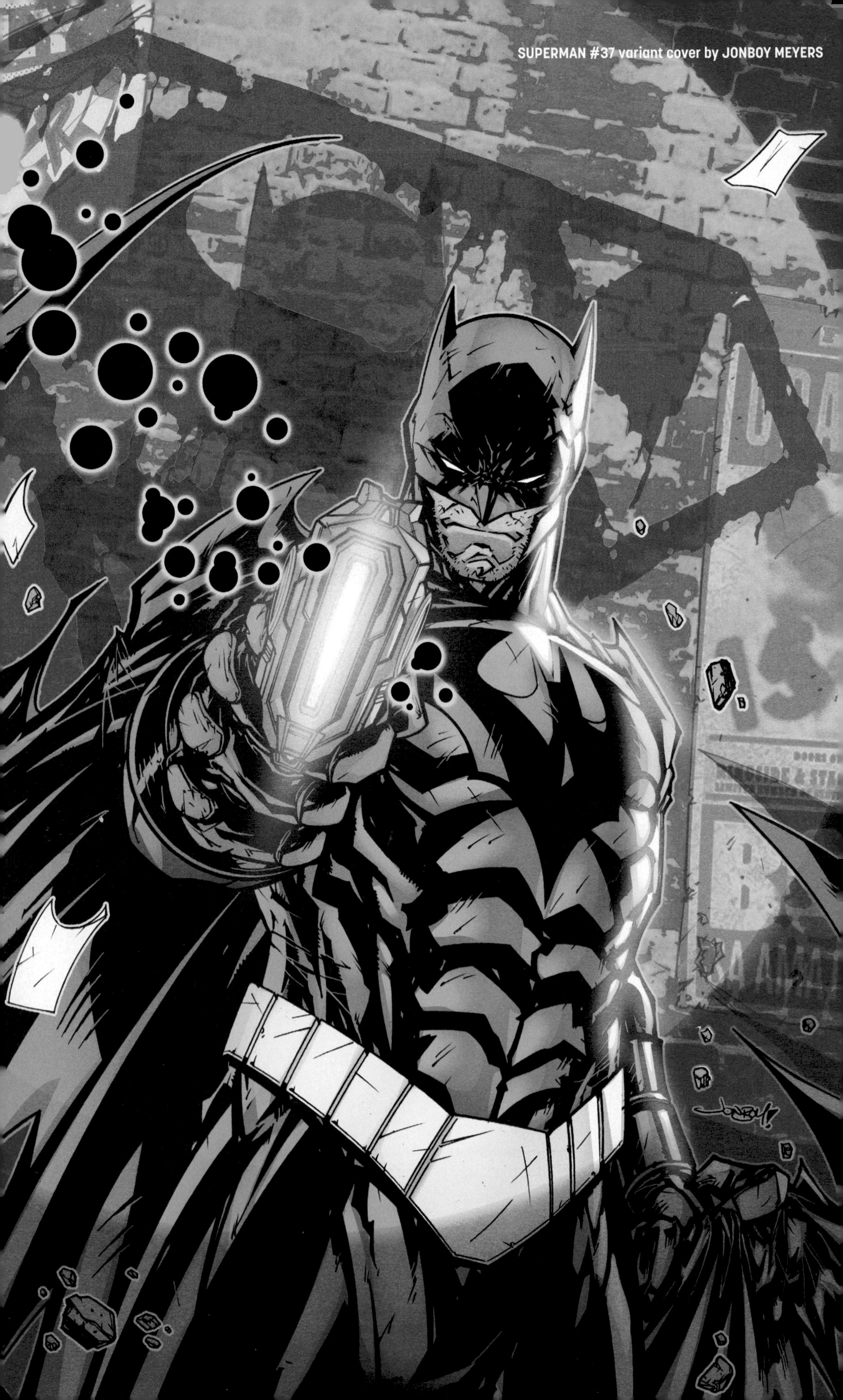

SUPERMAN #37 variant cover by JONBOY MEYERS

SUPER SONS #11 variant cover by DUSTIN NGUYEN

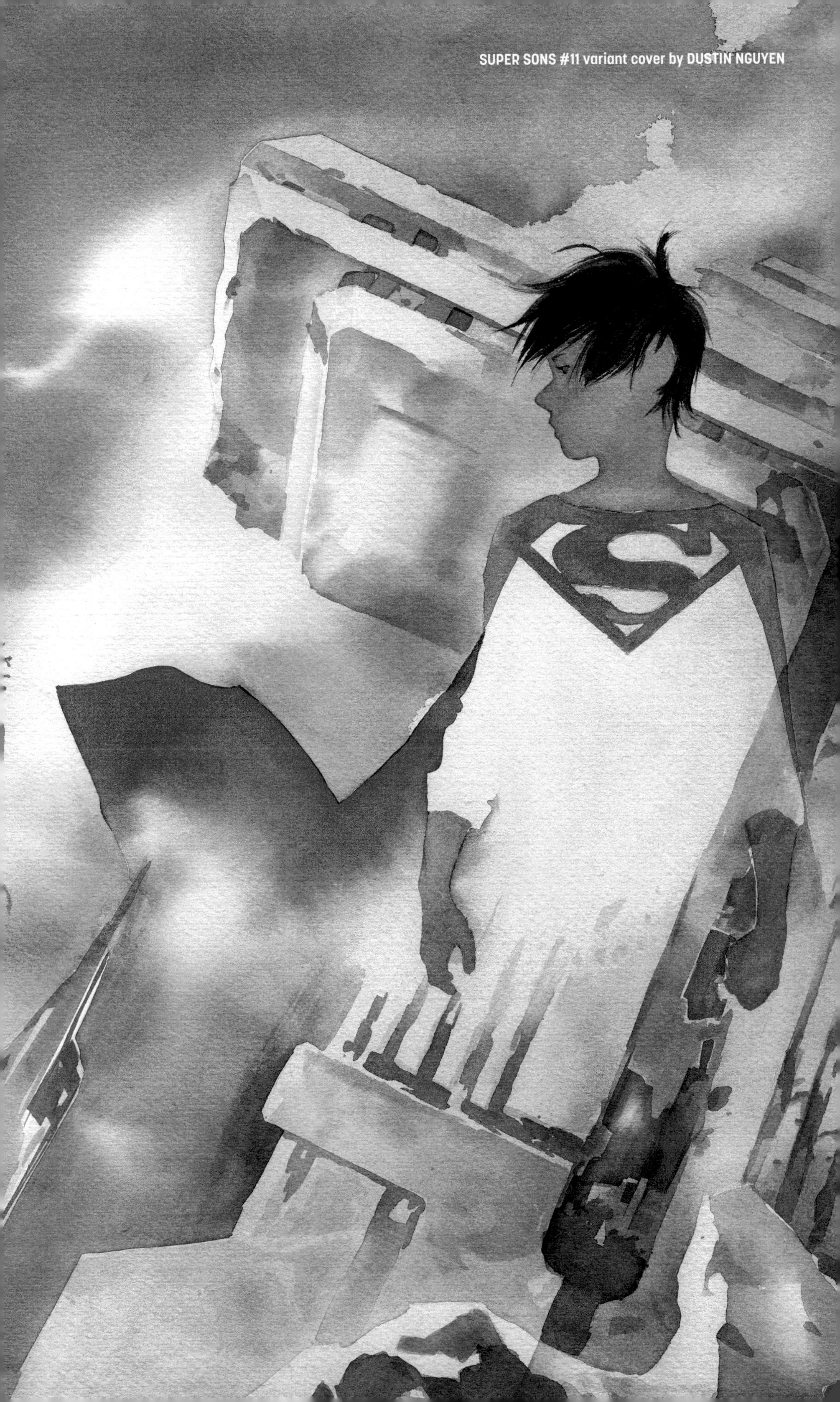

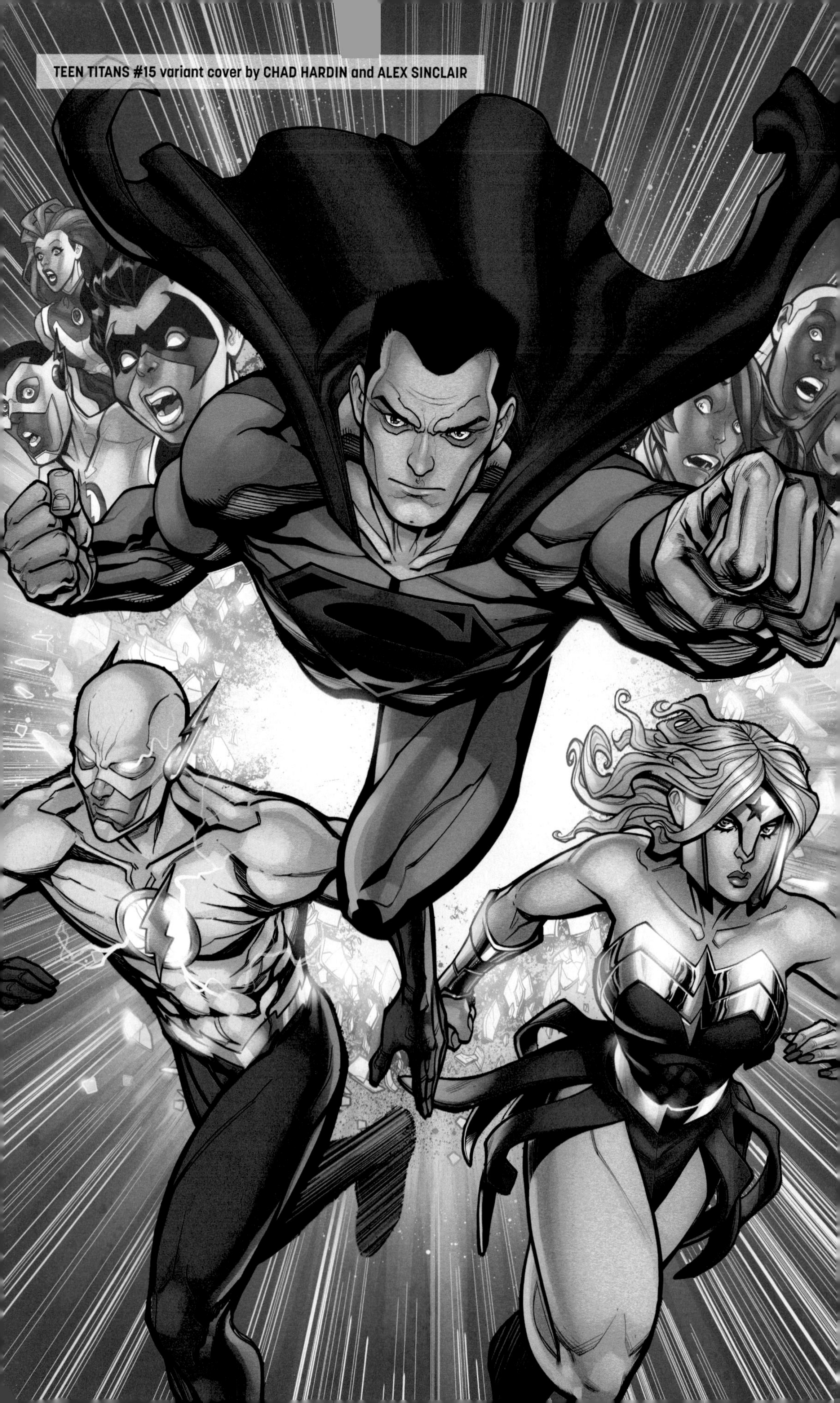

TEEN TITANS #15 variant cover by CHAD HARDIN and ALEX SINCLAIR

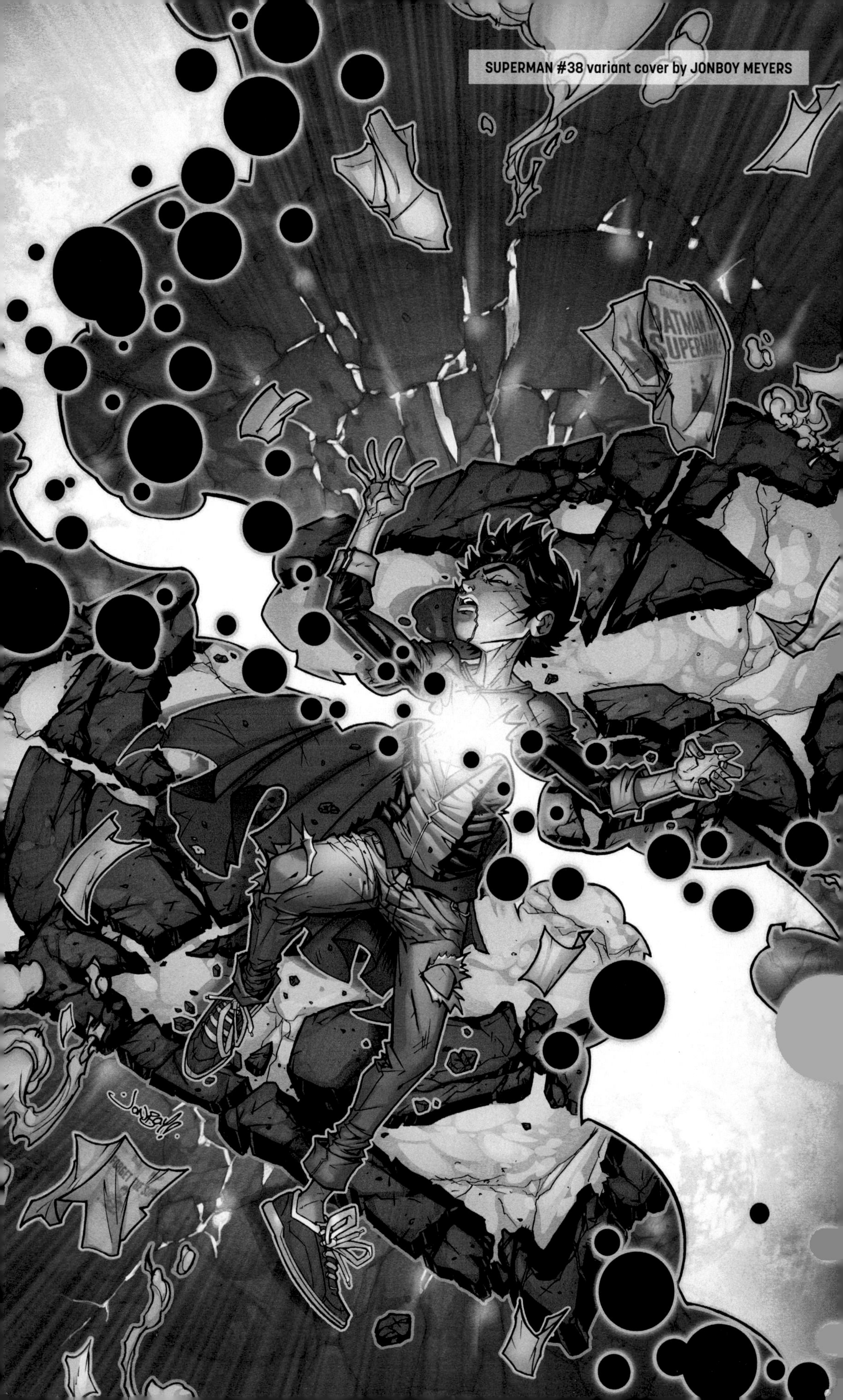
BATMAN
SUPERMAN

SUPERMAN #38 variant cover by JONBOY MEYERS

SUPER SONS #12 variant cover by DUSTIN NGUYEN

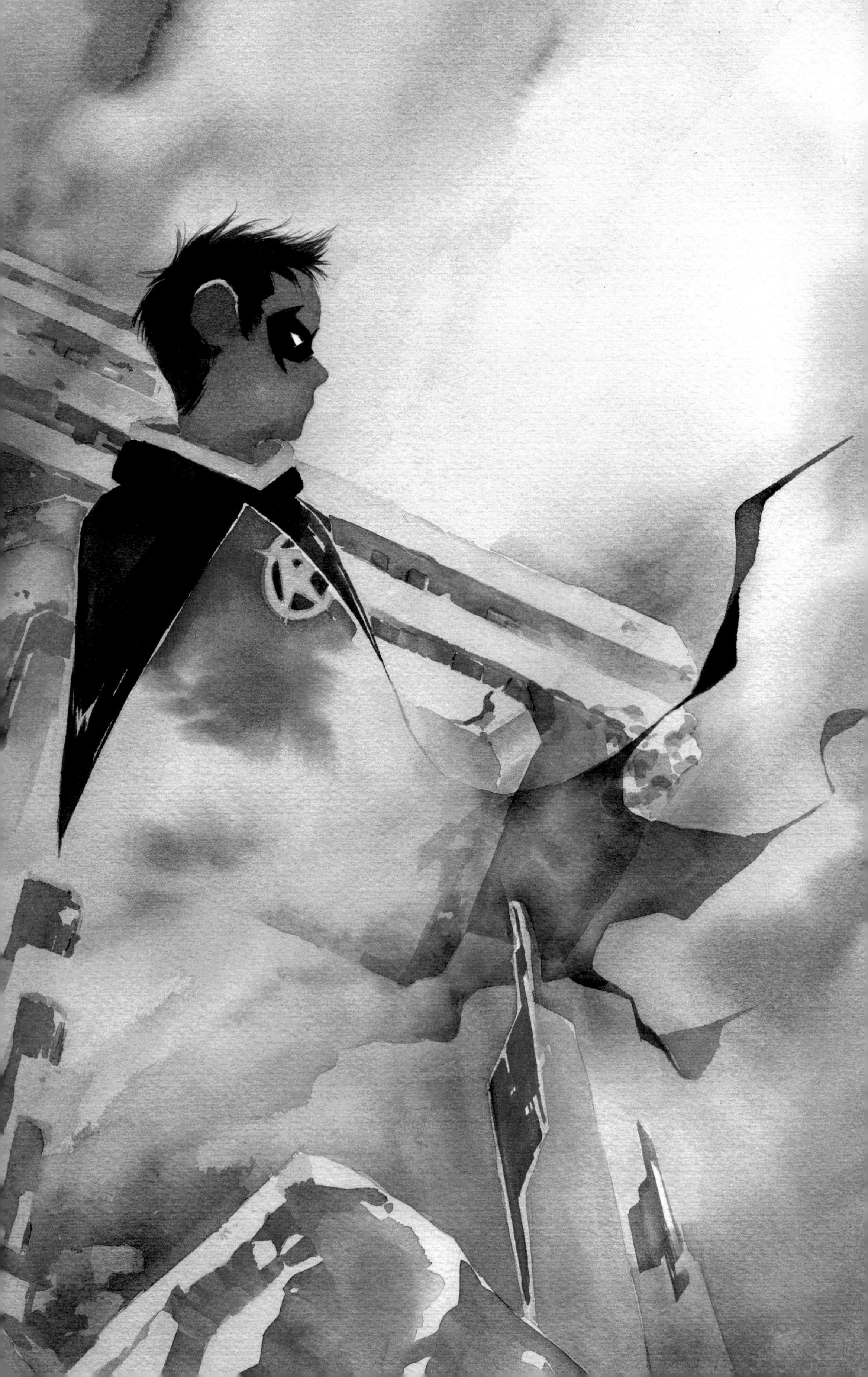

SUPERMAN #37 inks by JORGE JIMENEZ

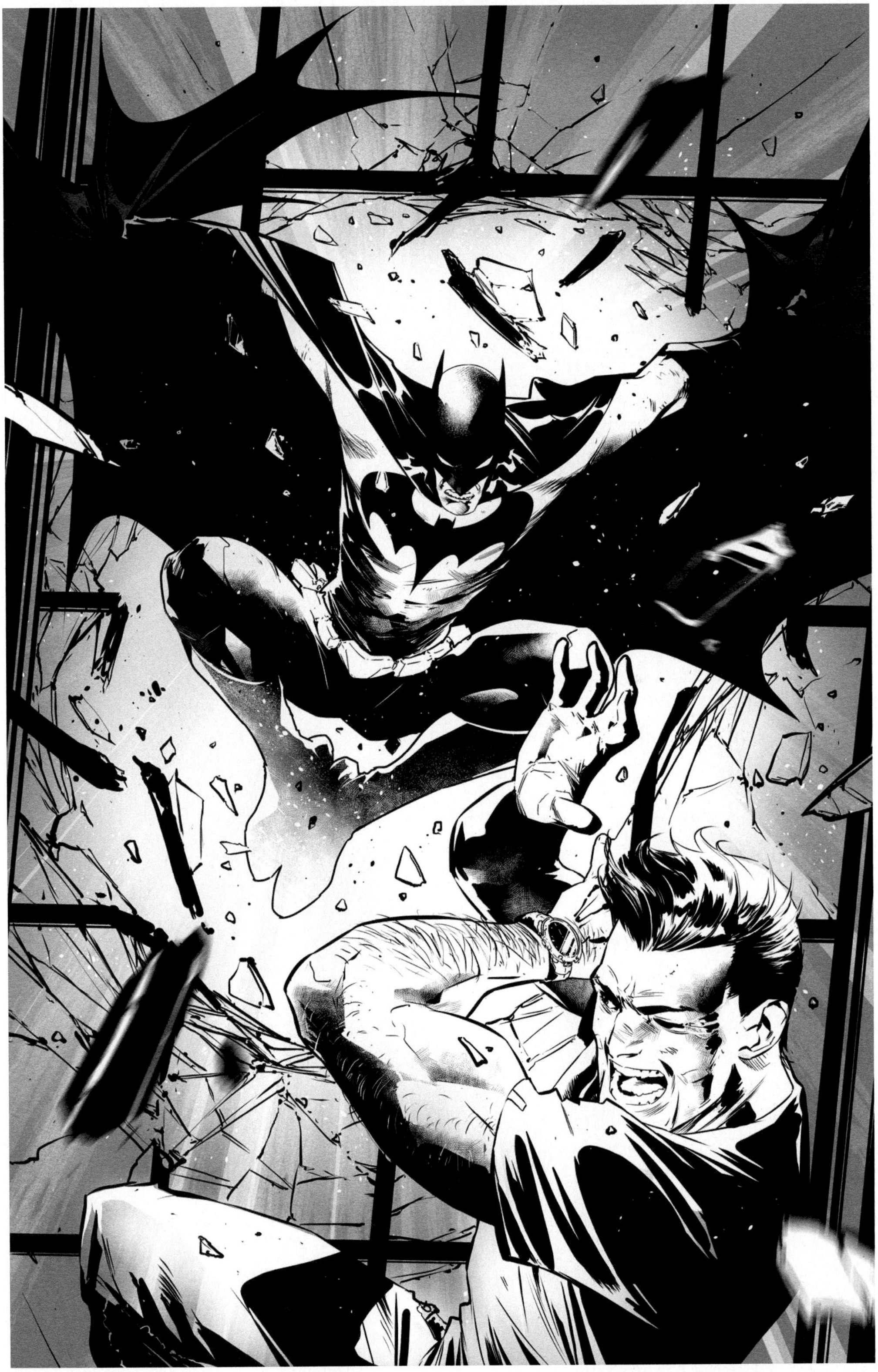

SUPERMAN #37 inks by JORGE JIMENEZ

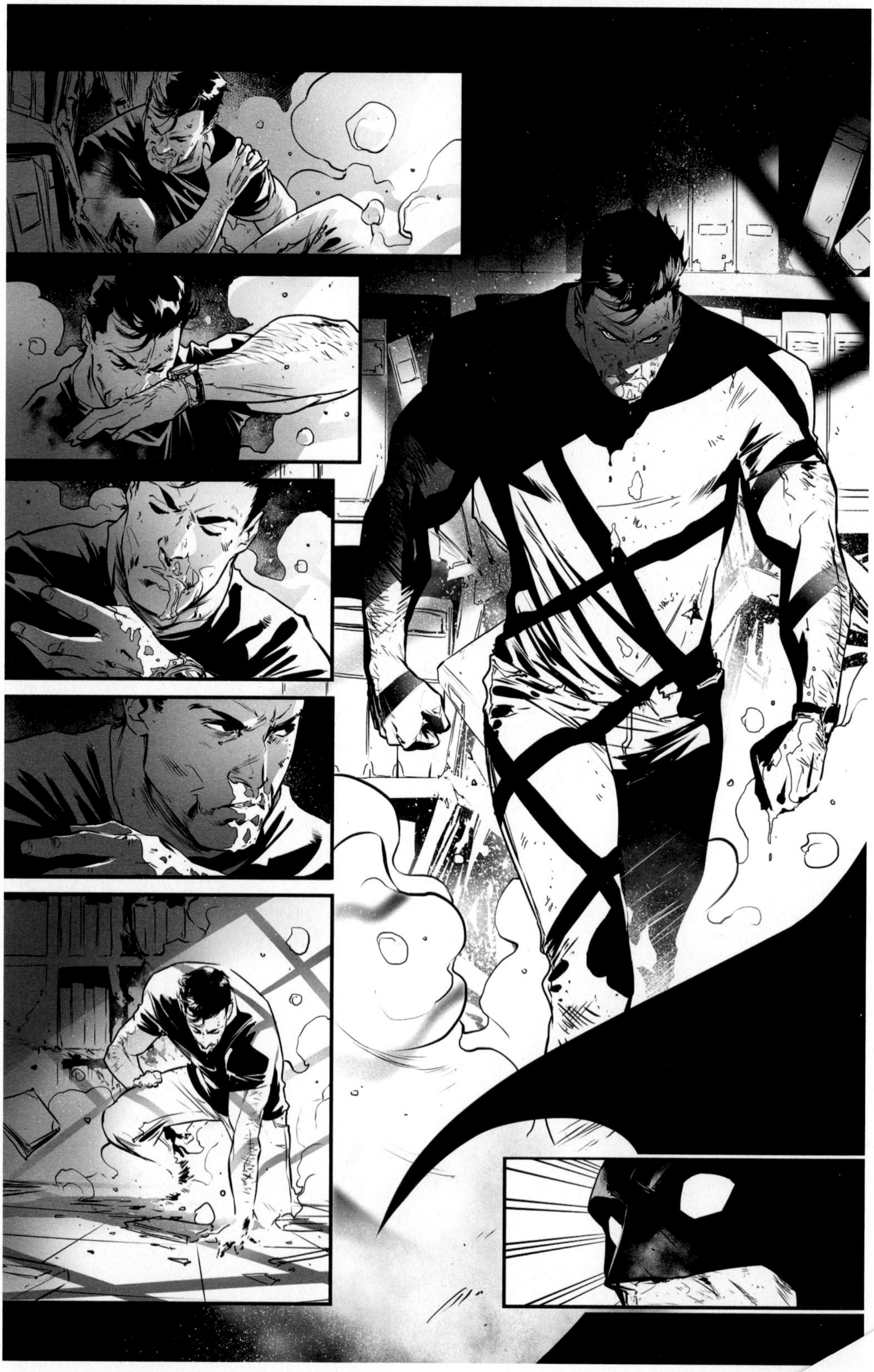

[redacted]

SUPERMAN #37 inks by JORGE JIMENEZ

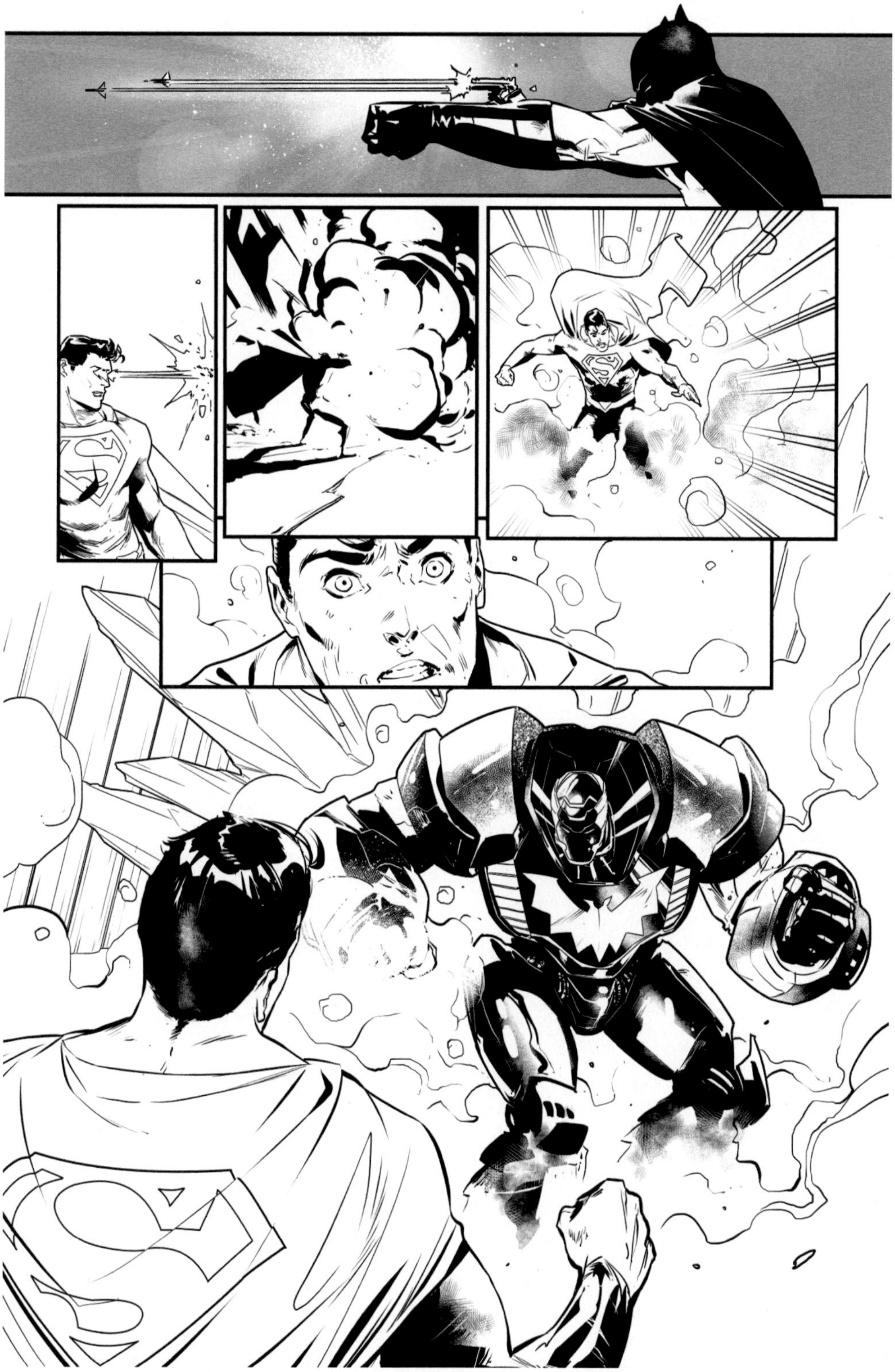

SUPERMAN #38 cover sketches by IVAN REIS

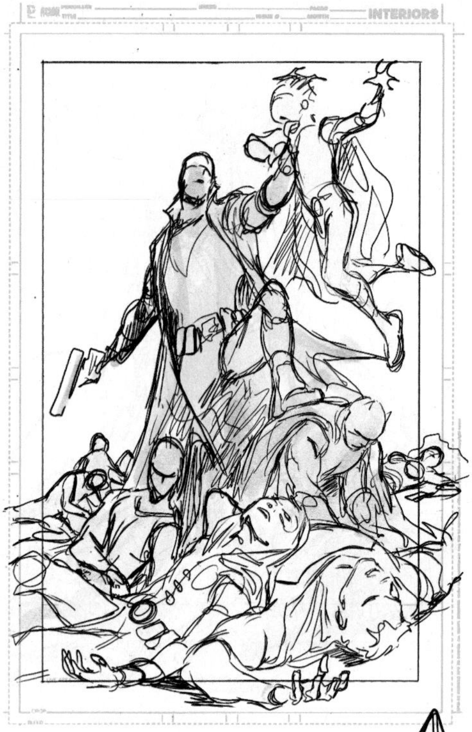
INTERIORS

A

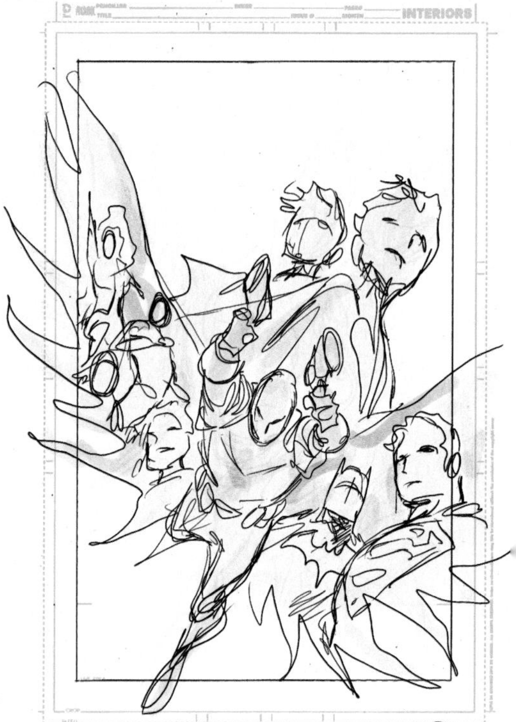
INTERIORS

B

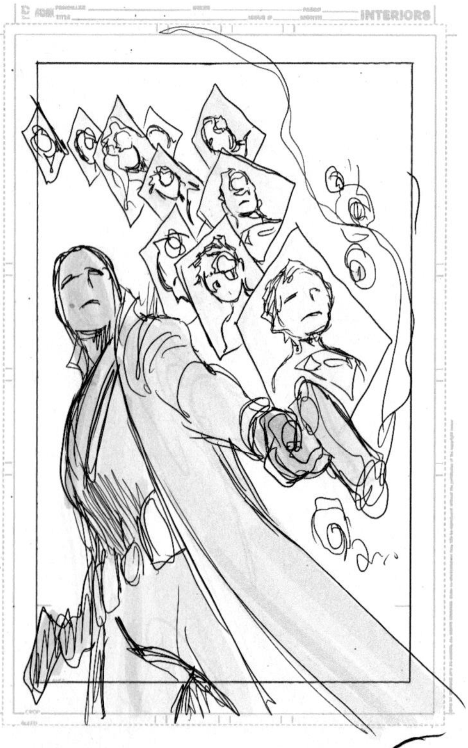
INTERIORS

C

TEEN TITANS #15 pencils by ED BENES

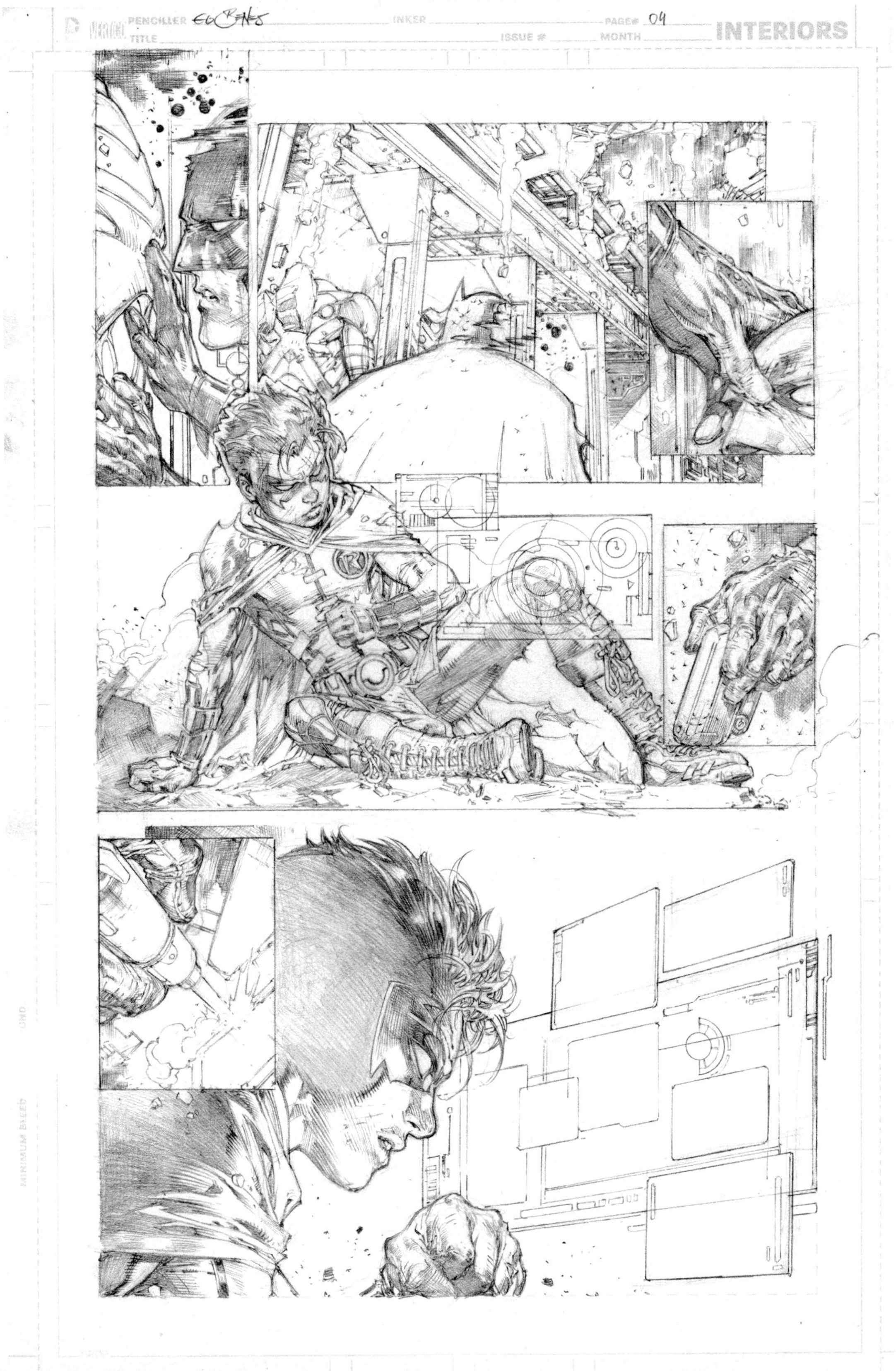
PENCILLER
INKER
PAGE# 04
INTERIORS
TITLE
ISSUE #
MONTH
MINIMUM BLEED

TEEN TITANS #15 pencils by ED BENES

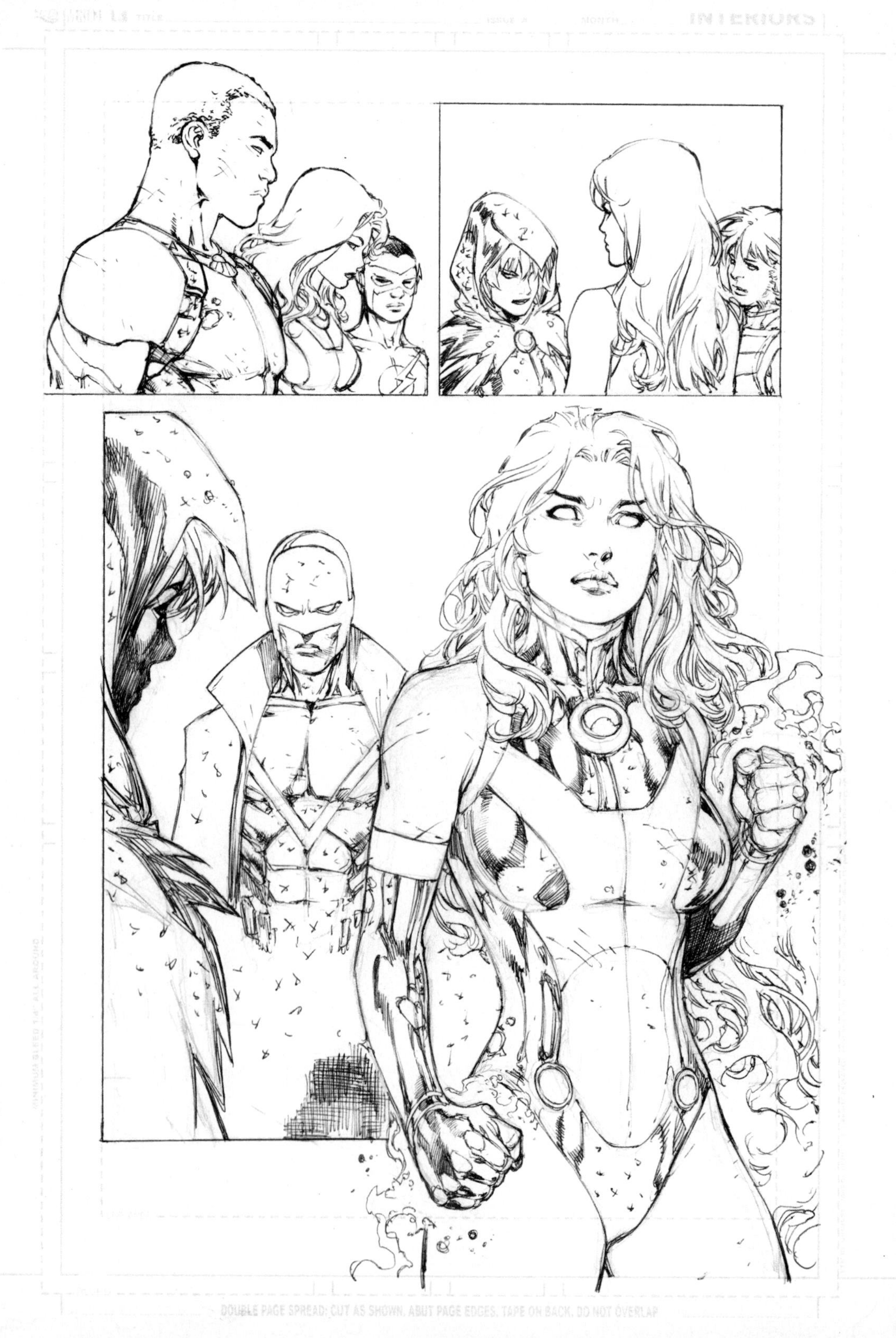
INTERIORS
DOUBLE PAGE SPREAD: CUT AS SHOWN, ABUT PAGE EDGES, TAPE ON BACK, DO NOT OVERLAP

TEEN TITANS #15 pencils by ED BENES

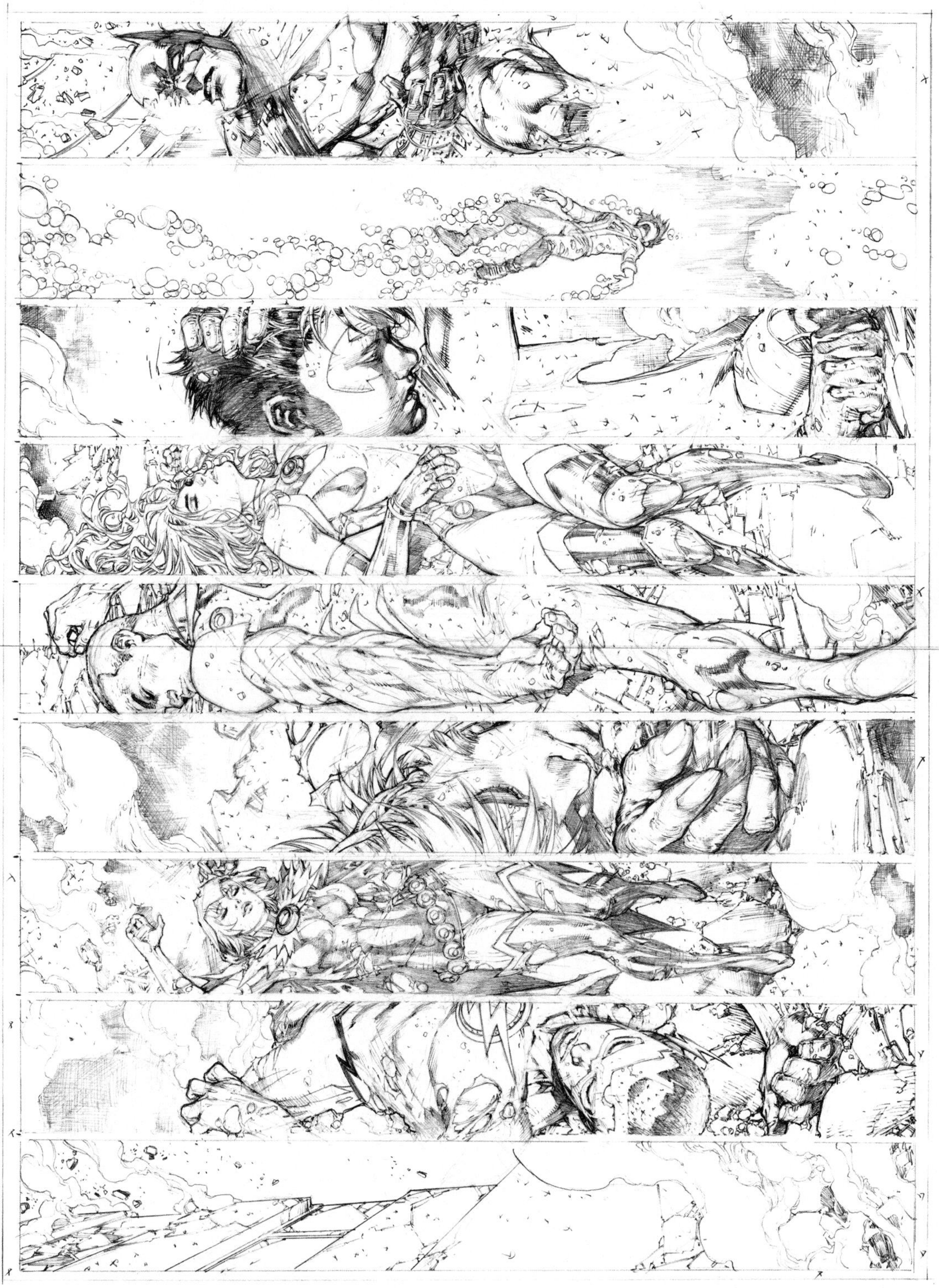

SAVIOR character design by JORGE JIMENEZ

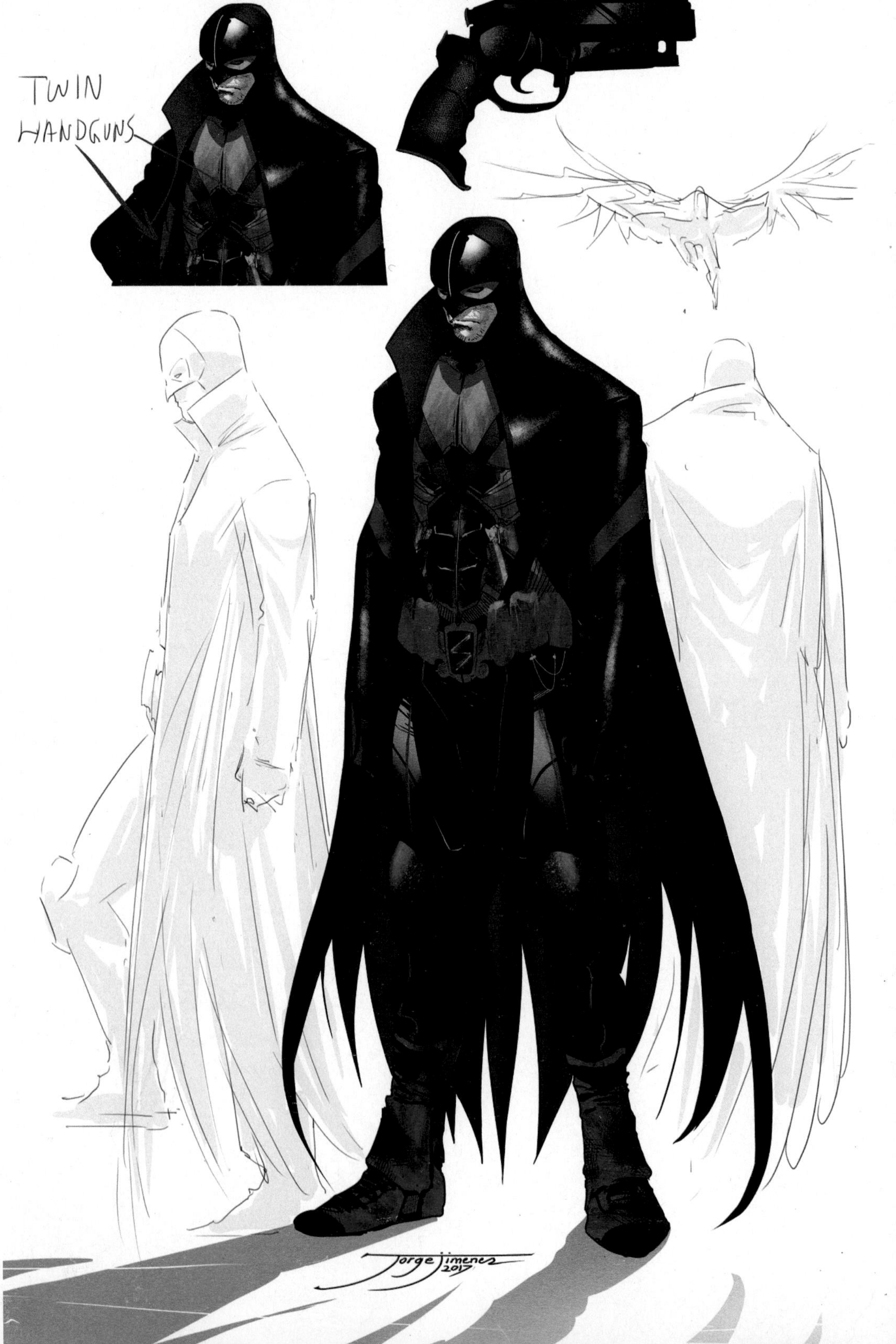
TWIN
HANDGUNS
Jorge Jimenez
2017